Revisiting "Our Forest Home"

Frances Stewart (1794–1872).
Photographer unknown.

Revisiting *"Our Forest Home"*

THE IMMIGRANT LETTERS OF
Frances Stewart

edited by
JODI LEE AOKI

DUNDURN
NATURAL HERITAGE
TORONTO

Project Editor: Jane Gibson
Editor: Allison Hirst
Design: Jennifer Scott
Printer: Friesens

Library and Archives Canada Cataloguing in Publication

Stewart, Frances, 1794-1872
    Revisiting Our forest home : the immigrant letters of
Frances Stewart / edited by Jodi Lee Aoki.

Includes bibliographical references and index.
Issued also in electronic format.
ISBN 978-1-55488-776-7

    1. Stewart, Frances, 1794-1872--Correspondence. 2. Frontier
and pioneer life--Ontario--Peterborough Region. 3. Immigrants--
Ontario--Peterborough Region--Correspondence. 4. Irish
Canadians--Ontario--Peterborough Region--Correspondence.
5. Peterborough Region (Ont.)--Biography. I. Aoki, Jodi, 1956-
II. Title.

FC3095.P47Z49 2011   971.3'67   C2011-901150-6

1   2   3   4   5   15   14   13   12   11

We acknowledge the support of the **Canada Council for the Arts** and the **Ontario Arts Council** for our publishing program. We also acknowledge the financial support of the **Government of Canada** through the **Canada Book Fund** and **Livres Canada Books**, and the **Government of Ontario** through the **Ontario Book Publishing Tax Credit** and the **Ontario Media Development Corporation**.

Printed and bound in Canada.
www.dundurn.com

Dundurn	Gazelle Book Services Limited	Dundurn
3 Church Street, Suite 500	White Cross Mills	2250 Military Road
Toronto, Ontario, Canada	High Town, Lancaster, England	Tonawanda, NY
M5E 1M2	LA1 4XS	U.S.A. 14150

In memory of

Amy Green
(1935–1995)

and

Shigeko Aoki
(1923–2010)

CONTENTS

LIST OF FIGURES

❧

NAMES FREQUENTLY MENTIONED

☙❧

A note to readers: Frances Stewart's family and friends are listed alphabetically by first name, as they commonly appear in the letters; acquaintances are listed alphabetically by last name. Some of the genealogical data was gleaned from *A Sense of Continuity: The Stewarts of Douro* by Elizabeth Shearman Hall and Jean Shearman, 1993, and the Jean Shearman fonds 02-001, TUA.

UPPER CANADA

Family and Friends

Anna Maria Stewart (*Birdie*): granddaughter (daughter of William and Louisa Stewart)
Anna Maria (Stewart) Hay: daughter
Anne (Traill) Atwood (*Annie*): daughter of Thomas and Catharine Parr Traill
Annie (Johnston) Stewart: daughter-in-law, wife of John
Betty (Moore) Taylor: a servant who accompanied the Stewarts to Upper Canada from Ireland in 1822. She returned to Ireland after only a few years. In the 1850s, after her husband, Peter Taylor, died, she once again moved to Canada, accepting Frances's invitation to take a place in the home of her son William's family.

Caroline (Mathias) Stewart: daughter-in-law, second wife of Henry

Catharine Parr (Strickland) Traill: friend and renowned published author

Catharine (Stewart) Brown (*Kate*): daughter

Cecilia (Ward) Stewart: daughter-in-law (first wife of George)

Charles Dunlop: son-in-law (husband of Ellen)

Charles Stewart: son

Charlotte (Ellis) Stewart: daughter-in-law (wife of Charles)

Edward Brown: son-in-law (husband of Bessie and raised by Tom and Frances from a child; brother to Robert Brown and Templeton Brown)

Eleanor (Stewart) Dunlop (*Ellen*): daughter

Eliza (Frood) Brown: niece of Frances and wife of Templeton Brown

Elizabeth Stewart (*Bessie*): daughter (deceased at the age of two)

Elizabeth (Stewart) Brown (*Bessie*): daughter (Tom and Frances had two daughters named Elizabeth)

Frances Brown (*Fan*): granddaughter (daughter of Robert and Catharine Brown)

Frances (McCormack) Stewart: daughter-in-law (second wife of George)

Frances Stewart (*Bun*): granddaughter (daughter of William and Louisa Stewart)

Francis Stewart (*Frank*): son

George Stewart: son

Georgina (Innis) Stewart: daughter-in-law (first wife of Henry)

Harriet Brown: granddaughter (daughter of Edward and Elizabeth Brown); Frances sometimes addresses Harriet with an alternate spelling: "Harriette"

Harriet Stewart: granddaughter (daughter of Charles and Charlotte Stewart); Frances sometimes addresses Harriet with an alternate spelling, "Harriette"

Henry Stewart: son

Joan (Brown) Stewart: daughter-in-law (wife of Frank)

John McNabb, Dr.: father of Louisa (McNabb) Stewart

John McNabb Stewart (*Mack*): grandson (son of William and Louisa Stewart)

John Stewart: son

Katherine Traill (*Kate*): daughter of Thomas and Catharine Parr Traill

Louisa (McNabb) Stewart (*Lou*): daughter-in-law (wife of William)
Maria (Frood) Reid: niece of Frances and wife of James Reid
Maria (Stewart) Reid: sister-in-law (Tom's sister)
Martha (Stewart) Fowlis: sister-in-law (Tom's sister)
Mary Dunlop: granddaughter (daughter of Charles and Ellen Dunlop)
Mary (Traill) Muchall: daughter of Thomas and Catharine Parr Traill
Robert Brown: son-in-law (husband of Kate and raised by Tom and Frances
    from a child; brother to Edward Brown and Templeton Brown)
Robert Reid: brother-in-law (husband of Tom's sister Maria Reid)
Stafford Kirkpatrick: brother of sister Catherine's husband
Sydney Bellingham: family relative and visitor to the Stewart's Douro
    Township home in 1824
Templeton Brown: brother of Robert and Edward Brown
Thomas Hay, Dr.: son-in-law (husband of Anna Maria)
Thomas Alexander Stewart (*Tom*): husband; Frances sometimes refers
    to him as "Mr. S."
Thomas Traill: husband of Frances's friend Catharine Parr Traill
William Stewart: son

Acquaintances

Armour, Reverend Samuel: Church of England minister who arrived in
    Upper Canada with his wife in 1826
Bethune, Mrs.: acquaintance who moved to Cobourg, Newcastle District,
    from New York about 1817, two years after the death of her husband,
    Reverend John Bethune
Fleming, Sandford: engineer, inventor, and surveyor; George Stewart
    apprenticed to become a surveyor under Fleming
Hall, Basil: Scottish traveller and author who visited the Stewart's Douro
    Township home in 1827
Hutchison, John, Dr.: the first doctor to settle in Peterborough, arriving
    from nearby Cavan in 1830
Reade, Dr.: doctor who accompanied Peter Robinson's 1825 contingent
    of Irish immigrants to the Peterborough area
Robinson, Peter: Commissioner of Crown Lands and Surveyor General

of Upper Canada responsible for settling two large contingents of
Irish immigrants in the Peterborough area in 1825 and 1827

Roger, J.M., Reverend: Presbyterian minister who visited Tom Stewart,
like Reverend Taylor, at his deathbed, causing some rift between
Reverend Taylor and Frances

Rubidge, Charles: a land agent who assisted in settling various immigrant
groups in the Peterborough area including the Peter Robinson
immigrants in 1825

Strickland, Samuel: brother of Catharine Parr Traill and friend of the
Stewart family

Taylor, Robert J.C., Reverend: Church of England minister who attended
Tom Stewart at his deathbed

IRELAND

Anna Maria (Noble) Browne: mother

Anna (Smythe) Stewart: sister-in-law (wife of Tom's brother John)

Anne (Garner) Stewart: mother-in-law (referred to as Mrs. Stewart in
the letters)

Benjamin Mathias, Reverend: brother-in-law (husband of Tom's sister Anne)

Catherine (Browne) Kirkpatrick (*Kate*): sister; while Frances sometimes
uses the spelling "Catharine," genealogical sources refer to her as
"Catherine"

Elizabeth (Sutton) Rothwell: cousin (daughter of Thomas and Mary Sutton)

Frances (Beaufort) Edgeworth: sister of Harriet Beaufort

Frances (Edgeworth) Wilson: daughter of Richard Edgeworth and
Frances (Beaufort) Edgeworth

Francis Beaufort, Sir: Harriet Beaufort's brother

Francis Browne, Reverend: father

George Kirkpatrick, Reverend: brother-in-law (husband of sister Catherine)

Harriet Beaufort (*Moome*): niece and housekeeper of Robert Waller;
governess and caretaker of Frances

Honora (Edgeworth) Beaufort: Francis Beaufort's wife

Jane (Stewart) Wilson: friend and cousin of Tom
John Stewart: brother-in-law (brother of Tom)
Louisa Beaufort: Harriet Beaufort's sister
Maria Edgeworth: daughter of Richard Edgeworth; novelist
Maria (Newcombe Noble) Waller: aunt (wife of Mungo Noble Waller)
Mary (Noble) Sutton: aunt (mother's sister)
Mary Wilson: daughter of Jane (Stewart) Wilson
Mungo Noble: uncle (Frances's mother's brother; assumed the name Waller later in life)
Richard Edgeworth: father-in-law of Francis Beaufort
Robert Waller: great-uncle who adopted Frances as a child (brother of Frances's grandmother Catherine [Waller] Noble)
Susannah Noble: aunt (mother's sister)
Thomas Sutton, Reverend: husband of Mary Sutton, and Tom Stewart's trustee

Genealogical Reference

The Children of
Thomas Alexander Stewart (1786-1847) & Frances Browne Stewart (1794-1872)

Anna Maria
(1817-1889)
m. Thomas Hay
21 Nov 1843

Eleanor Susannah
(1819-1907)
m. Charles Dunlop
25 Feb 1845

Elizabeth Augusta
(1821-1823)

Elizabeth Lydia
(1823-1893)
m. Edward Brown
24 May 1848

William
(1825-1864)
m. Louisa McNabb
31 July 1851

Francis Thomas
(1827-1910)
m. Joan Brown
24 May 1854

John
(1828-1917)
m. Annie Johnston
24 May 1854

George Alexander
(1830-1917)
m. Cecilia Ward
26 Aug 1856
m. Frances McCormack
25 June 1867

Charles Edward
(1833-1879)
m. Charlotte Ellis
9 Aug 1860

Henry Louis
(1834-1880)
m. Georgina Innis
3 July 1861
m. Caroline Mathias
21 Sept 1872

Catharine Mary
(1837-1924)
m. Robert Brown
4 Nov 1856

Legend:
m. = married

Genealogical Reference adapted from Elizabeth Shearman Hall and Jean Shearman's *A Sense of Continuity: The Stewarts of Douro*. Rev. ed. Toronto: Pro Familia, 1993.

Stewart family tree.

FOREWORD

ଔଓ

Several literary pioneers of central Ontario are well known. Personal journals, letters, poetry, travelogues, and botanical studies by such writers as Susanna Moodie, Catharine Parr Traill, and Anna Brownell Jameson were published either in their lifetimes or after. The letters of Frances Stewart are, however, unique. Frances is known to most people as the author of the letters in *Our Forest Home*, though she herself may not have readily recognized many of them. They were, in the first instance, private letters, written for family and friends, but subsequently published after her death in a heavily edited version by her daughter.

As Jodi Aoki notes, Frances Stewart, having immigrated to Canada from Ireland, was writing for a larger number of recipients than the addressees would indicate. Her letters were meant to be passed around amongst family and friends back home and she may even have had the sense that they would one day reach a larger audience. Frances Stewart clearly did not tell all, but, in spite of some reticence and evident self-censorship, we find a surprising degree of candour in many of the letters. One has the feeling that Frances hoped that her words would reach into the future and that, through those words, some vestige of her life would prevail over time. With the publication of *Revisiting "Our Forest Home"* we are now able to read those letters as they were originally written.

The experiences that Frances Stewart recorded in her letters remind us that women faced every tribulation which could beset the immigrant in a thoroughly alien environment. The exuberance with which Anna Jameson, for example, described Upper Canada can perhaps be accounted for by the fact that she was free to leave after only nine months in the country! Frances Stewart never saw Ireland again. She not only survived, but raised a family, supported an inept though well-meaning husband, oversaw the household, and reproduced, to the best of her ability with the materials at hand, her idea of what a "proper" life should look like.

Her letters describe the tasks which any female immigrant would be faced with: undertaking a plethora of household chores that she had never before attempted, and struggling all the while with the physical and psychological demands of the uncleared Canadian bush, the uncertain Canadian weather, the loneliness. It would be a mistake to gloss over or romanticize the circumstances of the immigrants without seeking to understand something of the trauma of their situation and the sources of strength that they called upon in order to endure the strife and isolation of their new lives. The letters of Frances Stewart help us to do just that.

Letters, daily journals, and diaries served a critical function for the radically dislocated immigrant. Recounting the circumstances of one's utterly changed life can be part of the process of reassessing and reordering one's hopes and fears. In addition to the obvious recording of news, events, and experiences, letters assist in clarifying life for the writer as well as for the reader, particularly when familiar places, spaces, and ties are absent. Memory is captured and recorded; events are recreated. Personal identity, assailed by change, can be claimed and reclaimed. Do we not all hope that our lives will be seen to have had substance and structure, and that our thoughts, fears, beliefs, experiences, opinions, and observations had meaning?

The stories that we tell about ourselves through letters, diaries, poems, works of art, and so forth, can anchor our identity. A coherent narrative of one's life can be constructed by employing bits and pieces of experiences arranged to inform loved ones far away. Letters, like journals and diaries, are both records and memorials, filled with contemplation, happiness, longing, or loss; cathartic, joyous, or morbid. Most immigrant experiences were riven with such competing emotions: longing for the past and hope for the future. Conflicting passions suffuse the letters of Frances Stewart and direct our attention to the circumstances of a life lived between worlds.

Jodi Aoki has worked for twenty years with the Stewart letters held in Trent University Archives. Her passion for understanding the life of Frances Stewart is perfectly understandable. Born and raised less than two hundred kilometres north of the Stewart homestead, she has some intimate knowledge of what a canopy forest, impenetrable underbrush, and stinging insects might have meant to a transplanted European immigrant. And almost two centuries later, it is still possible to understand, as Frances Stewart did, the necessity for self-reliance tempered by an appreciation for the companionship of neighbours.

Ms. Aoki has been able, through painstaking and skillful research, to locate, sort through, and separate from copied and edited correspondence, the original letters written by Frances Stewart, which we are able to read here for the first time. As archival research goes, the task was not an easy one. Original Stewart letters were interspersed with recopied fragments, some of which seem to have been written by Frances herself. Renditions of particular letters with slightly revised wording — additions, or more commonly, omissions — are also inserted into the collection. These reworded letters were written by Frances Stewart's daughter for the first and second editions of *Our Forest Home*.

Jodi Aoki set out to find the "real" Frances Stewart and in this endeavour called on her superior skills in deciphering indistinct postal marks, reading nineteenth-century handwriting, and tracking down leads to other Stewart letters in archival collections in North America and Europe. Determining definitive authorship involved much labour and great dedication to the task — and a good deal of detective work. The documents which Ms. Aoki presents in this volume give us a glimpse of a remarkable woman who was sustained in a difficult situation by her religious faith, female friendship a few miles away, assistance from Aboriginal neighbours, and her enduring hopes for a better future for her children. So far as it is possible to see the past, we may discern in these letters a remark-able woman supporting an invalid husband, raising children, cooking, sewing, reading, and writing in a small cabin in the Canadian bush, not with mere resignation, but with optimism and even humour.

Bernadine Dodge, M.A., Ed.D.
Peterborough, Ontario
2010

PREFACE

Frances Stewart's literary legacy poses a conundrum for readers. While the expansive archival holdings comprise approximately one hundred letters (four hundred if one includes the letters that Frances received from others) and extend over three-quarters of a century, many of the documents attributed to Frances could be considered problematic as they are not all *original* in the conventional sense. Hand-copied variants make up some of the collection. In several cases, the copies have been changed in small or substantial ways and are not in Frances's hand. Still other documents are extracted segments of larger letters or fragments which lack salutation or attribution. Evidence reveals that at least some of this material was created by the recipients of the original letters and sent on to others who had an interest in Frances and her life in Upper Canada. Yet other variants have proved to be the manuscript material prepared by Frances's daughter Ellen Dunlop for her book, *Our Forest Home: Being Extracts from the Correspondence of the Late Frances Stewart*.[1] Journal records dated 1822, documenting the details of the Stewart's trans-Atlantic voyage from Ireland to Upper Canada and their earliest immigrant experiences, further complicate the mix. Frances appears to have referred to these journals when composing the letters that she wrote soon after her family settled in the new world.

Once one has established provenance, the multifarious copies and extracts contribute advantageously to the substance of the historical resource as a whole. All based on the original letters, they present new or alternate detail that reflects the perceptions of those who knew Frances, and thus provide further insights about her. Over time, the copies *and* the originals made their way into the archival mix. The layered compilation presents a complex dynamic and poses not only a tremendous challenge, but also an uncommon opportunity for those attempting to understand the essence of the pioneer's life, especially when considered together with the many letters that Frances received.

As the transcriptions of Frances's letters are integral to *Revisiting "Our Forest Home,"* an explanation regarding my handling of them is necessary. First and foremost, they comprise the primary substance of this volume. Almost all are of original letters, although a few extracts, fragments, and copies have been included (and identified as such) if the subject matter is of considerable importance and is not represented in an original document. The archival source for each letter has been provided in the Notes. Work previously conducted by the late sisters Elizabeth Shearman Hall and Jean Shearman, great-great granddaughters of Frances Stewart, has complemented my transcription efforts and I am enormously indebted to them.[2]

Regarding the transcriptions themselves, they are exact except in Frances's use of punctuation. The multitude of dashes representing commas and periods in Frances's writings have been omitted and replaced with punctuation where appropriate. Capitals have thus also been inserted to indicate the beginnings of new sentences. The result is a text that is more easily read without having compromised meaning or intention. While nothing has been reworded or reordered, sections of letters deemed repetitive or inconsequential have been omitted; these omissions are indicated by ellipses. Likewise, some letters in whole are not included if they are largely similar in content to others that are included. For short forms of words, apostrophes have been supplied in some instances for the purpose of clarification: *Feby* has been changed to *Feb'y* to indicate *February*; *wd* to *w'd* to indicate *would*; *shd* to *sh'd* to indicate *should*; and, *thermr* to *therm'r* to indicate *thermometer*. Likewise, for the sake of consistency, I have provided apostrophes for *dont, cant,* and *wont,* and periods after *Mrs, Mr, Capt,* and *Dr.*

All spelling and grammatical anomalies have been maintained. Examples include *shewed* for *showed*; *&c* for *et cetera.*; *encreased* for *increased*; and *accross* for *across*. Abbreviated words, such as *affect'e, affect', affect'ly,* and *affec't* have all been maintained as in the original to indicate *affectionately*. Frances refers to her daughter(s), Bessie and Bessy, by both spellings. *Tho'* and *tho* both occur frequently, as does *oclock* and *oC*. I have maintained Frances's use of *DV* signifying the Latin *Deo Volente*, which means "God willing," and her non-use of the apostrophe to indicate possessive. Indecipherable words and missing sections of text due to torn or damaged letters are indicated with square brackets.

Readers will note that several letters not represented in *Our Forest Home* a century ago are now included in *Revisiting "Our Forest Home."* Comprised of those that Frances wrote to her friend Catharine Parr Traill, and Catharine's daughter, Annie Atwood, and one highly significant letter to Francis Beaufort, they have since fortuitously been deposited in archival repositories and meaningfully contribute to a plausible (re)construction of their author.

ACKNOWLEDGEMENTS

❦

I wish to thank Barry Penhale, Jane Gibson, Allison Hirst, and all the staff of Dundurn Press for their help and advice during the writing of *Revisiting "Our Forest Home."* It was a pleasure working with them to bring this book to fruition.

I am immensely indebted to Bernadine Dodge and Jim Driscoll, who read drafts of the manuscript and provided useful and constructive commentary. This project would never have been undertaken without Bernadine's unwavering support, encouragement, and enthusiasm, and I thank her from the bottom of my heart. I am grateful, too, to several people who provided me an opportunity to talk about Frances and nineteenth-century immigration during various stages of my research: David Bate, Carole Gerson, Joyce Lewis, Douglas McCalla, Michael Peterman, Joan Sangster, and the late Jean Shearman. I appreciate their insightful comments. From the outset, Carole Gerson and Michael Peterman supported this book idea and I am very grateful to them.

Without the kindness and co-operation of several institutions, this project would not have been possible. I wish to thank a number of people who provided me access to numerous pertinent nineteenth-century documents and permissions to reproduce them where appropriate: Janice Millard of Trent University Archives; Bernadine Dodge, formerly of Trent University Archives; Catherine Hobbs of Library and Archives

Canada; Mary Robertson of The Huntington Library; Tania Henley of the Toronto Public Library, Toronto Reference Library; Ian Montgomery of the Public Record Office of Northern Ireland; and Mary Charles of Peterborough Museum and Archives. Kim Reid, also of Peterborough Museum and Archives, was helpful in providing me access to several Stewart family artifacts, and to her I wish to express special thanks.

Lastly, my family and friends inspired, encouraged, and assisted me in a multitude of ways. To Naomichi Aoki, Naoto Aoki, Yoshi Aoki, Hiromu Aoki, the late Shigeko Aoki, Jim Green, Jim Green Jr., Kevin Green, Senaroun Tamkican, Mavis Amos, Cecilia Castillo, and Enid Gebbett, my love and deepest appreciation!

LIST OF ABBREVIATIONS

❦

LAC — Library and Archives Canada

PRONI — Public Record Office of Northern Ireland

TPL, TRL — Toronto Public Library, Toronto Reference Library

TUA — Trent University Archives

INTRODUCTION

☙☙

Woefully unprepared for an immigrant's life in the Upper Canadian bush, Frances Stewart, aged twenty-eight, left her beloved Ireland for the new world in the year 1822. Her life, spanning from her childhood to emigration and subsequent years in the colony, is revealed in an extraordinary assemblage of correspondence that, fortunately, has survived and been passed along through generations of descendants.

Born in 1794, Frances was raised by a loving and protective cousin in the home of her affluent great-uncle. Highly educated, she received instruction in several fields of study: botany and chemistry, music, Italian and French, contemporary and classical literature, and the Bible. Her extended family included the likes of Sir Francis Beaufort, the British hydrographer and inventor of the Beaufort Wind Force Scale, still in use today, and Maria Edgeworth, the novelist.

Sharing a perspective grounded in the sensibilities of Anglo-Irish Protestantism, Frances was supported and encouraged her entire immigrant life by her well-placed family and friends through their transatlantic shipment of letters, newspapers, religious volumes, and books of literature. Despite the physical separation, these writings provided her with a crucial sense of comfort, although she was sometimes in despair trying to find time to read them. She felt anxious, especially during the early immigrant years, about her children's education and their spiritual development. Believing that structured lessons and Church of England indoctrination

Thomas Alexander Stewart (1786-1847). Original is an oil portrait on ivory created by miniaturist Hoppner Francis Meyer assumedly prior to Tom's departure for Upper Canada in 1822.

(Source: Portrait of Thomas A. Stewart 1974.24.1. Courtesy Peterborough Museum and Archives.
Artifact photographed by Yoshi Aoki.)

were elemental to their futures, Frances worried that the absence of schools and churches would compromise her ability to raise her children as she and her husband, Tom,[1] aspired to do.

As she departed Ireland with Tom and their three young daughters, Frances could not have imagined the life before her. For the fifty years that followed her emigration, loneliness most of all was a close companion, and until her death in 1872, she was absorbed by memories of her past, holding on desperately to nostalgic recollections of her Irish loved ones.

The Stewarts were accompanied from Ireland by their two servants and Tom's sister's family. After arriving in Upper Canada, they resided for several months in Cobourg while Tom arranged for a land grant along the shore of the Otonabee River in Douro Township. On the evening of February 11, 1823, they moved into their new log home just north of the settlement that was to become Peterborough in the District of Newcastle.

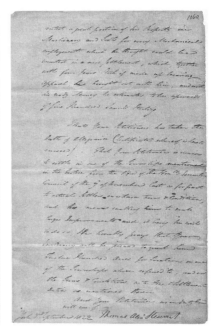

"*Land Grant for Thomas Alexander Stewart, York, 1822*"—
Tom's petition for a land grant of 1200 acres in Upper Canada.
For full transcription, see Appendix 1.

(Source: Executive Council Office of the Province of Upper Canada fonds RG 1 L 3, Vol. # 461, Bundle # S 13, Petition # 106, Microfilm # C-2814. Courtesy Library and Archives Canada.)

Despite the excitement and the intense relief at having finally settled after several months in transit, Frances was deeply unnerved by the step they had taken, and her thoughts were clouded by a pervasive sense of longing. She attests:

My own mind & heart were agonized with the constant dread of our taking this great leap. I did suffer more about this than about any other thing that ever happened, for who could help dreading such a step, so very doubtful in its consequences, besides the idea of leaving so many I loved so tenderly & knowing how much the step was disapproved of by those I valued & respected most. But I could not help feeling that Tom was right & I plainly

saw where "Duty" pointed so I tryed to smother every
other feeling but no one can tell the pangs I suffered. Oh
the bitter pang when I last parted from you all so dear &
from dear dear Merrion St. But why am I going over it all.
I am a fool.[2]

This passage represents a theme that was to weave through all
Frances's writings in the years that followed her immigration.

I first became aware of Frances in 1990 when I began working at Trent
University Archives where, thanks to the generosity of her descendants,
approximately four hundred letters that she either wrote or received were
deposited. While the fragile original documents generate interest among
researchers, much more has been made of the versions of the letters that
appear in the book *Our Forest Home: Being Extracts from the Correspondence
of the Late Frances Stewart*, compiled and published in 1889, and in a second edition in 1902, both edited by Frances's daughter Ellen Dunlop.

I was interested to learn that *Our Forest Home* was viewed with some
skepticism because of Ellen's editing decisions. I rather see the book as a
valuable textual artifact in its own right and a direct link to a real past life,
or rather, two past lives — Frances's and Ellen's — despite the evidence that
the letters were substantively altered by a loving and protective daughter.
Through the course of my work at the university I became increasingly
interested in the original letters and their multifarious layers and, understanding that they represent a remarkable testament to immigrant experience and a hitherto untapped resource, I undertook this study of them.

Frances's life may be loosely defined by three principal periods. The
first of these, the years of her childhood in Ireland until the time of her
departure for North America (1794–1822), is examined in Part One; the
second, her voyage across the Atlantic and her life in Upper Canada to
the time of her husband's death in 1847 (1822–1847), in Part Two; and
the third, the period of widowhood in Upper Canada until her own death
in 1872 (1847–1872), in Part Three. Each part includes, along with the

Introduction

Ellen Dunlop (1819–1907).

A page from Frances Stewart's letter to Harriet Beaufort, December 14, 1840.

33

transcriptions of letters, a contextualized overview of factors and contingencies that shaped that period of Frances's life. The overviews draw on letters written to Frances, including those from her friends and relatives in Ireland, her children in later years, and her dear friend Catharine Parr Traill. Such extraneous material, rich in detail and innuendo, provides context and contributes significantly to the reconstruction of Frances's life.

Frances's letters include details of her early years in Ireland and suggest a stark contrast between her pre-emigration experience and the life of emotional turmoil that she would eventually lead in the new world. They offer insight about her feelings and the day-to-day activities that she chose to divulge: her efforts to manage the household despite her inexperience; her worries about Tom and his general malaise; her concerns about her children's education and their futures; her interest in the Aboriginals who visited her home; her interactions with the servants; and her observations of the physical landscape about her and its comparison to the homeland. All these activities represented struggle as Frances endeavoured against all odds to maintain a genteel perspective in the forest. Her descriptions of her environment, both social and physical, clearly suggest that Frances's interests were focused on a cultured future rather than on one that merely guaranteed a material existence.

While emigration may be experienced as an opportunity to start a new life, it is obvious that Frances faced acute instability after arriving in the new world. Historian David Gerber, in examining the correspondence of nineteenth-century European immigrants, concludes that emigration particularly compromises feelings of continuity. He writes:

> Emigration puts a singular strain on personal identity, because it is a radical challenge to continuity. It may set individuals adrift by sundering their relationships to places, things, and people. Not only does it remove, if only for a time, practical, material, and psychological sources of support, but it also disrupts the emigrant's own self-awareness, for it is through this continuous relationship to places, things, and above all, to other people, that we know ourselves.[3]

Gerber claims that "immigrants have always risked a radical rupture of the self, a break in their understandings of who they are."[4] In light of this claim, it is significant to note that immigrant writings often reveal an interesting slippage between their authors' actual lived experience and how their memory transformed that experience in subsequent years. People's stories about themselves are often shaped by their *perceptions* of their pasts. As historian Bernadine Dodge argues, "Reconstructing the past from memory, text, or image, requires a narrative — a reconceptualizing of events and experiences to make them sensible, rational, coherent, and frequently to make past events serve a contemporary moralizing purpose."[5]

The study of immigrant letters is further complicated by the fact that authors, according to Jennifer Douglas and Heather MacNeil, "conceal and edit the self,"[6] omitting details and purposefully interchanging fact and fiction in accounts of their lives. Thus, past lives can never be definitively interpreted. The determination of meaning is compromised by a variety of factors, not least of which is that words are already imbued with ambiguity and nuance, rendering the examination of them complex and conditional. The difficulty of analysis is compounded again by the fact that there is no place from which to stand outside one's own life and context when examining another. Even with the late modern loss of confidence in objectivity, however, we can, with care and attention to context, study the past and explore its informative, redemptive, and enlightening possibilities while acknowledging that we can never unequivocally reconstruct an accurate past.

Archival research presents many challenges. While *Revisiting "Our Forest Home"* provides insight about the life of one Upper-Canadian immigrant, it recognizes that language, represented in the case of Frances through her writings, is governed by rules set by society and that different forms of consciousness are, in fact, regulated by historical circumstances. Words, such as those found in letters and diaries, in and of themselves, do not reveal the *truth*. Elements of history and the realities of people's lives affect and determine the variances of meaning that can be taken from any word or group of words. Historian Joan Sangster maintains, "While it is important to analyze the way in which someone constructs an explanation for her life, ultimately there are patterns, structures, and systemic reasons for these constructions which must be identified to understand historical causality."[7] In *Revisiting "Our Forest Home,"* while I examine Frances's immediate experiences, I also look at factors and contingencies such as class, gender, and ethnicity that affected her life, remembering Sangster's caution that "we do not want to lose sight of the totality of the historical picture."[8]

For nineteenth-century women immigrants, societal constraints imposed limitations on the way they thought about themselves and, thus, on the way they expressed themselves in their writings. Their letters and diaries and journals by their nature are more than just autobiographical and self-conscious representations. They are tied to the creation and pronouncement of identity. During the nineteenth century, such writings were an outlet for the expression of sentiments, worries, and ambitions. They provided a physical and tangible medium through which to fashion a personal storyline, allowing for the sometimes painful construction or reconstruction of the writers' sense of who they were and how they now saw themselves.

British sociologist Anthony Giddens believes that the act of writing helps to maintain a coherent narrative through periods of transition, and suggests, insightfully, that "a person's identity is [found] ... in the capacity *to keep a particular narrative going*."[9] As a matter of survival, keeping a "narrative going" was critical for Upper-Canadian immigrants, and the transatlantic exchange of letters, while providing a sense of continuity and shared community, helped in this regard by easing the transition to a new life. That Frances's letters provided her with immense comfort and a medium through which she could feel connected to loved ones is revealed in one succinctly stated testament. Her audience clearly defined, she writes, "I am always happy when I can write my letters at night for then I am with my friends."[10] The notion that Frances was driven by a nostalgic desire to retain the tenuous connections between past and present is substantiated by the large number of letters that she wrote.

It is conceivable that Frances, being one of the earliest women immigrants to arrive in the area, would have anticipated her letters becoming an important record for posterity; perhaps their composition was coloured by such forethought. Indeed, shortly after her immigration, Frances's relatives

Territory inhabited by the Stewarts, Reids, and Traills during the nineteenth century in the Peterborough region

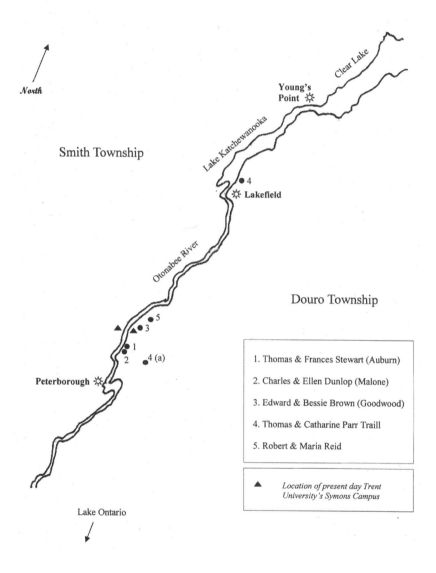

1. Thomas & Frances Stewart (Auburn)

2. Charles & Ellen Dunlop (Malone)

3. Edward & Bessie Brown (Goodwood)

4. Thomas & Catharine Parr Traill

5. Robert & Maria Reid

▲ *Location of present day Trent University's Symons Campus*

The Stewarts, Reids, and Traills in Upper Canada.

and friends in Ireland did impress upon her the importance of her letters and they broached the subject of publishing them. Their publication was never realized, however, until her daughter Ellen undertook the project several years after Frances's death. That Ellen was inspired by Catharine Parr Traill's several publishing successes is certain. Catharine had come to know Frances upon arriving in Upper Canada in 1832, living with the Stewarts for the first few months and becoming a life-long friend of the family. Several fondly written letters between Catharine and Frances and between Catharine and Ellen exist in archival holdings, establishing the close relationships between the women. Indeed, *Our Forest Home* includes a loving memorial about Frances that was written by the renowned author.

In addition to Frances and her friend Catharine Parr Traill, several other nineteenth-century British female immigrants — Susanna Moodie, Harriet Pengelley, Isabella Miller, and Anne Langton — also contributed to Peterborough's rich legacy of diaries, letters, and journals. Providing glimpses of their lives and experiences, the textual evidence attests that, faced with surviving — or not — these women learned how to cope and adapt to their lives in the colony, almost without exception. Immigrant women of the period had to assume positions of strength rather than weakness if they and their families were to survive. Frances knew at her core that her ability to cope was critical to the family's success in their new world. Stoic and principled, she could not give up. Through time assuming a position of quiet autonomy, Frances came to be deeply respected in the wider community as is evidenced in all external references to her. In Peterborough, many immigrants who believed they were elite were actually struggling to survive for many years after their arrival; unlike Kingston and York during the first half of the nineteenth century, Peterborough was not a centre of political or economic power.

In presenting Frances Stewart's letters in their original format, *Revisiting "Our Forest Home"* provides evidentiary testimony of early colonial experience in Canada. Through one female immigrant's letters, readers are accorded the opportunity to examine a nineteenth-century life and to consider it in the larger context of a nation's expansion during its formative years.

Part 1

❦

Ireland: The First Chapter in the Life of Frances Stewart,
1794–1822

Frances Browne was born in Ireland in 1794, at the onset of the Napoleonic Wars. The child of Reverend Francis Browne and Anna Maria Noble, Frances encountered sudden misfortune at the early age of two when her father died. In the interests of her daughter, Frances's mother, an invalid with little means to support her family, handed her over to the custody of a great-uncle. Till her marriage to Tom Stewart in 1816, Frances lived in Allenstown, County Meath, in mid-eastern Ireland, with Robert Waller, the affluent Anglo-Irish great-uncle. An older sister, Catherine, continued to live with their mother until Anna Maria's death in 1809, residing primarily in Bath in the home of her mother's sister, while another sibling, Maria, died an infant.

It seems curious that after Frances went to live with the Waller family, she and her mother may never have seen each other again, although a loving relationship is evident in their exchange of letters. Though both are known to have travelled to some extent during these years, the letters suggest that their plans to visit with each other may never have come to fruition. Whatever the case, it is Harriet Beaufort, a niece of Robert Waller who lived in his home as housekeeper, who figured most prominently in Frances's life prior to her marriage, becoming mother, mentor, and governess to her distant cousin. For more than sixty years, Harriet regarded Frances as a daughter and continued to counsel her through a succession of letters long after the two were parted forever when Frances left for Upper Canada.

Although eventually isolated from the learned relatives and friends who had shaped the course of her life, Frances continued to be influenced by their associations through all her immigrant years. Harriet's brother, Sir Francis Beaufort, was a father-like figure to her; accolades bestowed on him included having the Beaufort Sea named in his honour and receiving an honorary doctorate at Oxford alongside William Wordsworth. Harriet's brother-in-law, Richard Edgeworth, was a founding member of the Royal Irish Academy who organized plays and other literary activities for his nineteen children, including Maria Edgeworth, who became a well-known author. Frances began her commonplace book[1] while on a visit to the Edgeworth's and continued to write poems and literary excerpts in it for decades after she immigrated. Harriet, herself a published author, was well educated, and raised her charge in a

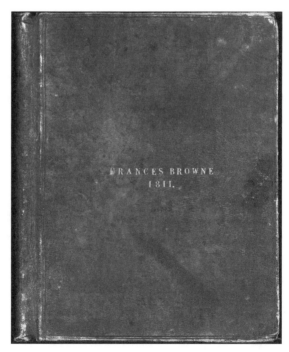

Frances Stewart's commonplace book, 1811.

(Source: Stewart family books 98-005. Courtesy Trent University Archives.)

manner and style that reflected her Anglo-Irish protestant sensibilities. Staunchly attentive, her letters to Frances reflect a caring individual of rigorous and authoritative temperament. She writes in one letter:

> Take care every day to be <u>attentive</u> & <u>considerate</u> … I hope you adhere to the custom of reading a little French or Italian after they leave the parlour after dinner…. Be steady about the time that you know ought to be devoting to acquiring knowledge … You are shockingly lazy … I suppose when you have done the *Iliad* you will be glad to continue the thread in the *Odyssy* … I wish you to … succeed in whatever you attempt — which you are perfectly equal to with a little regular perseverance.[2]

Others, too, took responsibility for ensuring that Frances received an upbringing to match their expectations. In a letter dated 1805, Francis Beaufort seems to have found grounds to admonish the eleven-year-old for acting impertinently, suggesting perhaps that Frances had indeed been spoiled as a result of having been sheltered and catered to by so many. He writes, "I have learned from various people, some of whom you may guess, that as you grow up and as your mind opens you increase in a certain quality called <u>Pertness,</u> this my dear little girl is what occasions me so much unhappiness at present, and if it was only to lessen that and thereby to oblige me I am sure you will endeavour to conquer this very bad habit."[3]

Frances had also been the cause of another type of worry during this period, although this time not of her own doing; on a trip to Dublin to have teeth extracted in the year 1804, she witnessed the now-famous Dublin Riots that were taking place in the streets, but came to no harm. There is little doubt that such an experience would have left a deep impression on a youngster just ten years of age.

It was on a visit to the home of her mother's sister, Susannah Noble, in 1816, that Frances met Tom, who had just returned from a tour of mainland Europe. Tom was related to Frances's aunt through marriage and was joint owner with his brother, John Stewart, of a linen and cotton

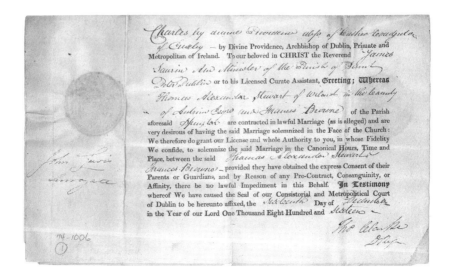

Marriage licence of Thomas Alexander Stewart and Frances Browne, 1816.

(Source: Frances Stewart fonds 74-1006. Courtesy Trent University Archives.)

manufacturing business, White Abby Mills,[4] which they had inherited from their father. He and Frances were married that same year. Anna Maria, the first of the couple's eleven children, was one of three born to them prior to their departure for Upper Canada. Anna Maria was born in 1817, Ellen in 1819, and Bessie in 1821.

Converging difficulties led to Tom's decision to emigrate from Ireland. Just a few years earlier, in 1815, as the Napoleonic War came to a close, much of Europe had become entrenched in an economic depression, resulting in a severe decline in the domestic linen industry and the impoverishment of the general population. These factors, along with the alleged destructive gambling habits of Tom's brother, John, are believed to have contributed to the 1821 demise of the family business. Faced with the reality of their straightened circumstances, Tom felt that emigrating would ensure the family's survival and independence, and he knew that he would be eligible to receive a large grant of land from the British government in the colony. Though he was lame from a childhood accident, and thereby compromised in his ability to do strenuous physical labour, he was comfortable in the knowledge that his able-bodied brother-in-law and former bookkeeper of White Abby Mills, Robert Reid, was planning to emigrate with him. Robert and his boys, ages nineteen, eight, and five, would help Tom clear his land and build his first log home. The Stewarts left Ireland despite the great misgivings of their families and friends. In later years Tom confided to Basil Hall that they made the decision to emigrate out of duty to their children.[5]

That the Stewarts were ill-prepared for the venture ahead of them can be easily concluded from an examination of the pre-emigration letters that Frances wrote, those during her childhood and adolescence, and in the months leading up to her family's departure from Ireland. Although they are few in number, the extant letters of this period provide a backdrop for understanding the difficult immigrant experience that their author endured. As would be the case in any human life, the circumstances of Frances's earliest years precipitated her values, judgments, and perceptions later on. There is much evidence to suggest that her privileged past coloured her views of the new world and, by association, her representations of her thoughts and feelings in her letters written over the fifty years that followed her immigration.

THE LETTERS

[1810]: May 16[6]
To Harriet Beaufort, Edgeworthstown, Ireland

[*an exercise of poetry preceded the letter proper*]

My dearest Harriet — As you desired me I wrote a little exercise to you but I think it foolish to write them in my letters because when you come home you will see every one that I write while you are away and therefore I think it foolish to fill up my paper with them. I was going to write to you last Friday but Bess said she wanted to write about business to you so now you see I have got a large sheet as you desired. I believe that when you desired me to buy Si: Di: you forgot that Anne Nangle has them all. So I have read the first con: on Gal: I myself tryed the experiment of putting a piece of lead under my tongue & a piece of silver over it & I perceived the change of taste immediately and very strongly....

Bess says she will buy the Ed: Review. She says also that she has a mind not to subscribe to it any more but to buy the numbers here for the expense is exactly the same. What do you think of this? Do you never walk in the evening? I have slept for these four days till past eight, but I assure you I try to be industrious & I am <u>always</u> down at the first bell as you desired me. When I get up I read my chapter (I am now in the 2d book of Samuel) then I dress quick, & as I never have fire you may suppose I am cold. So when I have written some Geo: I come down & read Plut: or Gal: or Spu: till the first bell rings & then I cut the bread & butter & after breakfast I practice as usual. When that is done I write & read & walk & eat & work & dress till dinner after which I water the Garden & walk & tea & play & bed or supper sometimes. Now you desired me in your last letter to Bess not to increase my practising but you know you told me your self that I might play half an hour longer. In general I play two hours & a half but one day when I was particularly anxious I did three, but only one day. Mr. Warren says I am improving. My Aunt made me play for [Dean] [William] Allot yesterday. He said I played very well & he came again <u>to hear me</u> but I was out. Warren asked me today whether I had played for him & when he heard I had he said he would ask him his <u>real</u> opinion of me. So I know I shall never have the satisfaction of knowing his real opinion for I think Mr. W. won't tell me. We have bought a nice good Piano forte from him & sent off the old one. Poor Mrs. Waller has, or rather is, sending me over two fine Lessons by Mr. Wm Waller. We are to go to Christ Church next Sunday again for the second time since you went. Poor Mr. Jager has been extremely ill so <u>dear</u> little Robinson supplied his place wonderfully last Sunday. I understood every word quite easily & liked it very much & heard an excellent sermon from Dean Allot. Do you know that there are a great many sweet peas up in our Garden & a great deal of Mignonette & the Siberian Larkspur has a bunch of buds. Bess says she asked two or three book sellers about the books & they all said they could do nothing or say nothing till they saw them....

I don't see any one, not even shop girls, wearing spencers so you know I have a piece of blue calico quite new & nice & it would make me

a very nice [ ] covered with a bit of muslin. A quarter of a yard of spot-
ted muslin would do very well & would not cost more than two yards of
cambric muslin for a spencer would do. Bess & I agreed this would be
better than a white spencer but nothing was to be done without asking
you. Answer this very soon. I have not a particle of cold & I always wear
my Velvet spencer. Good bye. Your own dear child, Fanny.

Write very soon.

Dinner is on the table so forgive scribble & the bad direction.

Bess wants to know what she is to do with Miss Quinns Handkerchief.

[1810]: July 3[7]
To Harriet Beaufort, Collon, Ireland

July 2nd–3d I mean
finished 4th

My dearest Harriet

I really do thank you greatly for your nice kind long letter and for all your
advice which you seem to be a little afraid of my not thanking you for. But
I know I always want advice & I like to have you give it to me. I feel so
odd without any one to advise or order me & I am sure I hope I am doing
without <u>orders</u> as you my dearest Moome wish me. But pray don't be too
sanguine & expect too much for then when you come you will be <u>woefully
disappointed</u>. I know I have been very idle whilst Lou was here but I don't
think I could have done much more. Now do pray imagine that I have done
hardly any thing and you will judge when you come whether you were right
or wrong. Very often when I began a letter to you I had determined to write
only very little at a time but some times when <u>they</u> saw me writing to you
they gave me things to tell you which obliged me to send it to you that day,
& at other times I got so <u>deep</u> in what I was telling you that I ran on without
considering. Now for the questions. 1st — it was in Percivals Ceylon that
we read the account of the Ichneumon, at least I believe & think so. 2 — It
was that every new language we acquire is like another eye.…

I admire Ellen, dear Ellen. I think the description of her amusement at the strangers awkwardness in rowing her little boat is very well

described. There were a good many parts which I unluckily missed when they were reading it out, but I intend to read it whilst the Society Lady is here & then I will tell you my full opinion. I think some of the, indeed, all the descriptions, are beautiful & I think Scott shines in description. I have at last very nearly finished the Lay which you may remember I began before you went away at the corner of the card table. As I don't sit there now I read it when I can between the first & second dinner bells. I admire it (if possible) more than ever. It comes first, Lady next & Marmion next. I intend to read Marmion again whilst I have the other two fresh in my memory. We, at least, I am greatly entertained with dear Ld. Nelson. I hear very little but what I do I like. He mentions Francises friend Hillyers & praises him <u>immensely</u>.

Oh! dear Harriet, I wish you joy of dearest Francis, both for his promotion & his prospects of (I hope) future domestic happiness. Is Miss Wilson pretty in her face. I know her figure is like Miss O'Beirnes. I suppose you have heard of Kitty Staples's choice. Bess Ruxton is very busy buying her wedding cloathes. Every body seems to me to know it for Mrs. O'Beirne mentioned today in a letter to Mrs. Waller and Miss Savage talked quite freely of it to us & all the Rosstown people seem to know it too. Mr. Barry is to be in town tomorrow to settle all his affairs & they are to be married at Rosstown as soon as possible. <u>Mrs. Ford</u> & all are in love with Mr. Barry. Margaret Barry is going to be married to a Captain Ammery of her brothers regiment. Tell Louise the backs of the Card cases are 10 ½ inches long by 3 ¾ broad, the pockets 2 ½ inches deep by 3 ¾ long. We have a fine patch of Mignonette blown in our garden & a good deal more coming. Every rose tree has three or four buds so I am at last convincing Bess that something will grow in it. My sweet peas are improving. Our Rockets are out of blow now. They were not quite to be despised. If I could once arrive at weeding up all the grass it would be very nice. Ask Uncle Beaufort what we are to do with Wms great umbrella. I will take care of his hat & coat. I am a goose — you need not ask him about the umbrella — I know he is to take it.

Love to all from your own child,

Frances Browne.

Bess is better. So is Anne.

[1816]: March 14[8]
To Harriet Beaufort, Collon, Ireland

Thursday March 14th

My dear Harriet

Now this is my third letter to you & you have written but one to me. I have been in expectation of one these two days. As you asked me to tell you every thing that I do I will now. I could not before as I was in such a hurry for my black petticoat for the ball that I could do nothing else. However, <u>Monday</u>, Catharine & I became very industrious again. I was up at 7. I had intended to practice before breakfast but as the drawing room was not done out I could not. So I sat down to read some of the fairy tales & just as I had found a dictionary & settled myself I was called to breakfast at ten minutes past 8. When I went down they were all there but the urn had not come yet so I sat down to read some of a pretty little story called "Education — or a Journal of Errors" which Aunt Susan begged me to read. I read it till breakfast immediately after which I went to play & that occupied one hour of my day, till about ten. I then wrote a letter to Aunt Rachel & walked in the garden till near one. We then went [on] a most <u>charmingly dirty</u> walk to the archdeaconry. We saw Mrs. De Lacy. Poor Mrs. Montray was ill with bile. By the time we got home again it was near three. I did more of my petticoat & read a little <u>mouthful</u> of "<u>Novelle Morali</u>" before dinner. After dinner Catharine, Bessy & I always retire to the drawing room. That is where we have sat a little while. Then Catharine & Bessy make me play all the waltzes, tunes & dances that I ever had for them. Then we go down to tea & after tea work or read till 10 oclock when we go to bed. I have been teaching Bessy music every day. When I have done playing I give her a lesson. She is learning a great long one of [Keyels] now which she began with [ ]. She plays very well indeed for so young a child. She is a nice little girl. Catharine draws every day. So have I these three days. She has some very good pencil things & sketches of [F-] which she has lent me to copy. At any rate they will teach me boldness for they are very bold. Now my [ ] Aunt Susan bids me lay a case before you viz: — she has the books for Kate & me. There are some very valuable she says & a number of imperfect sets & odd volumes not very valuable. Now, she says that they must be equally divided & that if we were to draw lots for them one might get all the valuable books & the other all the others. So Aunts Susan & Sutton said they w'd ask you & that perhaps you would be able to start a good method of dividing them. I have a list; shall I send it to you in my next letter? There is a beautiful edition of the *Spectator* I hear. I have not seen any of them yet as they are all locked up. Poor little Bessy has been plagued with headaches but she has taken some Calomel today & I think it will cure her. She & I have been very busy all day making crosses for Sunday.

Yesterday I saw Ellinor Wade. She came to see Mrs. Webb who lives next door you know. So she went out to the garden & we were all working in our garden & we had a great deal of conversation over the paling. She looks very well & not at all in low spirits. They are to go to England very soon but the time is not fixed as they must have an auction before they go. Mrs. Montray is quite well again & walked here yesterday with Mrs. De Lacy & Mrs. Tisdall who is staying at the Archdeaconry whilst her "caro sposo" is at the assizes. She asked me whether Mrs. Pilkingtons Moral Tales were ever published to which she subscribed long ago — answer this. Mrs. Montray bid me give her love to you all.

Aunt Susan has had a letter from Mrs. Stewart putting her in mind of her promise to go there in summer & so she gave me a most pressing & kind invitation to go too. What am I to say. If you go to Wicklow I will positively not go any where else — answer this too.

We have had two delightful days & have taken great long walks & I worked one whole day in the garden. Indeed I try not to be idle & to please you & every body. Uncle Sutton has had a very heavy cold but is better. I saw a house butterfly yesterday for the first time. What are you reading out & to yourself. Catharine heard from Aunt Rachel a few days ago. Poor old Uncle Latouche has been very ill but is better. Do now my dear creature write soon & answer all my questions — & about Mrs. Harrison — her name was Gale & she is mother to [ ] Allen. Pray say how Aunt Beauforts side is particularly. I have written out two tunes. They are very short. Tell me all about the Edgeworths &c. Where do Wm. & Emma go. Give my love to them & the children & to every one, not forgetting my [loves]. I forgot to ask Mrs. Martley about Susan but I will remember it next time.

Good bye my love — your own daughter from [F-] Fatlips

I try to hold up my head & never sit cross legs, not bite my lips. Did you see the thing in the newspaper about the flannel petticoat. Miss Vernon saw the whole thing & it was not the cleanest petticoat. She was at the castle that night.

1822: April 26[9]
To Honora Edgeworth, Edgeworthstown, Ireland

26 April 1822

My very dear Honora

We are now emerged in to the bustle of preparations for our departure which probably will take place about the middle of May. And you may suppose that all our ideas are in requisition to know what will be the most necessary provisions as to food & clothing for so large a party & during so long a passage, for I may call our progress up the river & Lake Ontario a part of our voyage or passage. We have 19 individuals belonging to our own party besides a family of six who are going along with us. This is the family of a sort of groom & labourer who has lived with Mr. Reid for above twenty years & who has actually saved enough of money within the last two years to enable him now to accompany his dear Master without being one Shilling expense to us. His wife was housemaid here & they have 4 fine little children. He says he could not live here after his master had left this place. Our party consists of 4 parents 12 children & 3 servants, one a young man & two girls, for women servants, grown up, are very useless & unprofitable in America as they require immense wages & do little or no work....

And now my dear Honora I must beg you will give my most affectionate love to all my dear friends, at home & abroad, if they care for me, & ever believe me

your affect' friend

F. Stewart.

Part 2

❦

Upper Canada: Immigration and Genteel Experience
in the Canadian Bush, 1822–1847

To the great advantage of the Stewarts, the British government, in attempting to address the problem of its excess officer complement in the aftermath of the Napoleonic Wars, was offering grants of land to those willing to move to Upper Canada. The War of 1812 had also long been over and there was concern that the resulting movement of United Empire Loyalists northward into Upper Canada from America was creating an unstable cultural situation that required monitoring. At particular issue was the notion that the migrating population, not all being of British stock, might pose a threat, even though, by all appearances, they were supporters of the British Crown. This perception of threat reinforced the desire of the British government to establish selected families in the developing colony.

At the same time in Europe and again to the advantage of the Stewarts, "a paternalistic style"[1] of gentry was becoming the established norm. This was a style that many believed would also suitably fit the bill in Upper Canada and the leadership roles were indeed taken up by educated and elite male settlers. Opportunistic, they set about instituting their own customs and manners and aspired to create country estates imitating those owned by the lesser landowners of Britain. Michael Wagner notes that the men considered most trusted to become the principal leaders were "retired officers on half-pay and gentlemen of moderate or fixed income whose status were endangered by a declining standard of living as a result of the post-war depression."[2]

Tom Stewart, a gentleman of a refined and cultured social class, represented the latter group. As a result of a letter of introduction to Lieutenant-Governor Maitland from the colonial secretary, Lord Bathurst, with whom Tom had a personal association through Frances's family connections, he was granted 1,200 acres on the east shore of the Otonabee River in Douro Township. In explaining the manner in which such a connection could effect a land deal of this magnitude, Selena Crosson writes, that "there was little demarcation between the 'personal' and the 'professional' in the colony" and that the "government functioned through the recommendations of 'friendly' acquaintances."[3] Frances, for her part, was heir to a small inheritance, paid out as annual stipends, and with this income to sustain them until such time as they could make a secure living in the new world, the family set out for Upper Canada.

On June 1, 1822, a contingent of 118 emigrants boarded the brigantine *George* at Belfast en route to the new world. Onboard ship with Frances and Tom were their daughters, Anna Maria, Ellen, and Bessie, their two servants, and Tom's sister's family, the Reids, along with their children and servants. It would still be three years before Peter Robinson, commissioner of crown lands, directed the first of two mass emigrations of Irish working-class immigrants to the Peterborough region. The family dog, Cartouche, also accompanied the family and took up a position amongst their several trunks of bedding, dishes, cutlery, candlesticks, farming implements, nails, and books, including an entire set of Shakespeare's plays.

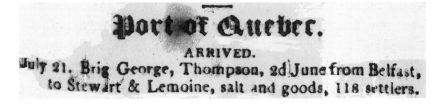

Arrival of the brigatine George in Quebec, 1822. Montreal Gazette, July 27, 1822: 3.

Pitcher.

Chamber pot.

Bowl.

Cup and saucer.

Plate.

Frances Stewart's brooch. A bog oak brooch carved with shamrocks and the words The Chosen Leaf.

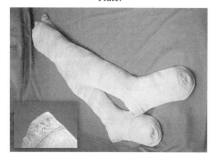

Frances Stewart's stockings. Note the embroidered date, 1816, the year of Frances's marriage to Tom, and the initials F.B. (Frances Browne).

Stewart family artifacts. Some of the family artifacts were donated to Peterborough Museum and Archives by descendents while others were located during an archaeological dig of the Stewart premises in 1973.

(Courtesy Peterborough Museum and Archives. Artifacts photographed by Yoshi Aoki.)

The voyage to Upper Canada from Ireland immediately presented Frances with a backdrop profoundly different from that under which the genteel immigrant had been raised. Sleeping arrangements aboard ship meant that she would share her cabin with her three daughters and the maid, while Tom took a cabin with the Reid family. Frances seems to have liked these arrangements, writing, "I am very comfortable here & quite independent & though I have only room to stand up & dress myself I am much happier than if we were all together."[4]

Frances suffered chronic asthma and headaches, and may have carefully arranged for the most comfortable crossing possible. Seasickness, however, was a matter not so easily accommodated. She notes in a letter, "We are beginning to rock about so much that I must stop writing. Though not sick, I have had some bad headaches & am sometimes stupefied & unable to fix my eyes on anything."[5]

Frances's acknowledgement of the class issues she encountered en route is revealed in her offhand comment that the captain is "just what you might expect to find a person who was raised from being a common sailor,"[6] although she tempers this criticism by recognizing that he "is anxious to pay us every attention in his power & is very good natured to the children."[7]

That Frances perceived herself a member of an elite class is obvious. According to Marilyn Silverman, "status-class hierarchy underlay people's experiences, forming the bedrock of their common sense, their individual consciousness, and their personal and collective perceptions."[8] Frances may have eventually acquiesced to the fact that her social space was to be encroached upon by more plebeian elements, although a short time after settling in Upper Canada she commented in one letter that at least in having contact with such gentry as the Rubidges,[9] she "need not entirely give up Society."[10] Through time, Frances sometimes did set foot across murky class borders, however, writing, for example, a long and newsy letter later in life to her former servant, Betty, tenderly inviting the widow to return to Canada from Ireland. She offered to pay her passage and told Betty that William, her son, would grant her a place in his home to care for his "chickens and children."[11] Frances had a long-standing companionable relationship with Betty and she sought to ensure financial stability for the newly widowed woman in her later years through finding her a station, a solution that would also benefit the interests of William.

Nineteenth-century immigrants, through necessity, often found themselves in association with classes of people with which they would not have associated in a like manner in the home country; boundaries were inevitably crossed. Depending on each other for basic survival, and sometimes for companionship and friendship, immigrants shared many of the same primary responsibilities and experienced aspects of pioneer life in comparable fashion, regardless of class or economic circumstance. The women became pregnant, gave birth, nursed, and nurtured. As wives and mothers, they were caregivers; they ran households, carried out strenuous and repetitive daily tasks both inside and outside the home, and they shared the joys and sorrows associated with bearing children and raising a family.

Despite the commonalities, however, at her core, Frances held tightly to views that differentiated her from those she considered to be of a lower class, a fact that is affirmed in several of her letters. A case in point is her references to the Aboriginals, whom she found "inoffensive people and very lazy."[12] Such literary representations about her adopted land reveal obvious built-in preconceptions and prejudices[13] and exemplify the prevailing Romantic notion that Aboriginals were aesthetic accoutrements to European civilization. According to W.J. Keith, "immigrants and travellers brought with them built-in cultural attitudes and assumptions, set ways of looking at the land and 'landscape.'"[14] Displaying the then-current Eurocentric racial discourse, her comments seem based more on her observation of a landscape that included Aboriginals, and whose lives and habits she found utterly alien and uncivilized.

Having been raised in the company of relatives who had invested a great deal in her education, Frances was aware that her depictions of the flora and fauna would be keenly received in Ireland. Her knowledge of botany allowed her to make reasonably reliable scientific observations and vivid accounts of her surroundings intersperse her writings. Indeed, the comparisons that she made with species of animals and birds and plants in her homeland may have contributed to a sense of connection with the land and people that she left behind. A few years after she arrived in Upper Canada, Harriet and Maria Edgeworth entertained the idea of publishing Frances's astonishing descriptions of her new life, but decided against doing so on the grounds that this would constitute an invasion of Frances's privacy.[15]

After a stay of several months in Cobourg in a house which was "as nasty & inconvenient a little cage inside as ever was,"[16] the Stewarts moved to the yet-to-be-surveyed township of Douro, approximately forty kilometres north of Cobourg. They arrived at their unfinished log house by horse and sleigh on the night of February 11, 1823. The letters reveal that, during the early years, even though they faced enormous challenges, the family at least had access to several varieties of food, many of which would have been unavailable to most other settlers. Frances writes that the merchant son of Mrs. Bethune[17] of Cobourg had taken it upon himself to help her family by ensuring ready access to a commercial supply of imported foods under his authority.

This important class connection had implications for the level of comfort that the Stewarts were able to attain. That Frances and Tom had the means to purchase food, especially in the years before they were able to provide for themselves adequately through farming, was critical to their survival. Frances refers to local purchases of barley, rice, potatoes, beef, mutton, bacon, buttermilk, milk, and bread.[18] Faunal remains found during an archaeological dig directed by Mary Lucyk Heaman in 1973 of the initial log house confirm pork, beef, fowl, and wildlife consumption.[19] The family was well off by pioneer standards, having had the means from the very beginning to augment their food supply. They also requested imported food directly from Ireland and this was sent to them by relatives in the annual commissions. Further supplements included venison and fish acquired through trade with the Aboriginals, as well as additional farm produce obtained through contracts with tenant farmers on their land.

The Reids built their home approximately one mile from the Stewarts, their properties separated by reserved lands. Evidence shows that the families regularly socialized, a contingent of Reids dining each Sunday with the Stewarts, and the children going back and forth, especially at times when their labour was required. It appears, however, that the sisters-in-law seldom visited each other despite the short distance between their homes. While Frances and Maria would undeniably have had little freedom or opportunity to socialize, they appear to have had quite different aspirations upon settlement and one wonders whether the two indeed had little in common.

According to John Mannion, Irish immigrants retained "much of the traditional social structure and communal consciousness"[20] in their new environments. Sydney Bellingham (1808–1900), a relation of the Stewarts who visited the two families in 1824, reports in his memoir that Robert Reid was "not an admirer of the aristocracy" and "prided himself on the dignity of labour," while Tom "had led a life of luxury and knew nothing of hard labour."[21] That such a perception of the two was recorded by Bellingham gives this comparison some credibility.

Descendents of Frances, the Shearman sisters, however, are skeptical of Bellingham's overall account of his visit, writing, "[It] was written many years later when he was an elderly man so it may have been clouded in retrospect."[22] Regardless, Frances wrote of her alarm at the Reids making little effort to educate their children and allowing them to grow up as uneducated farmers. She struggled to give her children an upbringing reflective of her own beliefs and values and abhorred the thought of them being raised in the same manner as the Reid children. Harriet Beaufort, ever attentive, was determined to support Frances's effort to educate her family and supplied her with useful texts in the annual box sent out from Ireland. She pressed Frances to make time to teach her children amid the hustle and bustle of running the household, writing, "I sent over a few little books for those dear children, & indeed I am growing very anxious to hear that they can read well & then write. You say nothing of arithmetic.... I am very sorry your hurry so much interferes with your teaching of them — but could you not continue to fix on even half an hour at a regular time to instruct them."[23]

Although compromised in her ability to provide the life she wanted for her children, it was, nevertheless, of utmost importance to Frances to separate her family from the labouring class through education, manners, and appearance. Marilyn Silverman's claim that class awareness is a response to "those commonplace, routine, and mundane beliefs and practices that people uncritically espouse"[24] fits well with Frances's elemental assumptions about education and manners.

Ironically, for Frances, it may be that the time spent on education contributed adversely to the economic success of her children in their adulthood. Few of them prospered financially, while the Reid children, who had focused more on hard physical work as a way of getting ahead, flourished, and several went on to professional careers. Harriet, ever cautioning Frances on matters of gentility, perceived the very notion of work as a threat and writes, "It makes me admire you more & more every day to see that you keep your elegant & civilized tastes in the midst of your present hard working life."[25]

Although Frances continued to be influenced by Harriet's repetitive and weighty expressions of concern and worry over several decades, she despondently acquiesced to the hopelessness of trying to maintain a real semblance of her former life. In one letter she states, "some times I am almost in despair about being able to do any thing but nurse or fuss a little about the children or housekeeping. Then when I have any time I write in such a hurry that I have no comfort."[26] She also despaired at not having time to further her own education, lamenting, "I scarcely even have even one half hour for serious reading. I am forgetting everything I knew & not gaining any new ideas — except upon housekeeping."[27] Family and housework conspired to limit the activities that she enjoyed most.

While Frances's letters reveal ample detail about her family, they are guarded in their references to household matters and only seldom provide specifics about the tasks performed. One is forced to draw inferences about her own culinary experiences, for example, from the silences around this subject rather than from anything concrete that she writes.[28] The following passage is as close as one gets to a discussion about food preparation methods:

> One night my poor little maid Betty slipped on the ice at
> the back door, fell & broke one of her ribs in two places
> as her side came against the handle of a tub.... I was able

to get a Scotch lassie to come to cook & finish the washing but she could only stay two days & after that I was cook, nurse, & everything myself for a few days. We had luckily a fine round of Beef which lasted cold for almost the whole time so I had no cooking except boiling potatoes & I got on finely & had neither fatigue or hurry of any consequence.[29]

Ellen, Frances's daughter, in *Our Forest Home*, too, leads one to believe that Frances did not normally assume the task of cooking. She avows, "As the maid was laid up for some time, [my mother] had to cook and, never having done so before, she was obliged to refer to her cookery-book for directions."[30] One detects a proud note in Ellen's statement. The claim that Frances only cooked when necessary holds consistent with upper-middle class sensibilities. Of course, Frances must have prepared food on numerous occasions, but she did not discuss this topic; rather, she focused on subjects relating to nature and to the daily activities of her family, subjects that would be of interest to the class-conscious recipients of her letters. The letters reveal that her daughters, in contrast, became proficient cooks; this is exemplified by passages that have them preparing menu items for elaborate family wedding feasts as they became older.

Frances was mindful of the paradox that she faced in trying to maintain an outward appearance reflective of her class. Misao Dean, in her examination of female labour and femininity in settler society, points to the fact that femininity, out of necessity, had to be redefined for pioneer women. She looks at Catharine Parr Traill and Susanna Moodie, Frances's contemporaries, and argues that the two women, despite the so-called demeaning physical work that they did, were held in high regard by those who read their books, due to the fact that they were seen to be contributing to the very survival of their husbands and children. Because of the sheer volume of work in a pioneer home, settler women had to perform hard physical tasks, even if they were so fortunate as to have servants. Dean suggests that the British acceptance of the publications by Traill and Moodie shows that the "extraordinary strength and persistence"[31] of the two women was a qualifier that allowed them to maintain their class status while performing manual labour more commonly considered appropriate to the working class. That the two women would sacrifice themselves to such a degree for their families was perceived as commendable. According to Barbara Maas, such sacrifices provided settler women with "new sources for prestige which enabled them to relinquish former patterns of female prestige,"[32] and that this, in turn, effected positive changes in self-image. Despite the seemingly limited choice of roles open to them, settler women exhibited considerable agency on the farm and in the household.

In the case of Frances, although careful in her depictions of her onerous daily tasks, it is evident that she was proud of the tangible results of her labour. She writes, "Oh, I am become a famous Tailor. I have just made up a nice pair of Frize pantaloons for Tom & am to make him a waistcoat of the same materials.... He is so fond of this frize that he is determined to have a whole suit."[33]

Frances knew that she walked a tightrope when revealing to her upper-middle-class correspondents that she performed tasks normally considered labourers' occupations. It was important that they understand that she had maintained her class sensibilities despite the fact that she performed tasks directly related to the physical survival of her family. She wrote of the tasks without complaining, tempering her depictions with acceptance, appreciation, and resignation, and glossing over the details while still baring her soul to her readers. Her family and friends were awe-inspired by Frances's accounts of her life and consistently commented on her ability to maintain a cheerful countenance under such demanding and laborious circumstances.

Frances seems to have seen her own life, too, as a remarkable testament. In a language couched within the constraints of her humble demeanour, she writes, "Indeed all my pursuits are so completely changed that I scarcely can help thinking I have been changed by some Evil Fairy, for no people could be so totally different as Fanny Browne of Dublin & Fanny Stewart of Douro, except that my dear friends are the same & equally fond & tender. Oh this makes me know most exquisitely that I am Fanny Browne still."[34]

Like all upper-middle-class immigrants, Frances exhibits a radical ambivalence. She is aware of her double identity, torn between pride at her perseverance and fortitude and in her newly learned accomplishments, and shame and humiliation at having to do such work at all. The passage poignantly reveals that she saw her life as having been usurped by an "Evil Fairy" and that she viewed her physical household tasks as sharp contrast to the pursuits that she enjoyed most. It also reveals that by 1829, the date that she wrote the above passage, she envisioned herself a survivor, viewing her life within the new delineations of the changed social and physical environment in which she lived.

Remarkably, in 1827, the gift of a piano from Maria Edgeworth made a precarious journey from Ireland to the log cabin in Douro and Frances was able to resume her passion for music, a factor that may have slowly contributed to her recovery from a long period of depression. The letters around this time suggest, too, that Frances had undergone a deep religious conversion and that she had begun to feel more confident and stronger in spirit.

A letter that Catharine Parr Traill, who had immigrated to Upper Canada from England in 1832, wrote to Frances establishes that over time Frances came to be regarded by her friend as a wise and experienced mentor and that Catharine looked to her for spiritual and emotional support and sound practical advice. With affection, Catharine writes, "Your loving-kindness in word and deed has ever been a balm to my spirit.... Your nice letters are so precious to me that I feel happier for having read them for days afterwards."[35] Supportive female friendships amongst immigrants were integral to survival and the letters between Catharine and Frances contain several such passages expressing affection for one another and suggest a deep friendship between the two. Missing in the letters between the friends, however, are the comparative references to the pain and anxiety they must have endured as a result of their relationships with husbands, both of whom were often despondent and prone to bouts of depression.

Critical to Frances's immigrant experience was her relationship with Tom. Her letters give the impression of mutual trust, respect, and dependency. Early on, she writes of Tom's efforts to provide her with every possible comfort as they struggled to begin a new life in a challenging and unfamiliar environment. It is apparent that she deeply respected the strength of character that he manifested as he conducted his arduous daily activities, and that his firm religious bearing gave her comfort and a sense of security.

A careful reading, however, reveals subtle evidence of marital strain. Frances had not fully agreed with the decision to move to Upper Canada, although she admired Tom's reasons for doing so and felt duty-bound once the decision had been made to concur with his plans; that she was a devoted and obedient housewife is apparent. Frances fits well, in fact, Jane Errington's description of Upper-Canadian society's ideal woman. Errrington writes, "First and foremost, to be a good wife, a woman had to be a 'good' woman. This meant that she had to be a devout Christian. Young women were advised to 'labour under the grace of God,' to study the Scriptures and to apply them in their daily activities. A good wife also had to be 'amiable,' with 'goodness of heart and purity of manners' so as to be able to 'impart a moral excellence to all around her.'"[36]

Barbara Maas attributes such gendered assumptions and expectations to the Victorian era in which they flourished. She says, "British-born women had fully internalized that part of the Victorian code of womanhood which declared marriage as woman's highest destiny and wifely obedience as woman's foremost duty within marriage."[37] It is of some significance, therefore, that Frances may have breached this code in 1826 by writing to Harriet's brother, Francis Beaufort, on an undisclosed matter relating to difficulties that she chose not to share with Tom. This particular and significant letter reveals that Frances grievously regretted having written in an earlier letter in the manner that she did, knowing that Tom would have been displeased with her had he known of it and pained had he been aware of her unhappiness. Feeling desolate about the matter, she writes, "You unmasked very justly that in all my complaints I mentioned my husband very little. It was because I knew very well he would not approve of my writing in that strain & therefore I wrote without consulting him. If I had opened my mind more to him, I should not have been so silly but I did not like to let him know how gloomy I was as I knew it would only add to his pain."[38]

Frances's worry about Tom's frequent bouts of depression and her knowledge that he felt her to be inept and ignorant in her performance of household duties most certainly would have contributed to the difficulties that she endured after immigrating. Because of her lack of experience, she was disadvantaged in circumstances that demanded that she work long and strenuous days at varied domestic chores. Accustomed to having been cared for by servants in Ireland, she had little direct experience at organizing and managing a household. Her feelings of inadequacy caused her much unhappiness and this in turn resulted in negative self-assessments. The letter to Francis seems to have been written during an extremely low point in Frances's life. It is plausible that, in addition to their fundamental differences in thinking, she and Tom compounded each other's feelings of unhappiness as each suffered debilitating periods of depression. Their second year in Upper Canada had been sadly marred by the death of their youngest child, Bessie, and it is conceivable that Bessie's death, along with persistent feelings of loneliness and ineptitude, and probably physical and emotional exhaustion from bearing and nursing a succession of children (five between 1817 and 1825), all contributed to the despondency that Frances experienced.

By baring her soul to family and friends, such as she did in her letter to Francis Beaufort on matters relating to Tom, Frances in effect nurtured her extended family relationships. Writing in such a manner encouraged their support and, indeed, in times of need, she turned to them for help. She directly sought Francis's assistance in procuring a position for Tom, for example. In an attempt to enhance her family's economic position, she writes, "I cannot tell you how deeply we feel all your active kindness about the Land Company & the other appointments you & kind Maria E. [Edgeworth] have been endeavouring to procure for Mr. S. [Tom]."[39]

Nancy Christie notes that, "The fear of imminent destitution … pervaded all social groups and was a much recorded and discussed subject in familial correspondence."[40] She would consider such a communication from Frances to Francis Beaufort a "begging" letter, corroborating her claim that "the hierarchical features of gender, age, and wealth were reinforced within the extended family economy of obligation."[41] She mentions the gendered "rhetoric of need"[42] and the emotive language used in nineteenth-century letters, arguing that "there were powerful conventions surrounding the definition of respectable poverty, which were policed within families, and that these codes of deservedness were well understood by poor relatives."[43]

Frances would, at least subconsciously, understand that a letter written from a gendered and subordinate stance would elicit positive response from relatives, who would feel a sense of familial obligation to assist her in finding a position for Tom. She would know that it would be in the wider family's interests for Tom to secure a respectable appointment befitting the family's social position in Upper Canada.

Although the Stewart family did not prosper financially, Tom became successful, to a point, in other ways, and would be considered representative of the immigrant gentry, as defined by Wagner, that is, that "the gentry became local leaders, ardent supporters of economic progress, and officers in the local militia."[44] Tom was appointed to the Legislative Council of Upper Canada, he was a proponent of the development of an inland waterway, and he led a company of two hundred volunteers in the 1837 Rebellion, although this company was not called to action. We learn from the family research of the Shearman sisters that, by 1827, Tom had given up farming himself, distributing his farmland to four or five tenant farmers,[45] and one year later, claiming, that of his 1,200 acres, he had seventy under cultivation.[46] This figure far exceeds the rate by which land was cleared and cultivated by peasant settlers, who, on average, according to John Mannion, owned one hundred acres and cleared less than two acres per year.[47]

This point is significant in that it proves that, although Tom had conceded that he himself was not a farmer, he had adapted to a new way of life by taking on tenant farmers. Wagner claims that the rate by which the gentry cultivated their land is an indicator of their adaptation.[48] Against all odds, and even, on occasion, while drawing no rent from his more destitute tenant farmers,[49] Tom had successfully devised and legitimized a means to support his family in line with traditional gentry sensibilities. Nevertheless, he remained attuned to the scale of achievement of most other Upper Canadian gentry in that he was ever only moderately well off.[50]

One can never definitively know the ways in which Frances conducted her daily life or moulded the lives of her children as they grew and had families of their own. It is apparent only through their letters to her and to others that they cared for her tremendously. She seldom divulges any detail about the many pregnancies or the births she endured. Amusedly, her reservedness in one letter, although following convention of the period, caused a mirthful response from her correspondent in Ireland:

> And behold, there was a real treasure, a copy of your letter with an account of the birth of your dear child, but my dear, we really could hardly help laughing at your beginning your letter so composed telling of common occurances, & then nearly at the bottom of the page, comes a paragraph of how the lady of T A Stewart Esq had a Daughter! Really it put me in mind of a history of some travellers in some hot country, who missed one of their females for an hour, but she came up at last with a Bairn in her arms, whose birth had delayed her.[51]

Frances's references to her children are as with mothers everywhere. In 1826, her young charges were "great wild racing creatures. Anna is up to my shoulders, Ellen about a head lower, Bessy very amusing and engaging, Willy a great stout laughing fellow."[52] Decades later, she avows, "I think you would love these dear children of mine if you knew them."[53]

As with any large family, the Stewarts coped with illnesses, scandals, and financial woes. They also enjoyed the arrival of grandchildren as their daughters and sons begat a new generation. Evidence suggests that mother and grandmother stoically took this all in stride.

THE LETTERS

1822 [journal][54]
[To Harriet Beaufort], Ireland

Journal kept 1822

On Saturday morning June 1st <u>our</u> family accompanied by some of the little Reids & our dear sister Mrs. Mitchell left White Abbey in the Barge accompanied by our kind friend Mr. Quin. We soon reached the Brig *George* which was at anchor nearly opposite to White Abbey & which was to convey us to Quebec. About two hours after we had come on board Capt. Thompson arrived & gave orders for sailing immediately. This gave us some uneasiness as not expecting to sail till the next day. Mr. Reid had gone to Belfast & had not yet joined us. At 1 o'clock we set sail. It was a charming day. The Cave hill & the shores on both sides of the Lough looked more lovely than ever. After we had proceeded beyond Carichfergus we saw Mr. Quins boat following us & gaining on us rapidly which set our minds at ease about Mr. Reid. But a sad trial awaited us for the same boat which brought him was to convey back our dear friends the Mitchells, Alex'r Wilson & Mr. Quin, as well as several other people who had accompanied us so far on our voyage.

2d June Sunday. A fine day. After breakfast, not being sick, I went on deck. I saw the fine Northern coast of dear Ireland in beautiful blue distance & the Island of Rathlin, but I was soon obliged to shut my eyes as the motion of the vessel, tho' very smooth, made my head giddy & gave me violent pains in my eyes. We all went to bed about 9 but in the middle of the night a great swell came on & such a roll that I could scarcely keep from tumbling over my little bedfellow Bessy. About 2 o'clock in the morning the carpenter came into the cabin to put in the dead lights, & just then the vessel gave such a roll that all our trunks, boxes & baskets came sliding down to the leeside of the vessel. Towards morning the swell abated a little & after breakfast I went on deck to see the last view of dear Ireland. It was a grey dull morning but I watched the last glimpse of land as long as I could see it.

Tuesday 4th June. We met a Balbriggan fishing boat by which T A S sent a letter to Mr. Black.

Wednesday, Thursday & Friday were fine days.

Stormy Pettrel or Mother Careys chickens

It is about the size of a Swallow & in its general appearance is not unlike that bird. In June & July it comes near the rocky shores to breed but at all other times keeps far out at sea. Multitudes of them are seen all over the vast Atlantic Ocean especially before stormy weather. They often skim with incredible velocity along the hollows of the waves & sometimes on the summits braving the utmost fury of the waves & tempests. The inhabitants of the [ ] Isles draw a wick through the body of this bird which is by the process so covered with grease as to burn when lighted like a candle & serving the purpose of one. We saw numbers of Birds called Mother Careys chickens — also sea gulls. These birds are never seen <u>very</u> distant from land at this season.

Tuesday 11th. Cold and dark but a nice steady breeze.

Wednesday 12th June. At 5 oclock a fine handsome vessel passed near us. "We spoke her" & found it was a Glasgow ship called the *Trelawney*. On the evening of this day we saw a large fish following our ship. Some said it was a shark. At last it made a bound out of the water & rose several feet so that its whole form could be seen & then they said it was a Sunfish. From this time till 7 July nothing new occurred. We saw several seabirds called shearwaters or cutwaters & numbers of porpoises. We always observed that these porpoises appeared in numbers before a breeze came on. Some nights the sea was illuminated with phosphorous which was very beautiful. On fine days we sat on deck most of the mornings & in the evenings the sailors danced. Whilst we were passing the Banks of Newfoundland thick fogs prevailed & the weather was very cold & it became <u>tormentingly</u> calm.

7th July. We heard the welcome news that land was seen, 5 weeks after our departure from Ireland. It proved to be part of the Southern coast of Newfoundland. In a few days we saw the two fine headlands of Cape Breton & Cape Rage & passed between them just at sunset. All this week we proceeded slowly up the Gulph of St. Lawrence, the weather remarkably pleasant & fine but too calm for sailing. Several of the people amused themselves in fishing & caught some fine mackerel & codlings & 2 Dogfish. The water from the time we entered the Gulph had a brown colour quite different from the fine dark blue of the Atlantic. On the 7 July a thick fog came on about noon. When we went up on the deck after having prayers in the cabin we learnt that we had a narrow escape, for in the thick fog a very large vessel had nearly run us down. Fortunately the danger was perceived just in time to be avoided by great exertion.

On the evening of Saturday 13th we took a pilot on board. It was a most lovely evening & the dark purple tints of evening on the hills on the Canadian side of the river formed a beautiful contrast with the red tinge of the setting sun on the Nova Scotia coast opposite. All seemed now to promise a prosperous passage to Quebec. Our pilot said we had not yet come to Bic Island. Capt. Thompson said that according to his calculations we had passed it.

Sunday 14th July — A fine warm morning but so thick a fog that we could not see land on any side. Capt. T. wished the pilot to anchor till he could see whereabouts he was as there are many islands in this part of the river & the navigation requires some skill. The pilot assured him there was no danger as he was sure we had not yet passed Bic. But a few hours proved he was wrong — & also too rash — for about ½ past 12 when we were all assembled in the cabin we felt a dreadful shock & a strange & horrible sensation as if every piece of timber in the side of the vessel was tearing out. We all ran out as fast as possible & found the ship had struck a rock & was sticking fast on it. The tide was ebbing so that nothing could be known as to the state of the vessel, nor could anything be done as to removing her till the tide flowed again. In the meantime all was a scene of confusion & terror. The passengers in the hold became very clamerous & the Capt. with difficulty prevailed on them to wait in the vessel till he could ascertain whether there was much danger.

About 1 oclock in the afternoon the fog cleared off for about an hour & we found we were lying close to a small bare island with large stones all round it & reefs of rocks stretching from it like the rays of a starfish. Our ship had got in between two of these reefs in a most extraordinary manner & had struck on one reef, upon which she was now fast, and as the water became shallower we c'd see the rock under the ship. The pilot now pronounced this to be Red Island & said that we must have passed Bic island long before. We saw some people on the island & heard a shot. Capt. Thompson, Mr. Reid & some others went off in a small boat to learn what could be done in case we sh'd find the ship had been impaired. They soon returned accompanied by 4 men in a Canoe. They were all Canadians & spoke only French but I could not understand it. It was very different from what I had been accustomed to. They had been out shooting seals which are very numerous here. These men are dark coloured with dark eyes & long noses, rather handsome men. They wore Mocasins, a kind of shoe made of Deer skin or Calfskin without any sole & ties up round the ankle.

When our passengers found land so near they wanted to swim or wade to the shore but the Capt. prevailed on them to wait till the change of tide enabled him to find out the state of the vessel & promised that in case of danger they should all be safely landed on the Island. We continued in the state of suspense till the tide enabled the ship to move a little, when she was towed round the reef of rocks, & after one dreadful scrape we set sail. But as it was dark & as the tide had again changed the Capt. thought it best to anchor till the next tide. Next morning we set sail again & at low water anchored at Green Island.

Monday 15th July. We all liked to see everything we could on shore & accordingly the small boat was prepared for a party to go to the opposite shore, part of Nova Scotia. Mr. Reid, Mr. S. & myself together with some others set out & soon had our feet once more on dry land. The ground along the shore was covered with white clover & blue Irises which looked charmingly gay & glowing to our eyes, so long accustomed to the sameness of the Ocean view. We saw some Indian huts or Wigwams near us & went to them. The Indians looked inquisitively at us but yet seemed to wish to keep at a distance. The men were employed making Brooms. The women or Squaws were making Baskets. They use little Hammocks for the Infants or Papousies & suspend them from the roof of their huts.

The Indians make Brooms of wood, generally a Sapling or pole of Blue beech or Basswood or any tough wood & strip off the bark. Then they tear the wood in thin stripes from one end to within a foot or so of the other end & when they have the pole reduced by doing this & a large quantity of striped pieces they turn them down over the end of the pole so as to make a brush when lapped round with some narrow stripes of the wood, leaving the smallest & longest part of the pole for the handle of the Broom. These are very coarse but answer for sweeping floors & may be had for a trifle from the Indians.

The Squaws make Baskets of the same tough wood cut into stripes which they weave together & dye of different colours with the juices of plants. They also manufacture dishes & baskets of Birch wood & bark & Butternut.

We saw a path through the woods & were tempted to explore a little way into these great forests. We had not proceeded far when we came to a paling beyond which was a small space of pretty open country with rich meadows & corn & potatoe fields & several houses, some in clusters, little hamlets & some detached, all made of logs. We crossed two fields & reached the nearest house. The inhabitants were all French Canadians. The family consisted of a man & his wife & mother in law & a beautiful child about 3 years old. He was a fisherman & had a house for smoking the fish filled with fine salmon hung in rows along the roof.

1822: July 1–21 [journal][55]

July 1 1822

We are now on the Great Bank of Newfoundland & have just dined heartily on a most excellent Cod which Tom caught yesterday evening. We have hitherto had a most prosperous & even rather pleasant passage. I have not been the least ill, though we have had some very sickening nights. For the first fortnight we got on very fast indeed & hoped to have reached Quebec by this time, but for the last ten days we have had a great deal of calm weather & when there was any wind it was not quite favourable. By [tacking] constantly we have arrived so far. I have much reason to be thankful that we have had so safe a voyage & that I have escaped sickness. We are as comfortably settled in this vessel as such a number could be in so confined a spot. We have one very large cabin in which all the Reids sleep, Mr. R. & Tom swinging in the middle in cots. In this we eat & in bad weather we sit there. I have the little state cabin for my party. There are two good & very wide births in it. I sleep in one with my nursling & my maid, Anna Maria, & Ellen in the other. I am very comfortable here & quite independent & though I have only room to stand up & dress myself I am much happier than if we were all together. I am very glad to have it to retire to whenever I like. When the weather is fine I sit on deck all day except at mealtimes. For the last week the weather has been foggy, damp & cold. On Midsummer day the thermometer was only 42 at Noon. This weather is very common in this part of the Atlantic & is disheartening just now as I am in a state of feverish impatience which I cannot conquer to get to the end of our voyage & be settled in our own log house. We have no passengers whose society could be the least pleasure to us. The Captain is just what you might expect to find a person who was raised from being a common sailor. He is rough & vulgar but is anxious to pay us every attention in his power & is very good natured to the children. We are beginning to rock about so much that I must stop writing. Though not sick, I have had some bad headaches & am sometimes stupefied & unable to fix my eyes on anything.

Wednesday July 10. Ten days have passed my dear friends since I wrote the latter part of this & yet we have made very little progress in this tedious passage. However, for two days we are cheered by being within sight of land, a delightful sight after having seen nothing but the boundless ocean for 33 days. This land was the southern or south Eastern part of Newfoundland. We saw land on each side of us on Monday when we were between Cape Raye in Newfoundland & Cape North in this island of Breton. They are a very pretty chain of hills ending in abrupt headlands. Today we have been for the most part out of sight of land but now & then had a very indistinct view of the island of Anticosta, a large island 130 miles long & 30 broad, covered with stunted trees, but uninhabited. We have several times seen whales at a distance spouting their jets d'eaux into the air but they have not been very near us & we could only distinguish the immense body of the creature. But we have often seen a smaller species very near us which spouts in the same way.

In the very middle of the Atlantic we were accompanied by little birds of the swallow tribe but webfooted. They are called Mother Carey's chickens & are very pretty little birds. When in the middle of the Atlantic a poor little House swallow flew into the rigging & was caught. We have seen numbers of a sort of puffin I believe called <u>shearwaters</u> because they skim on the surface of the water & seem to cut through the waves. About a week ago a little bird was found in one of the boats & I took it to nurse as it proved to be a land bird & we were not near land at the time. It is very like our grey linnet but the bill is very long and crosses over at the point like the crossbill. I have kept it in a basket. It is going on very well & is so tame that it eats out of our hands & sits on our shoulders. Yesterday it sat on my head all the time I was at dinner. It is a dear little thing but does not attempt song. We are now in the gulph of St. Laurence, the weather extremely cold.

Sunday July 21, <u>Quebec</u>. Here we are at last safe & sound after a passage of exactly 7 weeks & one day. We reached this new world at about eight oClock this morning. All our passage up the river has been most interesting. The views on both sides (since we have been able to see land on both sides at once) have been the most beautiful I ever saw. For above 200 miles along the coast of Nova Scotia we were within sight of the finest mountains covered with trees from the highest point down to the waters edge. As we approached the Canadian coast the headlands were equally beautiful & surpassed anything I had ever seen except Killarney. Some of the views reminded Tom very much of the [ ]. Altogether I was delighted more than I can express and Oh how often did I wish that I could share my pleasure with you, all my dear friends. We came on slowly. On Saturday night last, we came to that part of the river where pilots are taken. Our pilot came & we thought ourselves secure against the rocks & banks, but how ignorant were we of our fate! Next morning we were surrounded by a thick fog & even the pilot was at a loss to know whereabouts we were. Fortunately there was so little wind that the ship scarcely moved on. At half past one just as we were assembled for prayers in the Cabin, we felt three great stokes & the whole ship trembled Oh most frightfully. We all remained panic struck for a moment. You may imagine our fright when we heard that we were striking on a rock!! Exactly as we struck the fog cleared off & we then saw that we were close to Red island. Some French Canadians happened to be on the island fishing & as soon as they saw us they came off in their Canoe to assist us. They were very active & very good natured, particularly one old man, who really was most benevolent & never left us till one the next morn'g. We struck there for 6 hours before we moved or could feel sure that the vessel was safe. At last she moved round, the pumps were tried, she made no water. All seemed safe, when bump we came on another rock. Soon, however, after several bumpings & scrapings we got off most providentially. No bad consequence except two of the sailors were hurt, one of them rather severely by the Anchor, & we had the pleasure of nursing him in our cabin all night & the next day & have made him nearly well again. The next day was lovely & as we were obliged to anchor for tide, we had time to go on shore but I have not room in this letter to enter into the details of our excursion on shore, our first landing on American ground. I will keep it for a letter to Kate which I will tell her to send to you. I cannot cram all I want to say into one sheet, and besides I am surrounded by people — 19 in this little cabin at once. I scarcely know what I am about, for Bessy is roaring for me too, but notwithstanding all my confusion my heart is steadily, warmly & gratefully devoted to my beloved friends. Give our kindest loves to Ma & Lou, Upton, E'town, Allenstown, &c.

1822: July 10[56]
To Catherine Browne (Kate), Ireland

Began Wednesday July 10th [1822]

My dear dear Kate

I suppose you have long [before] this received a horrid scrawl which I sent by a vessel to Ireland some weeks ago....

The day after our exploit of Red Island we were obliged to stop till the tide changed & we amused ourselves in the intermediate time by taking a row to the coast of Nova Scotia where it first begins to be inhabited & where we saw two or three Indian Huts and a few houses here and there. Our eyes were gratified by seeing a nice bed of white clover just growing on the edge of the sandy shore along side of the clover & near a little inlet of the sea water was a brilliant patch of the pretty blue Irises which we used to have in our Irish flower gardens. These grew in patches all through the trees and looked very gay and pretty. We saw numbers of our dear old Irish weeds, Docks, wild sorrel, yarrow and many others, but along with these are mixed many beautiful kinds which are new to me. On Sunday morning we all got up at 4 oclock to see the waterfall of Montmorenci which is a very grand thing but we were too far from it to see it as well as I wanted. The water falls 245 feet, quite perpendicular & is a great body of water. The foam rises far above the tops of the surrounding houses. We were thinking of going there before we leave this but I am afraid we shall not be able as we have many things to do & we are to go on to Montreal tomorrow (Thursday 24th) — but I must go on with my journal. We arrived here about 8 oclock on Sunday morning and breakfasted on <u>fresh bread</u> & <u>fresh milk</u> which I think was enjoyed more than anything I ever tasted in my life. The milk is excellent … seems perfectly pure, 3d a quart, the bread very nice, 8d for good … loaves. After breakfast we dressed ourselves and proceeded to walk about the streets which are very ugly indeed, narrow and crooked and full of rubbish and chips and shavings. The houses are in general very good and very clean as far as I have seen yet. We went to Church which is a very neat plain one, pretty large and very full of respectable genteel looking people. We had a very good sermon from Mr. Mountain, the Bishops son, but … such a monotonous melancholy service … made me very sleepy. There is a very good organ and a very sweet choir, some delightful <u>young</u> voices. After Church we walked a little more and enjoyed the lovely views which surround us on every side. The sun was so hot that we could not walk long. The next morning Tom had some enquiries and arrangements to make. About 12 o'clock we set out to visit Mrs. Mountain to whom Miss Wren had given us an introduction … whilst I was enquiring if she was at home she walked to the Hall door, so I presented Miss Wren's note & told her who we were. She then shook hands in the kindest way and said they had almost given up all expectation of us. The Bishop was not at home nor the young ladies but Mrs. Mountain invited us to breakfast there today. She is a very respectable looking old lady but nearly as deaf as Mrs. Montray. There is something about her face that reminded both Tom and me of our dear Aunt Bess. She was as kind as possible and really seemed quite tender. How very much we are indebted to Miss Wren for have introduced us to such agreeable <u>friends</u>. She asked us in the most earnest manner to tell her if there was anything we wished to have done or anything she or her family could do for us. She procured us a Ticket of admission to see the Citadel. This is a curious place & wonderfully strong. I am sure I hope its strength may never be tried during our term here. It certainly has been a happy undertaking in one way, as it gives employment to some hundreds of poor Irishmen. There is a very fine view from the Signal post where there are Telescopes. It was dreadfully hot walking up to Cape Diamond, the height on which the Citadel is built. For it is an ascent all the way and not the least shade from the burning sun and you may guess how hot the sun must have been when the thermometer was up to 80 in the shade, but this is nothing like the heat we shall have as we go further up the river. We were so fagged after crawling to the Cape and back that we were glad to stay in the cool shade on deck till after dinner. Then we took [a] boat and went to the opposite side of the river. There is a very pretty road along the shore close to the water and on the other side is a steep rocky and woody bank which rises above a hundred feet perpendicularly. We saw a great many Indian huts. The poor Indians were employed in different ways, some making little baskets of shavings … various colours. Others were preparing Bark of Birch trees [ ] canoes. They seem inoffensive people and very lazy.

Wednesday 25th, no 24th I believe. Yesterday morning at half past seven we, that is, Tom and I, set out to go to the Bishops, 8 o'clock being their breakfast hour. We found the old lady ready to receive us in the dining room. She ushered us into [ ] a bookroom or study where his Lordship was sitting. He is a fine white headed old man of 70, quite patriarchal in his appearance. He came forward and shook hands like a kind old friend. He seem quite interested [inquiring] in the most kind manner every particular respecting our plans and intentions. After talking for a short time we went back to the dining parlour where we found the two Miss Mountains seated…. At one o'clock, Tom, AM and I set out so thought it better to meet them at their house than to bring the carriage here for the streets are so very bad for driving. We found the two young ladies bonneted and ready to accompany us. They seem to be all enthusiastically fond of children & Mrs. M. took AM away to shew her to the Bishop & he was so delighted with her that he brought her back in his arms and kissed her over and over. When the Barouche came round we went off and took a pretty drive to a sweet place about three miles off on the bank of the river. It belongs to a Mr. Percival who came out here with his wife & family some years ago. He struggled against difficulties like all other Emigrants at first. He is now collector here & very rich & possesses one of the prettiest places in Canada. It is laid out with great taste — the woods so judiciously cleared that his lawn has the appearance of a fine Park. Mrs. Percival is a most Charming woman who is accomplished and cultivated enough for a count, but she lives here quite happily and educates all her children herself. She has eight children & lies in every year regularly. You will be surprised amongst all our visits that Tom has not waited on Lord Dalhousie. But the most provoking thing in the world has happened. Tom has put up all his Quebec letters of introduction so carefully that he cannot find one of them now. Where they are we cannot find out but it is of less consequence than it might have been as Lord Dalhousie is in the country about a hundred miles off & we could not see him. Besides we know that his Lordship would only refer us to Sir Peregrine Maitland & we have numbers of letters to him....

Montreal, July 28th. I intended to have finished this letter at Quebec, but every time I was writing the latter part of this letter, my poor sweet Bessy grew very ill with a vomiting. I think she was ill teething ... the extreme heat affected her. She continued very ill indeed ever since. Today she is a little better. Her eyes have rather a more lively look & her food has remained on her stomach. She is terribly changed. She bore her voyage as well as possible and was fat and lively a few hours before she grew ill, but the weather at Quebec that one day & the night before was so hot & our cabin so close & hot that I could scarcely breath. She is a sweet dear child but God keep me from repining at his will for she & all other blessings are but <u>loans</u> & he may take but I trust this trial may not be given me now, but if it is His will to take her or prolong her sufferings, Oh may I submit with full security that <u>all is right</u> that He sends or wills, and if her present amendment continues may I not be unmindful of this mercy. You will say I am in a very preaching mood but dear Kate my mind has taken a [bent] from having suffered a good deal & I always try to view all with reference to the Giver of All. I hope I don't appear <u>Methodistical</u> for indeed I dislike <u>canting</u> or talking much or unnecessarily on religious subjects.

We are very comfortably settled here in a most excellent house, nice clean airy rooms and quite enough of them, a sitting room, a kitchen and 5 bedrooms, but no furniture, all for fifteen shillings a week!! As we arrived on Saturday we could not procure any meat, it was so late in the day, but we have most excellent bread and delightful milk, good butter, fresh eggs & some hams of our own, so we are in no <u>great</u> danger of starving.

This town is very clean as far as I can see. The surrounding country is very beautiful, but we have not been able to walk about much yet as it rained all night & all the morning & we had awful thunder & lightening. It is now fair but the streets are too wet for walking. Dinner is just coming on the table so I must stop at present. I will despatch another letter from York. So do believe me my dear dear sister, here or elsewhere, ever your truly affect' sister

F. Stewart

Tom joins in long kind love to all your dear dear party. Tell [ ] Sutton that Tom thinks it will be most convenient to send the Somerville money & [ ] [ ] interest altogether as it is troublesome to send the small [ ] separately.

1822: September 11[57]
To Louisa [Beaufort], Ireland

Wednesday night Sept'r 11, 1822

My dearest Louisa

By a letter which reached me on Monday the 9th from dear Harriet, I find it probable that this letter may come to you at poor old 37.

This letter of Harriet's had a very quick passage. The last date was June 29. It was the most delightful, cordial to my spirits which were beginning to droop at the length of time which had passed since I heard of or from any one creature. Oh how I did devour it & how I have read and re-read it. The excellent accounts it contained of Bess & of the improvement in her own health are delightful.

But my dearest Aunt Beaufort seems to be the stoutest of the 31 party now. This does truly rejoice my heart, & that she may be blessed with that strength of mind which helps to support herself, as long as she is permitted to remain with those to whom she is so dear is my constant prayer.

What horrible accounts there are in the newspapers of the sufferings of the people in the west of Ireland! I am sure a number of people will come to this country which is truly a land flowing with milk & honey. There is no such thing as poverty. We have had very good opportunity of judging of this, as during our passage up from La Chine to Kingston, a distance of 173 miles, we slept every night, or at least several nights, at farm houses, & during the day, sometimes called at cottages to procure bread or milk. The week which we spent in this part of our travels was I think the most interesting of the whole voyage, & therefore I will give you a history of it.

The first day nothing particular happened, except that it was the hottest day we had during <u>our lives</u>. No day has been half so hot since.

We were in 4 open boats, sitting perched on our luggage exactly as soldiers wives sit in baggage carts. The Reid family filled two. We occupied a third, & a poor family who accompanied us from White Abbey were in the 4th, so that we were a formidable party, 27 in number.

About 6 in the evening we reached "Les Cascades" 24 miles from La Chine where the Rapids began. The scenery all along was very beautiful but here it was magnificent, the water rushing over the great stones in that great river & appearing between different wooded islands was most beautiful and formed such a contrast to the smooth glassy Lake (I may call it) through which we have been sliding all day. Our boatmen were all French Canadians & could not speak a word of English & their language was so different from the French we are accustomed to, that we found it very difficult to understand anything they said, but they always understood our French. Whenever they came to a shallow place they stopped rowing & all took long poles with which they push the boats on by sticking one end into the ground or against a stone. When rowing they sang a great deal. Their songs had a very wild sound, not a bit like our old "Canadian boat song."

There was an Inn at "Les Cascades" to which we all went & where we dined. The Innkeeper was an Irishman but indeed his accommodations were very bad. He said his best bedrooms were engaged by an officer & his family so our whole party were to divide two very small rooms between them.

The female Reids 8 in number took one, we, the other. The male part of the Reids went to the hay loft which they said was clean & cool. The poor people slept in another hay loft. The officer who turned out to be Capt. Melville, an acquaintance of Tom's, told us that the beds were swarming with bugs, so we spread mattrasses of our own on the floor & lay down, but not to sleep, for not one of our party, from Tom down to little Bessy, could bear the bugs which we found crawling all over us & all over the walls & floors. Tom said he would go to the hayloft, so I did the same & had all the wee'ans carried out there, & never was a bed of down so delightful, nor never was sleep more refreshing than ours that night, on nice clean hay with our cloaks about us & the sweet air & the sound of the cascade which lulled me to sleep in the most charming way you can conceive.

The next day we were to travel 4 miles by land as the Rapids were too violent for us to remain in the boats. We hired a waggon in which Mrs. Reid & four of her children, Tom & I & our 3 children, all stuffed. A cart containing the rest of the children & servants followed & the men & boys walked. Waggons are the sort of carriage generally used by gentlemen's families in <u>Upper</u> Canada. They are just a very large four wheeled cart with 2 seats like Gigs placed one before the other. The driver of course sits in the foremost & takes as many beside him as there is room for.

We womankind took boat again at the end of 4 or 5 miles but the men & <u>even Tom</u> walked the whole day as we had a strong current against us, & the boatmen required to have the boats lightened. Tom walked that day <u>twelve miles</u> & was the foremost of the party the whole way.

Our progress was very slow that day & we stopped at "<u>Coteau du Lac</u>" where there is a Port. We were advised to apply to Col. Nicholl who lives there for leave to spread our mattrasses in some military store room or some such place. So Tom & Mr. Reid introduced themselves to him & made their request. He was excessively civil & said that he could give us a room in his house which had been built for a kitchen but which was not used for one. So he shewed us into a nice clean light room more like a parlour than a kitchen.

Here we were settling ourselves & giving the children their supper when Col. Nichol sent to beg that we would open a door which was between our room & another & make use of that other room also, as he saw how much too large our party was for one room. This was particularly amiable of him, for upon opening the door, we entered a very nicely furnished drawing room carpeted, curtained, sofa'd & book'd in a very pretty manner. The gentlemen & boys slept there & we females kept possession of the other room.

I always placed my Mattrass exactly at the door that little Bessy might be cool, for she never could sleep unless the air was <u>actually blowing</u> on her. She was very ill & feverish poor little dear & generally started crying every half hour.

The next morning we got up at half past three & were glad to lose a few hours of sleep that we might gain a few hours of coolness, for the sun was very very hot though not half so bad as the first day. We had a heavy shower about the middle of the day which cooled the air & drenched us completely, though we covered ourselves as well as we could by lying down under the tarpaulins that covered our luggage.

We stopped for shelter at a post office, I forget where, & found shelter, but no fire was in the house at which we could dry our dripping garments, so we read a parcel of Kingston & Montreal newspapers, & when the rain ceased, returned to our respective batteaux & when we got to Charlottenburg we stopped at an Inn & dried our clothes, but there was great scarcity of fire every where, for in this hot season people keep their fires lighted as short a time as possible. Having dried ourselves we once more went to our batteaux & went on & on till nearly dark in the evening, & the boatmen at last stopped, but, alack a day, no house was near enough for us to sleep at. There was one in sight, but there was a marsh between us & it, & it would have taken up too much time to go round this marsh. So we determined to lay our mattrasses on the grass which was nice & smooth & to keep company with our batteau men who always sleep either in the boats or just beside them on the shore. They had already a blazing fire at which they were busily engaged cooking pea soup for their supper. Our party had another fire, not for cooking, but to keep the flies & insects from us which by the way never annoyed us much except one day before we came to Quebec. We laid our beds all round the fire. Over mine Tom made a sort of little tent of a sail & 3 of the long poles the boatmen use. This kept us quite dry & comfortable. But the Reids would not make a tent though they might have done so as easily as we did, & I think both Mr. Reid & James got colds which they still feel the effects of. Poor Mr. R. has been ill which has greatly altered his animated keen eye & energetic manner.

All the Reids have been ill more or less of the same complaint, but nothing alarming. Thank God our family have escaped all sorts of illness. Except little Bessy, we have all been <u>perfectly</u> well since we left Ireland & she is now well again & regaining her good looks & spirits. But I must return to our travels.

We all slept well & arose early to renew our tedious voyage of which I began to grow tired. The next morning we went on as usual passing along a country not so pretty or so interesting as that we had for some weeks been accustomed to. The banks of the river about Cornwall & for two or three following days was common land with a few loghouses & comfortable farm houses & some fine walnut & Hiccory trees, but I have not yet seen any of the magnificent trees I expected in this country where everything is on so great a scale.

The day after our night spent on the grass grew very rainy & we were wet through all our clothes. I never was so wet in my life, so completely soaking with wet. However, the rain began towards evening & we had not long to sit in the wet boats.

Even <u>under us</u> was all wet. I never saw such awfully heavy rain. About 6 in the evening we came to a little village, the name of which I forget. We found that the walkers of our party had gone into a house to dry themselves, so we all fled to the same house in a great hurry and found a most beautiful fire, but such cross people that they seemed quite angry at our going in the way of their tea making & venison frying, which occupied the entire attention of the very crusty old dame & her maid. They <u>pushed</u> us away from the fire whenever they wanted the kettle & did nothing but complain of the dirtying of the floor & the noise of so many children.

At last after waiting a tedious quarter of an hour our gentlemen came with the good news that they had found <u>hospitality</u> & lodgings. It was now very nearly dark & we had to walk a good way splashing through the puddles & wet, & then up a lane full of cows & <u>growling</u> bulls. But we at last got to the farm house of Mr. Marsh & here we found Oh! such true hospitality. He was blowing up a fine fire to warm & dry us & was so active & thoughtful about all our little comforts that he left us nothing to wish for. He spread our bedding before the fire to air & his wife (who seemed, poor woman, in the last stage of a dropsey) brought us pans full of nice new milk & very excellent loaves of her own baking, the only bread we had tasted since we left Montreal, for I own, though bread was plenty in every house, it was not good in general.

I was the only one of the party whose clothes were still wet, & my shift was clinging to my skin. So I retired to Mrs. Marsh's nice tidy little closet within her bedroom & changed all my habiliments. They have no family so the house is very small & they could only spare us the tiny kitchen floor to sleep on. But it was given with such a good grace that it made us all contented.

My mattrass was very wet so I left it airing all night & went with Tom to the barn where there was plenty of clean straw upon which we spread our blankets & cloaks, & lay down as usual, without undressing which none of us has had the comfort of doing at night since we left Montreal. Maria & her children slept in the kitchen & she said that good natured Mr. Marsh got up every now & then to watch & turn the bedding at the fire. The next day he insisted on driving as many as liked to go in his waggon to the far end of the "Longue Saut." This is a rapid which lasts for 3 miles & very few pass up there in the batteaux. I preferred walking but sent Betty & the children with Mrs. Reid & her squad in the waggon. This day was not at all too hot. It was early & our walk was delightful, part of it through cleared farms & part through the woods, where we gathered quantities of nuts. When we slept in this manner at farm houses we had nothing to pay except for milk & bread which were the only provisions we required as we had cold meat with us & dined & lunched every day in the boats, so that our lodging cost us nothing. In our walk we had peeps of the river which were most beautiful.

I find I am at the end of my paper long before I have come to the end of my week, so I will keep the rest for Anne Nangle. It is impossible to put so much in one letter so I will only say that we are all well this 13th Sept'r. Tom & Mr. Reid are gone to Douro to see whether they like it enough to settle there. I hope they are safe & well.

I am living alone without any companions but the children for the first time in my life. I find every day much too short. I have often dined & drank tea with the Fosters who are really the kindest people that can be. Mrs. F. takes me out to drive whenever I can join her & I have gone 3 or 4 times. I wish you could all have the pleasure of seeing how very comfortably we are fixed & how very well & comfortably we live.

Oh how completely happy I should be if — you may guess that if — but I know it is indulging weakness to wish for impossibilities, or to expect perfect happiness here in this world.

God bless you all. Give my most affectionate love to all my dear friends, beginning with the 31 party & extending any where that you know I love.

Yours, F Stewart

[1822: September 11][58]
To [Harriet Beaufort], written from Cobourg
Fragment

I have seen several crows and wood peckers & Eagles flying far above my head but we came too late to see Humming birds, of which I hear there are numbers in summer.

You asked me in one of your letters if there was any thing I wanted. No thank you dearest. My wants have been fully supplied by all my dear good friends already. But indeed any newspapers would be a great pleasure to us & I fancy could be sent by post open at the ends. But you could learn this from some one conversant in the rules of the Post office.

Apropos, Col. Foster advised me to tell my correspondents to pay the postage of all letters to Quebec as it would make their coming more certain. Then we pay the inland postage up here & from this I always pay the postage to [ ].

You cannot think how comfortable I found the wrappers on ship board, nor how often I thought of dear Bess & Anne who made them. At York, I wore my puce sarcenet every day & my beautiful cross barred washing silk when I paid visits. I take care to be always dressed nicely & am so well supplied with beautiful clothes that I should have no excuse. I have just made up a grand assortment of very nice caps I assure you with lace borders or quillings. I hate to be caught untidy at home. Since the weather has grown cold I have begun to wear my pretty purple bombazine. I am very careful of it. I have a great deal of work to do, such as baking & other such operations not fit for such a pretty gown. On those occasions I wear one of my wrappers....

We are in treaty for a cow. We have got a goose & gander to make a beginning & a little puppy dog for watching & keeping the wolves away from our cattle, for there are some wolves always in the woods when settlers first go into them, but they soon retreat. There are a great many Deer at Douro I hear. We are laying in salt pork & pease & various sorts of provisions for our winter store. But I hope by next winter we shall have them of our own....

There are very pretty roads here, pretty to my mind from the novelty. There is such a wildness in the general appearance of the country, the cleared part open at each side to the road, like & common, then wood again, then a part of it half cleared with the stumps sticking up & fallen trees lying all about. The roads are in many places, where the ground is swampy, made by laying trees across, close together. Those are called corderoy roads, & you may imagine what jumbling ones bones get in a waggon bumping over these trees. In general the roads are made by clearing a passage thro' the wood, & if it wants repair it is just ploughed up & then harrowed & left for driving on. So you may guess what bogs these roads are in wet weather & then in frost all rough. But when snow is fairly on & frozen over, then they are delightful for sleighing.

Yesterday Tom, the children & I took a nice walk of above a mile along the lake. The shore is very pleasant. It is smooth hard sand. The view of the village & its white houses & church made me wish that I could make a little sketch to send you.

1822: December 14[59]

To Mrs. Waller and Maria [Noble], Allenstown, Ireland

Cobourg — Newcastle District
Upper Canada
Saturday 14th December 1822

My dearest Aunt and darling Maria

I am sure you have heard all about us & our proceedings from Clongill & Merrion Street, but you cannot hear from any creature how often I think of you all nor how sincerely I love you. You may guess how impatiently I watch for the arrival of English mails. But this month has hitherto been blank & no letters have we received since the 5th November when I had one from dear Kate dated 17th Aug't mentioning the intended trip to Cheltenham & also one from Harriet telling of their safe arrival there, & giving so very indifferent an account of our beloved Bess that I am miserable for the next letters. From what Harriet said I much fear she was not able to return to Ireland before winter. It must have been very disagreeable as well as inconvenient in every way <u>wintering</u> at Cheltenham.

I dispatched a long letter to Catharine from Montreal, Ditto to Bessy from York, a short letter to Catharine from York, and a long one to Aunt Sue from this, all which have I hope reached Clongill long ago. So of course you know that we have long reason to hope for success in our undertakings here. So far we have succeeded to the full extent of our wishes and expectations & our prospects look well as far as we can see. There are certain "<u>Settlement duties</u>" such as clearing a stated number of acres & making roads which must be done within two years, which (on so large a tract of land) will be rather expensive. But when these are performed & the Government fees paid, we shall have only our own wants & comforts to satisfy & I expect to enjoy more comfort than we have had yet since our marriage.

The first two years after Emigration are the worst because of being obliged to buy all sorts of provisions as well as having to build and clear land & pay Gov't fees & perform settlement duties, all which are greater in proportion as the number of acres is greater. But we are unusually well off, for the land is remarkably good & the situation one of the most whole-some in Canada as well as beautiful. It is a new township which is not yet surveyed & we are the very first settlers in it. But we have neighbours very near us, not any of our own class, however, nearer than 6 or 7 miles. There are a great many farmers from England & Scotland in the two adjoin-ing townships & there is a Flour Mill & Distillery within three miles of our Loghouse, so that we are not like our curious countryman Col'l Talbot, 180 miles from any European. I regret that we have not become acquainted with this oddity but indeed I am rejoiced that we are not set-tled in his District which tho' fine land is so far back that I should indeed have felt in banishment. Here we are between Kingston and York & in a very few years a public road will pass close to our land from Kingston to Simcoe which will be a great advantage to us. There is a constant inter-course between this village & the settlers up there & we can have frequent opportunities both in summer and winter of receiving letters &c from this place which will be our <u>post town altho' 35 miles from us.</u>

About 6 miles from us there is a family of whom everyone speaks the highest terms, & I expect to have a great deal of pleasure in the society of Mrs. Rubidge. Every one says she is a most charming woman & a perfect gentlewoman. Since our arrival here we have met with great civility & attention from everybody. Indeed I never met with kinder or more truly friendly people. Mr. McCauley our own clergyman is a most excellent young man. He is Canadian & was educated by Dr. Strachan but went to Oxford to study there & take his degree & is a very well educated & I believe a clean man but very diffident. He has 5 or 6 young men who live with him as pupils & he is most active in doing good in every possible way. When Tom & Mr. Reid came first here <u>to explore</u> & visit Douro you know poor Tom was taken ill. He was at an uncomfortable noisy inn but our good friend Mr. McCauley sent his waggon for him & had him removed to his house, where he had every comfort & atten-tion that could be. He had a very severe bilious attack with a high fever & was so ill that the Doctor visited him twice a day for some time but I never heard this till lately as he never told me how ill he had been. He is now perfectly well again & only impatient to get to our own house but we must wait patiently till the snow comes & till the sleighing begins as no waggons can run on the roads in their present state. We were to have gone a month ago but we were prevented by poor little Anna Maria's being ill with I believe a worm fever. She is now a great deal better & able to walk out but looks miserably pale & thin. However, I trust the bracing winter weather will bring back her chubby cheeks & strength. Ellen is a going Lioness & as rosy & stout as possible & very bold. Bessy is grown very fat & strong. She can walk very well when she has anything to hold by & is very amusing for she imitates everything she either sees done or hears & she is a great coaxer but very passionate. In this little bill of health I suppose you would be very mad if I did not mention my own ladyship, so I must add to it that I am perfectly well now & have quite regained my strength. Indeed I find the frosty weather agrees remarkably well with me & I have never yet felt it as cold as I have often been at home tho' in reality the air is much colder than it ever was in dear little Ireland. This morning the thermometer was down to 8 & a few days ago it was 10. Between these two days we had some very warm delightful weather, so warm that on the 12th of Dec'r we breakfasted with the window open from really finding the room too hot. The weather has been very changeable all this Autumn & winter & there has been more rain than ever was known before in this country. We have had some snow too.

I generally contrive to walk a little every day & when the roads & fields are too wet I walk up & down our little court by the door. The country about here is very thickly inhabited for three or four miles on every side & there are a great number of half-pay officers, both Naval & Military, who have brought their families here, so that civilization is very fast spreading & this nice little town is increasing in a wonderfully rapid manner. Since we came here in the beginning of Oct'r, 5 houses have been built & are now inhabited & there are 3 more building now & in this village which is not larger than your Greta or Gretagh there are three very extensive shops or stores, a post office, a Cabinet Maker, shoemakers, tailors, Butchers, Smiths, Carpenters, who all carry on their respective businesses. Besides, we have the Sheriff & two Inns & two Schools so you see what a busy little spot it must be. We have been visited by two or three families but as we don't like to hire a Waggon we don't keep up any great intercourse beyond a walking distance. Mr. McCauley & Mr. &

Mrs. Henry & Mrs. Bethune who all live about a mile or a mile & ½ off are our principal friends & we go there very often & find them friendly and pleasant.

15th Dec'r Sunday evening. Tom has gone to dine with Mr. McCauley who carried him off after church. I was too lazy to accompany him so here I am seated in my odious little den of a parlour which, however, is very snug this cold evening — thermometer 12, but we have got a stove which heats the room delightfully & sitting at the far end of the room we are as warm as near the stove. The heat spreads so equally all over the room, which is not the case with a fire, for at a fire your face may be nearly roasted when your back is freezing. In our kitchen we burn very great fires indeed sometimes & we keep on a good fire there all night notwithstanding this one night last week & last night too. Indeed, water in a pail at the opposite side of the kitchen was frozen over & our kitchen is not more than 10 feet across, but we take good care to keep ourselves warm & we all wear flannel next our skin.

How often do we talk of all our friends & how often do I wish to know what you are all doing. If there could be some kind of glass to see how you all go on, how delightful it w'd be. But I try to prevent myself from regretting what cannot be helped & I try to look forward with a hope that we may be allowed the happiness of meeting again in four or five years. In the meantime I must turn my mind to the many blessings I enjoy & be thankful for them, & surely few have more reason to feel grateful to the Almighty than I have, who have so many sources of happiness, & tho' I have been surrounded by adversity in many of our connections & have had some trials ourselves, yet I cannot say I have met with one real <u>misfortune</u>, for even in the midst of these trials I have seen good arise. The greatest trial I ever met with was leaving my friends but I believe in my heart it was the best thing we could do & I am sure it was a right thing to do & this alone ever could reconcile me to it. I must now feel rejoiced for I see every reason to hope that we shall be very comfortable & quite independent & we need not entirely give up Society for in a year or two we may enjoy & amuse ourselves as much as we please. I wish some of your <u>idle boys</u>, James or [Wm], w'd come over next summer & pay us a visit. I am sure they would like it & they could give you a good report of us. I almost come to the end of my paper long before I have said half what I want to tell you but now I must end as I cannot cross this for I am sure you find it quite hard enough to read without it. Adieu then my dear dear friends. Give our fond love to your fireside & to Clongill & ever believe me your affect' child & sister — Fra's Stewart

[1822 or 1823][60]
[Journal]

June is the best time for a summer burn…. When the ground has cooled so as to be able to walk on it the men come for "Logging." They draw the Logs into heaps with oxen & pile them up with poles or "hand spikes" used as levers, & skids for supports to raise the heavy Logs to the top of the heap. These "skids" are poles placed with one end on the Log heap, the others on the ground on which they roll the logs till they are at the top of the heap. The logs are [ ] by a strong iron chain 10 or 12 feet long or more. One end is fastened round the log. The other end hooks into a ring in the yoke of the oxen. Every evening these log heaps are set on fire & it has a beautiful appearance, perhaps 20 or 30 immense fires blazing & sparking up & illuminating all the surrounding forests. When the log heaps are all burnt the ground is ready for any seed or crops you choose to put in.

Indians

The wigwams are formed of several slender poles stuck into the ground & brought together at the top, covered with pieces of Birch bark. The fire is sometimes lighted inside in the centre. In summer they cook out of doors. The Indian women or Squaws carry their infants in curious little cradles made of a board rather longer than the child with a small hoop at one end which comes over the childs forehead & protects it, sometimes two or three hoops all round the head & sometimes they ornament these hoops with Porcupine quills dyed different colours. They lay the child on the board with its head under the hoops & strap it down tight & swath it up, so that they can place the cradle on one end without the infants slipping in any direction. In these cradles they keep their infants always

& carry them about so on their back or in the arms. When the child crys instead of rocking they put one end of the cradle against or on their toes & jump it up and down gently.

The Indians and Squaws are much improved in dress since they have mixed more with Europeans. The men now generally wear European clothes, hats, trowsers, long coats, &c but when they retire to the woods to hunt they wear their own dress which is merely a shirt, a sort of frock coat made of Blanket & fastened round their waist with a belt. On their head they wear a hood or cap of coloured cloth bound with some different colours & with two points sticking up at the top like ears of some animal. I wish I could give you some idea of it [*a tiny diagram is included in the original*]. This is the back & it falls over their neck like a cape. I cannot make any scratch. [Like] the front at the points they have a little knot of ribbon & a tassel. On their legs they wear leggings or stockings of coloured cloth tied at the ankles & knees, on their feet moccasins of Deer skin. The squaws have not yet adopted European dress except that they put up their long hair behind & some of the educated girls wear stays. They wear a Bedgown of coloured cotton, generally from it [ ] cotton or larger pattern & bright colours, petticoats of green or purple cloth bound round with ribbon of different colours in rows round the tail & often ornamented all round with silver buckles or broaches put close together which look very pretty on the dark cloth [*a tiny diagram is included in the original*] — that way. They always wear a blanket for a cloak or shawl & go bareheaded, the stockings & moccasins like the men.

They encamp in parties in the woods near settlements but are always shy & never encamp in clearings. The men go out hunting & leave their families at the encampment. If an Indian sees a Deer or Deer track, he will follow it for 2 or three days together & do without food all that time. He will go on & persevere till he hunts it down & kills it. Then he opens it, takes out its entrails & eats them raw, he is so hungry & exhausted. He then returns home marking the road as he goes along by breaking twigs or other little signs which he tells his Squaw & she sets out & follows his marks. She knows his from all others & will not touch a deer sh'd she see it on her path till she comes to the place he described where he had left his Deer concealed in a safe manner. She then ties it up with bands of Basswood bark & fastens it on her back by a band round it & round her forehead. In this manner they carry immense loads, 100 lbs or 150 lbs. The Squaws always carry burdens as the Indians think it beneath them.

In summer they don't always make wigwams but turn their canoes bottom upwards & sleep under it.

They light their fires very expeditiously. They always carry about with them a store of dry cedar bark & spunk which is knots of maple become quite rotten. It grows dry, light & spongy & is used as tinder. When they want to light a fire they powder some dry cedar bark & mix a little gunpowder with it. They put a bit of spunk along with this which has been set on fire with a spark from a flint. They then whirl it round & round when the gunpowder explodes & the cedar bark takes fire & blazes instantly. If they are in a great hurry for a fire they find out a dry rotten stump & log of which there are plenty everywhere in the woods. Into this they fire their gun, then pile up dry sticks & have a fire directly.

1823: February 24[61]
To Maria Noble, Allenstown, Navan, Ireland; also addresses Harriet [Beaufort]

Douro Loghouse Feb'y 24, 1823

Well my dearest friends, here we are at last <u>at home</u> and although we must bear a good deal of inconvenience for some time, yet we feel real enjoyment beyond any we have had for many a long & weary month. Before I say anything more about this place, I must go back a month to Cobourg & tell you about what passed then. I wrote to you the 7th of Jan'y which letter I am afraid is in the dead letter office as it was directed to Merrion Street. The 18th of Jan'y I wrote to Catharine so you know by my letter to her that yours of Sept'r 30 reached me safely. Ah dear Harriet, you cannot conceive the comfort it is to think that you do not deceive me about my dear Bess. Thank you for giving me such a minute detail of her sufferings which must be most trying to her & her dear nurse tenders. I will not say anything now about the anxiety I feel about you all. You know what one feels at a distance from a beloved friend in such a state but you cannot well conceive how this anxiety is encreased by such an immense distance as that which separates us & by the length of time which there must be between letters. But this cannot be helped so I will not dwell on this painful subject any longer. I may, however, say that I do think this is the only source of painful reflection that I feel here. We have the prospect of possessing everything to make us comfortable & happy except the company of those we are most attached to.

In my letter to Kate I believe I mentioned a nice drive we had with very nice people called Mr. & Mrs. Faulkner on a very delightful day to a beautiful village called Port Hope, about 7 miles from Cobourg.

Nothing happened for some time after worth mentioning except that we had very cold disagreeable weather, a good deal of snow, & very little sunshine in the day, & most intensely cold nights, so much so that water was frozen in our kitchen which is only about 9 or 10 feet square, where we kept a good fire all night. In our room where we & the children slept & where we had a fire constantly day & night the therm'r was down several mornings to 30 before we got up. One night my poor little maid Betty slipped on the ice at the back door, fell & broke one of her ribs in two places as her side came against the handle of a tub.

Tom & I laid her on a matrass in our room & had her bled & early next morning had the Doctor to see her, who ordered low diet, saline draughts & quiet. So she lay there for some days. I was able to get a Scotch lassie to come to cook & finish the washing but she could only stay two days & after that I was cook, nurse, & everything myself for a few days. We had luckily a fine round of Beef which lasted cold for almost the whole time so I had no cooking except boiling potatoes & I got on finely & had neither fatigue or hurry of any consequence. And poor Betty was able to assist me a little in a wonderfully short time. I think these little vanities are very useful for people don't know what they can do till they are tried. Betty is now quite well & useful & willing as ever & a great comfort to me.

Well one fine day soon after this adventure our friend Mr. Bethune called to take us all out in the sleigh. He begged that A.M. & Ellen might be of the party so we all drove to the township of Haldimand the next township on the Kingston side & after a drive of 7 miles we turned. The country is very pretty & very hilly, beautiful undulations & steep rugged vallies. Coming home it was desperately cold & snowed a little & we were very glad to get into comfortable houses.

We called on Mrs. A. Macdonald who had removed to her own house a few days before. If you received my last letter you know something of her & the Boswells. We also called on the Boswells who we found very friendly neighbours during our sojourn at Cobourg. They said they wished very much to take us to see Mr. and Mrs. Sowden that we might see how very comfortably people can live even in an indifferent loghouse. So we appointed the following Tuesday evening for our drive. It was fortunately sunny & mild altho' the therm'r stood only at 10° & in the morning at ten, was 11° below zero!! At half past one Tom, A.M. & I set out with Capt. & Mrs. Boswell & drove 8 miles, mostly through woods, to Mr. Sowden's farm. His loghouse is the oldest in the township of Haldimand & has been built for 25 years. It is black & shabby looking at the outside but I never saw more comfort & cheerfulness than there seemed to be within. There was a larger fire than my poor British eyes had ever before seen within the walls of a house. I am sure the logs on the fire were 8 feet long!! but since that I have seen many such.

I must tell you a curious romantic history about this family. The father & mother of Mr. Sowden had been attached to each other in their youth but for some reason or other could not marry. They each married other people & afterward old Mr. Sowden's son was married to the daughter of Mr. S's former flame. Sometime afterwards, old Mr. Sowden became a widower, the lady a widow, & as nothing was in the way then, they were united in their old age & came to this country with their son & daughter about 3 or 4 years ago. Old Mr. S. died about 3 months ago. Old Mrs. S. lives in the loghouse with the young couple & their children. She is more like a picture of an old lady than any one I ever saw. She was of course in [ ] but all her clothes were made & put on in the stile of 70 or 80 years ago. She is a fine looking old lady. Her face & complexion reminded me a little of Mrs. Montray.

On the whole we were well pleased with our evening & had a very pleasant ride home. The following Friday was appointed for leaving

Cobourg. We were up by cock crow & had all our affairs in readiness, bonnets & pelisses all ready to clap on, but we waited & watched in vain. Our sleigh never came. At 2 oclock the man whom we had engaged to drive us sent word that he could not come till Monday so we were obliged to wait very uncomfortably. We had left out a couple of mattresses for sleeping on the night of our journey, as we divided our journey, & we made use of these to lie on & borrowed plates, dishes, cups & saucers &c as all our things were packed up, & we did not like opening them again. Friday & Saturday were most charming days, the sun so bright & warm & we were quite provoked at losing them & were all out of sorts.

On Monday morning Feb'y 10 at ½ past 9 oclock we left Cobourg, Tom & I on one seat with Elly stuck between us, Betty, A.M. & Bessy sat before us, & Mr. Parker our charioteer in front of all. We had besides 3 blankets to roll about our feet & knees, a great many coats & cloaks & a bag of bread & a basket of cold meat so we were pretty tightly packed. We had another sleigh full of luggage of all sorts, bedding, trunks, tubs, baskets, & on the top were 2 baskets of live stock. In one were a goose & gander, in another a pullet & kitten, our servant boy set to take care of them & Cartouche & Douro, another dog, sat beside him. We formed a very ludicrous cavalcade I assure you. We went 20 miles that day & had a very pleasant drive. We passed through miles & miles of forest & I was delighted with this new scene. Every now & then we came to small clearings with loghouses & generally a good stock of cattle & poultry near the houses. At 4 we reached Page's Tavern where we were to pass the night. There was one very decent clean bed room but as it had no fire place we preferred sleeping on the floor in the sitting room where we spread our mattresses & blankets & coats & cloaks & slept soundly & comfortably.

Page is an Englishman who has been only 3 years here. His inn is a loghouse & we found it very comfortable & everything tolerably clean. The next morning soon after daylight & breakfast we set out again on our journey. Pages is 18 miles from this, all our road through thick woods. Indeed the <u>road</u> scarcely deserved that name for it was merely a track through the snow where one or two sleighs had lately passed. We [ ] & turned through branches & between trees & often had showers of snow from branches above us which our heads touched.

The boughs of the beautiful Hemlock pine were loaded with snow & often they bent down so low that we were obliged almost to lie down to be able to pass under them. We were 2 or 3 times obliged to stop & cut a pass for our sleighs where trees had fallen across the road. This day we drove the distance of 9 miles through woods without seeing any habitation except a few huts of Indians. I told you in a former letter that the Hemlock pine of this country was the same as our Arbor Vitae but I was mistaken. Arbor Vitae is called <u>Cedar</u> here & is common in marshy ground & on the banks of rivers. They grow large & spread their branches to a great distance. The Hemlock pine is a much prettier tree. Its leaf is a dark green & when rubbed has a sweet smell. It grows very high & is feathered down to the ground & is quite a pretty evergreen here. Indeed this & Cedar are the only trees I have seen here that can be called evergreen, except the different pines.

Feb'y 27. I have just heard that one of our workmen is going to Cobourg tomorrow so I will finish this to send by him & I am in hopes he will bring back a packet of letters with him. Last week Mr. Bethune sent us some New York & Montreal papers but I did not see anything of the arrival of a British mail.

I must go back to where I stopped in my journal. 14 miles from Pages we arrived at the river Otonobee. This is our river. We reached Scotts Mills 2 ½ miles from this. Here we found that we could not cross the river as we expected, the ice having given way & Scott's boat could not ply because there was a broad border of thin ice on each side of the river. So we sent a man across on foot to tell Mr. Reid to send his oxen & sleigh to the opposite side of the river, 2 miles lower down, & we determined to walk across at a place called the "Little Lake" about 2 miles lower down. This delay was a great disappointment to us besides giving us much trouble, but this day was to end all our travels & that gave us spirits to proceed with vigour. We walked to the <u>Little Lake</u> & across it through deep snow which came above our ankles. John Reid carried Ellen, & Mr. Reid, Bessy. The workmen carried our bedding, bags & provisions. Everything else we left at Scotts Mills. At this side of the lake we found the patient oxen. Our luggage & ourselves we packed into the sleigh & we proceeded in the shades of evening to Douro, drove nearly 5 miles thro' woods &

at last heard voices crying out "here they come" "here they are" & all the little Reids came out to meet us. We soon saw our loghouse whose windows were quite illuminated by the glare of the charming fires Maria & the children had prepared for us, & even had there been no fire I think we must have been warmed by the joy every one shewed at seeing us here, from Mr. Reid & Maria down to the youngest. Indeed it was delightful to be received so affectionately.

Our house was in a very unfinished state, the doors <u>laid to</u>, not hung & worse than this, the upper part of the chimney was built with boards as the frost made it impossible to go on with mason work. But we are now safe for Tom had it built up with stone last week in a temporary way & in Spring we must have it built over again as it would not do as it is & it smokes. The first night we found it rather cold but every day since we have made the house more & more comfortable. We have got a great large kitchen with a huge fireplace, 8 feet long. One other room is smaller & within it is a little store room & a room for the children. At present we sleep in our sitting room but in summer the children are to move upstairs where we shall have 2 good rooms and 2 closets & then we are to sleep in the room they occupy now. Our books fill up one entire side of the sitting room & give it a very comfortable look. We have 2 windows, one to the south & one to the west, so that we have now fine warm sun shining in from about ten till near 6. I think this is one of the prettiest places I ever saw. You would be delighted with it. Even now it is beautiful when the ground is covered with snow. The river is nearly twice as broad as the Boyne at Navan & at this place rushes on with great noise & carries large lumps of ice down from Mud Lake 20 miles above. The current here prevents it from freezing over but 2 miles below it is quite still. It winds beautifully & the edges are fringed with fine spreading Cedars & Hemlock Pine.

Will you let dear Mrs. Stewart know that we are here, all well & happy. The Reids never passed a winter without any colds or illness of any kind, but this one, & they have lived nearly in the open air all through the winter. But certainly tho' the cold is so intense, I never have suffered from it as I frequently have at home. Tell Mrs. S. we will write to her very soon & give our affectionate loves to her, also to Clongill, Allenstown, E'town,

Black Castle. Tell Uncle Sutton with our love that we hope he will be so kind as to send the [ ] as soon as he can. It will be very acceptable by the time it arrives. Tom begs him to send 3 bills for Security. Dublin bills will do very well.

Now dear give my fondest love to my beloved <u>Bess</u> & Anne, Aunt B & Louisa whom I often thought of when they were travelling through the rebellious regions in the South.

Ever yours most affect'
F Stewart
Tom sends his kindest loves too....

1823: March 11⁶²
To Catherine Browne [et al], Clongill Rectory, Ireland

Douro <u>Cottage</u>!! 11th March 1823

My beloved Sisters & Aunts of Clongill

Yesterday morning we had the delightful [feast] of 2 mails from England, 2 sets of letters from Clongill, 2 sets from Cheltenham & 2 from dear Mrs. Stewart, the first we have yet secured from [ ]. You may guess how we felt at this most unexpected & wonderful account of our dear Aunt Bess's <u>Accouchement</u> for I can call it nothing else. I had formed very gloomy presentiments from the former letters & had been preparing myself & trying to <u>arm</u> my mind, feeling sure of much worse accounts. You may then judge of the delightful sensation I felt at reading so many accounts of her amendment from different quarters & finding that all agreed. I read the letters over & over & never closed my eyes all last night with thinking over all their contents.

Our letters from our much loved Mother were not so cheering as they contained the news of the death of poor dear Anna Mathias, who we all loved extremely & little Lucy Bellingham, who has been a favourite of mine ever since the time of our beloved Eliza's death when this little girl shewed such strong affection for her Mother.

Besides all these letters Tom received Uncle Suttons enclosure of a Bill of Exchange for £55.7s.1d British which George Kirkpatrick

enclosed to us & mentioned in his letter the safe arrival of the poor
old Montreal letter which indeed my dears was not worth wishing &
watching for so long. I wrote it in hasty moments & when my mind
was in a state of [ ] about poor weeny Bessy who I thought at the time
was [in] a very hopeless state. She continued very delicate all summer
& all the time we lived at York but grew better in a miraculous manner
from the time we left that vile place. The Garrisson indeed is healthy
but York is an odious place tho' not at all dark or gloomy for we saw it
in hot sunny August & Sept'r when gloomy would have been refreshing. My beloved Catharine you never before your last letter told me
of that pain in your side. I hope that [those] all powerful waters of
Cheltenham have been of permanent service to you [ ] now my dear
dear child always tell me the truth about your health & every body that
I love for it is indeed mistaken kindness to put off mentioning illness
or to deceive a friend at a distance. Your two letters were dated Oct'r
& Nov'r. Mrs. Stewarts Ditto, Harriets latest was 4th Dec'r so you may
circulate this news to the different houses. I wrote to you last 18th Jan'y
& to Harriet from this house on 28th Feb'y which letter I directed to
E'Town as I knew they could have it forwarded to her in [ ] to any part
of England & I was not sure of its arriving at Cheltenham before May. I
think I will pursue the same plan till I think I may direct to Merrion St.
again for her letters are so long coming & mine going that I never feel
sure of their reaching her safe.

Your list of marriages amused us very much, none of the parties
mentioned more than poor little "Skinny." I dislike calling names &
saying anything severe but I cannot resist in the present instance for it
puts me in mind of our little snug suppers in the [ ] at Wilmont, that
time when the rest of our time was passed rather unpleasantly. Oh dear
Catharine, the happy gay time I passed at Wilmont before I was married & for nearly a year after is now like a dream. It was very delightful but it was a useless time. I was indeed living like a butterfly then.
Then came the very very unhappy time which I try never to think of.
Then came dear Lakefield where we lived so peaceably & comfortably
with that kindest & best of Mothers. I like thinking of Lakefield. We
lived there nearly two years & indeed it was a happy time. Then came

White Abbey where we were with dear good friends too, but it was not like Lakefield & all the time of our abiding there our minds were harassed by that nasty old Thomson & besides my own mind & heart were agonized with the constant dread of our taking this great leap. I did suffer more about this than about any other thing that ever happened, for who could help dreading such a step, so very doubtful in its consequences, besides the idea of leaving so many I loved so tenderly & knowing how much the step was disapproved of by those I valued & respected most. But I could not help feeling that Tom was right & I plainly saw where "Duty" pointed so I tryed to smother every other feeling but no one can tell the pangs I suffered. Oh the bitter pang when I last parted from you all so dear & from dear dear Merrion St. But why am I going over it all. I am a fool. I must come to the present time & tell you about our nice territory here. You will have learnt from Harriet that we arrived here the 11th Feb'y. I believe I forgot to describe the place as it is now. Our clearing is at present very small as the snow prevents much from being done at this time of year. Our opening around this house is about as large as FitzWilliam Square. You may imagine the houses of that little square, all very tall trees. Our little clearing is in this shape. I find I have turned this very nice

A changing landscape, Douro Township, 1823. Note Frances's observations: "thick wood all round here," "cleared but full of stumps," "road to Reids," "road," "road," "road to Cobourg," "cleared," "wooded bank down to river," "River Otonabee." (The drawing is upside down to Frances's text).

drawing upside down. So you must turn it. The trees are very high, higher than any trees I ever saw in Ireland but in general they are not surprisingly thick for they grow so close that they have a drawup look. The river runs at that front of the house from which it is about

as far from the house as the road is from Clongill [ ]. The bank is a
rapid declivity but not so much as to be ugly. At present there is a
thick border of wood between us & the river through which we have
made some openings & we can see the rushing water in two or three
places from the window. The river here has a strong current & it rages
away carrying huge masses of ice down from the Lake about 20 miles
above us, called Mud Lake. The Otonobee river is a very winding one
which adds much to its beauty. Here it is nearly twice as broad as the
Boyne is at Naven. Altogether as to beauty of situation & fertility of
soil, we could not have been fixed more completely to our satisfaction.
The house is in an inconveniently unfinished & unfurnished state but
as we are to be our own carpenters &c this will reconcile us to the
inconvenience of waiting sometime longer than we should otherwise
do. The frost interrupted the building of our chimnies & we have had
them put up in a temporary way just to do till Spring when we must
have the present chimney taken down & another built. The floors are
also to be laid in summer as at present the boards are only loosly laid
down to season so that we can't do any thing to the inside of the house
till Autumn or next Spring then (probably in Autumn we shall plaister
our walls neatly & make them fit for papering). We shall also plaister
& whitewash the outside but now we have the rough Logs outside &
the Logs smoothed down at the inside of our house. Our kitchen is
24 feet by 18, our sitting room 17 by 15, little bedroom inside 12 by
8 & a tiny storeroom within it or rather between it & the kitchen. At
present we sleep in our sitting room, & the maid & children in the
inside room, but in summer they are to move upstairs where we shall
have two good rooms & a closet & then we shall take possession of
the room next [to] this. The Reids house is the same size as this but
the inside division will I believe be differently arranged. They have
the hall door at one end. Their clearing is twice as large as ours which
gives their place a more chearful appearance but ours will be opened
more as soon as the snow is off the ground when Tom will hire men
& get it done quickly. He intends to have ten acres cleared this spring.
Tom is busy all day making shelves & tables. We have got a bedstead
but it is only a temporary one as he has not any seasoned timber yet.

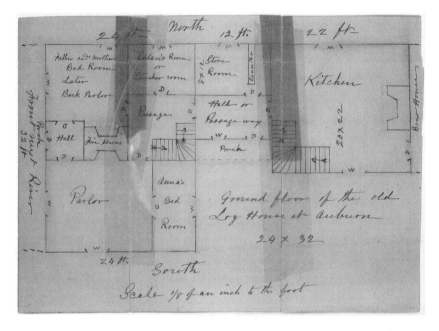

"*Ground floor of the old Log House at Auburn.*"

(Source: Frances Stewart fonds 97-023 Folder 5. Courtesy Trent University Archives.)

March 13. I have just [ ] [ ] that our neighbour Mr. Scott the Miller is going to Cobourg tomorrow so I must [finish this] letter [forthwith] to send by him to the post office. (Pussy has walked [ ] my paper & dirtied it all). Thank dear Bessy for her letter & Aunt Sutton for her note & tho' last not least darling Aunt Sue for her <u>Scrap</u> which is very precious to me. I lay by all my letters from home by themselves & read them over & over again. You all managed very nicely, not one of your party told the same news so that each contribution seemed as if they had come from different houses instead of different parts of a room. I pictured you all to myself, Aunt Sutton on the sofa with her writing desk before her, [Bessy at hers] in the corner, you at yours opposite [ ], & the dear Mamsey at her table in the window next the Piano. Now is this right?

Oh these were lovely letters & I felt so happy reading them. I just then forgot that <u>3,500</u> miles separates us!! One cannot have everything & I really do think that we only want our friends & <u>church</u> here to make our happiness complete. The latter I think we shall have in a year or two as there is a village plot laid out at Scotts Mills 2 ½ miles from this & I think there will soon be a church, for the township just at the other side of the river is thickly inhabited at this end & every month increasing in Settlers. [ ] township will be settled immediately as already numbers of [ ] [have] fixed on it & are only waiting till it is surveyed to come & built & clear. [Last week] [ ] just at breakfast time by two sleighs full of Strangers driving up to our door. One of them, a very nice gentleman-like elderly man, handed a letter to Tom & the 5 others (who were not very like gentlemen) set about helping us to make up a good fire for they were very cold. This elderly man was introduced to us by our friend Mr. Falkener of whom I told you before & he wishes to take land here & came to see what "The Bush" looked like. He had never been really in the woods before. He seemed delighted with the beauty of the spot here even at this dreary looking season & will probably draw his land in this township. He is a Quaker & has eleven children. He is an Englishman & Mullet is his name. The other yahoos (for indeed they were very uncouth animals) said "they could not see what enducement any gentleman could find in such a place." So I am in hopes they will not return tho' of course we need not visit them if we don't like them. Mr. Reid thinks some of his family will come here next year & perhaps some of ours. I believe I mentioned before that Gov't have promised that ten thousand acres should be reserved for 2 years in case our friends should join us. I do wish greatly that some of our friends who have small incomes & large families were here for it is the best place in the world for them, but I will never advise any one to come. It is like matrimony. We have been most prosperous in every thing. Our voyage & journey were performed most astonishingly when the number of little children are thought of & the dangers & hardships they were exposed to & Maria Reid & Nancy Bailey so near being confined & yet no accident or unpleasant circumstance occurred. When I look back & think of all we have "gone through" since we left home I cannot help feeling surprise & gratitude to that Merciful Being who has watched over us & protected us all. Twenty families might come & not one so prosperous as we have been. I had no idea of the arduous undertaking. Even at the time I did not perceive the trials nearly so much as I now do when we coolly talk over & when I think over every part of our voyage from Ireland to York & from thence to Cobourg, for we were in some danger in that short passage of 70 miles.

You ask how high your three nieces are. Anna Maria is 3 feet 7 inches. Ellen is 3 feet 1 inch, & <u>Bessheen</u> 2 feet 4 inches & a quarter. I found your present of the nice greenstuff frocks most useful, dear Kate, for washing is so troublesome at this frosty time when every thing must be dried within doors & then the danger of burning is so great when children or old people either wear muslin clothes, besides which the coldness of the weather makes stuff the pleasantest & best material for winter gowns & frocks. I have worn a black stuff gown all this winter & the chicks their little greeny's. In summer cambric muslin or English fine ginghams will be the pleasantest & coolest every day coloured gowns, & calico for frocks. I have not worn any additional clothing this winter more than I did in Ireland. The only difference I made was wearing a flannel chemise instead of a flannel petticoat & then my other chemise over the flannel & one upper petticoat & my gown. The great secret is wearing flannel next the skin & I have found this quite enough. Out <u>walking</u> at Cobourg I never wore more than my old grey cloak. Sleighing, my dear <u>Plaid</u> & my [-coat] over it, was the greatest muffling I ever found necessary even at night. Here I seldom put on either cloak or bonnet when I go out to take a race which I do every day two or three times. The cold is sometimes very extreme but I have never found it disagreeable. On the 4th of March at 5 in the morning the thermometer was 18 below zero & for three days was always 5 or 6 below zero at seven in the morning but we had good fires & when I went out I ran & never felt cold.

Pray remember me to all my friends & tell Mrs. Stewart we got her letters & thank her & the rest of the writers from our hearts for them. Tell her she did not tell us her present direction. So you must tell us soon. Tell her I am going to write by this post to Mrs. Mitchell but do you write dear for fear the other letter sh'd be lost. Reids all well.

Bessy's extract from Mrs. O'Barnes letter was indeed gratifying tho' my conscience told me at the time that I ought to feel ashamed for I know how little I deserve such praise. I don't accuse dear Mrs. OB of being a <u>flatterer</u> but I think her warmth leads her to think too highly of people or at least of me. Pray give my affectionate love to her in which

I am joined by Tom, & Mr. Reid who is just come in desires his kindest regards may be added & pray to her you write to her tell her to forward our kind remembrances to Enniskillen. I have a great respect & esteem for Doctor OBeirne, not much for his wife, entre nous — but you need not tell this.

I am glad you have got the Montreal letter. I believe I told you in it of the great kindness of the Mountain family. Indeed I never can forget the interest both the Bishop & Mrs. Mountain expressed about us nor the affectionate manner in which they took leave of us. I have been waiting till we came to our land to write to Mrs. M. for I think I owe her that slight attention & my letter shall go tomorrow I think if I can possibly make time to write tonight. Pray thank Miss Wren for having introduced us to such a very friendly & agreeable a family. Remember me to the [ ] family & particularly to dear Mrs. Montray. You are very welcome indeed to send my letters to darling Aunt Waller & my beloved Maria who is in deed & in heart my sister. [*A line that follows has been heavily crossed out*]. Pray give my tender love to Aunts Sutton & Sue & Uncle & Bessy & ditto to my dear Allenstown Aunt & Uncle & sisters & brothers, & ever love your doating & etcetera sister & brother. Fra.S. & TAS

[1823][63]
"Extracts from Canadian Letters"

Douro, 1823

"In the autumn of our first year in Douro our youngest little girl of not quite two years old was [ ] with Dysentery. I was quite ignorant of the disease & there was no Doctor within reach, the nearest being a good many miles distant. We had as yet no canoes on the river & were often depending on chance visits from the Indians for a passage to the other side. One of our hired men, a faithful Highlander, seeing how very ill our darling was, volunteered to swim across the rapid stream & walk through the woods to the Doctor, promising that if I wrote the particulars, he would bring the necessary medicines. He started early in the morning of a cold October day & returned about midnight with some powders & a message that the Doctor would come up the following day. But no improvement & the day passed in great anxiety for the Doctor did not come. On the third day he came having left at the promised time, but lost his way in the woods & hence the delay. The next day she appeared more lively, but refused to take the Arrow root & sage which I offered her. She asked for bread & of this alas we had none of it to give her, having for some time been unable to procure good flour. It was a bitter trial not to have what she seemed to crave for. The next day she fell into a stupor & towards midnight her angel spirit passed away to the immortal land." 20th October 1823.

On the 27th of October, there assembled together the whole of the settlement including the six Highlanders employed in clearing the land, in all numbering twenty seven souls, the only Christian inhabitants in that vast forest stretching for thousands of miles unbroken east & north of the Otonabee & the little Lake to follow to the grave the youngest & most endearing of the little band of Pilgrims, who had arrived on the shores of the Otonabee the previous year. The spot settled as the last resting place lay midway between Mr. Stewarts clearing & that of Mr. Rieds on a sloping ground known as "Hemlock Bray," beneath four [ ] hemlock pines, whose interwoven & spreading branches found a perfect canopy, & whose huge tough dark gray trunks & stems with their spiral tops towered far above carrying ones heart & eyes far away in the clear vault of heaven.

No human architect could equal in design the somber grandeur of the [ ] [ ] under whose somber shade this sorrowing group were gathered together in mournful silence. Strong & hardy men stood there breathless beholding the scene which lay before them rendered the more sublime by the knowledge they were assembled there alone in the midst of the noble works of God untouched by the hand of man.

The generous & stalworth Donald who had risked his life so lately in procuring remedies to relieve the little sufferer, whose remains were now in the midst of this solemn scene being consigned to the earth, was powerless to restrain the outpouring of his swelling heart. Deep & lasting the memory of that day sank into the hearts of all who joined in the beautiful & touching burial service of the Church of England heard for the first time in the midst of the little band of Pioneers who founded the settlement in that vast wilderness. No hallowed spot was ever dedicated with more heartfelt prayer than that where little Bessie was laid beneath those noble "Hemlock trees."

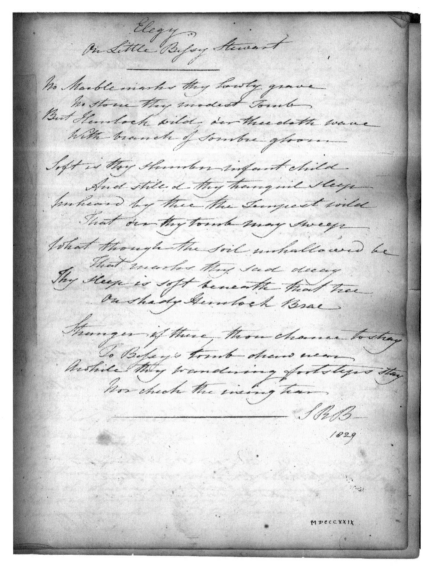

"Elegy on Little Bessy Stewart," 1829. A poem dedicated to the memory of Frances Stewart's daughter, Bessie, who died in 1823 at the age of two. Original located in Frances's commonplace book.

(Source: Stewart family books 98-005. Courtesy Trent University Archives.)

1824: January 27 and February 5[64]
To Harriet Beaufort, Ireland
"Extracts"

Douro, Jan. 27, 1824

My dear Harriet,

I began a long letter to Louisa on New years day which I have never yet had time to finish from some unforeseen circumstances which have added a good deal to my domestic employments, & which make it necessary that I should now begin this new sheet to you without waiting to finish hers. Well then I must begin <u>regularly</u> & tell you my circumstances which are these. My <u>paragon</u> Betty, the maid who was so useful & such a treasure, has turned out (like all other <u>paragons</u>) to be a most abominable little animal & has left me against our consent & after <u>pouring out</u> such a heap of the most abusive lies as you could never imagine any one could invent. I have found that she has been for months deceiving me. I need not enter into the detail of her artifice & ingratitude but will proceed to state my <u>necessities</u> to you, in hopes that you may in some time send me the remedy. Here I am without any maid. I cannot in this busy country get a servant girl without paying wages much too high for our means, as the lowest wages given are from 4 to 5 dollars a month, or £12 or £15 a year. So I must do without one till you or some one else can send me out two little girls. I should like to have 2 if possible as I can find abundant employment for them. I wish to have the oldest not more than 14 or 15 years old, but strong for that age & healthy, clean & good humoured. I should wish that they had never been at service & should be unacquainted with the ways of servants. Perhaps you might find such as I want at some school. I should like that she should know how to <u>spin</u> well, for spinning will in a short time become one of our household employments. Indeed spinning & washing are the only accomplishments that I am particularly anxious these girls should have, for cooking, baking &c I can easily teach them after they come. As for needle work I don't expect them to do much but if they are good workers <u>it will be no objection.</u> I should like to have them bound to me for 4 or 6 years. They should be

bound in Ireland & I can have indentures drawn up & signed here likewise. Perhaps Mrs. Stewart or Mrs. Wilson might know of a family going
who would take charge of them.

Your Sept'r letters reached me last month so I may reasonably soon
expect more. I hope you had Mrs. B. & Lu. with you at Christmas. Ours
passed cheerfully & our new year begins pleasantly. At least we have no
reason to think that our expectations of success will not be realised, but
we find that everything must go on "step by step" as you used to say to me,
& we do not raise our expectations too high. I believe when I last wrote in
Dec'r Tom was just going to Cobourg by the new road. He found it rather
a tedious journey as his sleigh was drawn by oxen & the new road was so
bad that he was all the first day going 9 miles. It was Saturday. That night
he slept at an old highlander the husband of my femme sage, as he took
the old lady home with him. They live within 2 miles of Mr Rubidge's &
on Sunday Tom went there & spent the night & day there. Tom reached
Cobourg quite safely & crossed Rice Lake in his sleigh for the first time.
He returned in Mr. Henrys sleigh as far as Rice Lake & it left him on the
other side of it where he was to wait till his own [ ] sleigh came up. This
was so slow that he waited & walked about on the lakeshore for a long
time, & then he thought he would go back part of the way across the lake
& listen if they were coming. When he had proceeded some way from
the shore one of those sudden thick snow showers came on which you
sometimes have at home accompanied by high wind. Poor Tom could
not see land on any side nor could he hear any sound to direct him which
way to steer his course. He was surrounded by an atmosphere of snow &
the wind was most intensely cold. He tied down the ears of his cap & but-
toned his coat tight round him & tried to gain an island which he knew
was near. At last he became uneasy for he did not know where he was,
or how to find his way back, & he was growing too cold for pleasure. In
this very uncomfortable situation he was considering what to do, when
he thought he heard some one call out. He lifted up his cap & distinctly
heard a call which he answered & very soon a man came up to him &
told him that Major Anderson (who lives on this side of the lake) begged
he would come to his house as he would certainly perish if he staid out.
He very kindly sent his sleigh out for Tom & brought him safely to Terra

Firma once more. Major A. did not know where the person was, he had just distinguished a figure & guessed that it was some poor passenger who had lost his way. He was very kind and hospitable. Tom soon saw his own equipage arrive & he proceeded to Mr. Rubidge's where he slept & came home safe & sound next day, heartily tired of his oxen sleigh & of the new road, which was so badly made that no horse sleigh can come up here without great difficulty for in consequence of the snow & frost there are many trees lying across the road uncut. I mean by this very confused sentence that in consequence of the snow, the men could not cross cut the logs which had fallen across the road & every sleigh has to jolt over them. Some of them are I daresay 2 or 3 feet in diameter. These nice little jolts we called Hop overs, & they are very common I hear in the roads thro' the woods. But indeed the best of our "Bush" roads scarce deserve the name for they are but paths.

I am sure you are in misery about me now, my dear Mamma's & think I am killing myself with all sorts of hard work now that I am without a maid. But you need not be uneasy for I do not <u>indeed</u> do anything more than my ordinary business, or at least nothing fatiguing. Mr. & Mrs. Reid have very kindly given me their eldest daughter Mary & she is very good natured & know how to do every [*sic*]. She is excessively anxious poor little girl to save me & is always trying to get everything before me, that I may have nothing to do but nurse my "Papousie." Maria, besides sends the servant girl here every Monday to wash, so you can see I am well off only that I feel quite ashamed to let poor Mary do all Betty's work & I know it must be very inconvenient to Maria to give her to me, & it must continue for so many months, before any of your little girls could come. But both she & Mr. Reid are very good natured & assure me they are very glad that Mary should be here. She cooks & cleans the kitchen & washes the eating utensils. I bake & make the beds & sweep the <u>two</u> rooms, which with my care of the little buntling & my constant supply of needle work fill up every moment of every day, & at this moment I am sitting up waiting for my bread to be baked & taking advantage of the silent midnight hour to write to you my dear. I generally read a little to myself while I am nursing babe, the only time I have now to read. Sometimes I get a good deal of time for this indulgence as she has not yet taken any thing except what I could offer her & consequently is very often with me. She thrives fairly & is strong & fat & sleeps well in general. She has been my bedfellow since her birth & I have taken the entire care of her since she was a week old. It seemed very odd to me at first & I trembled every day when I was washing & dressing such a tiny creature, but now I am become quite expert & am a very good nurse. She was vaccined on Sunday when our little Doctor paid us a passing visit. He improves on acquaintance very much & we like him better every time he comes. I have really told you all my occupations so don't be uneasy for constant employment is very good for me. The servant boy who we brought with us was very bad, idle & impudent & at last ran away, but in a month he came back & is now much better & is improved in many ways. He carries in all the water for our cookings & washing, cleans the pans & kettles & makes up fires & when we want assistance in lifting any heavy thing, he & his master are always near & willing to help us. I never half thanked you my dear for all your delightful presents which are & were & will be most useful. They were just in time for my Papousie who has some frocks of the pink gingham & nightcaps &c of the longcloth. Tom admires the bombazine very much. Even the linen covering of the box was most useful for [ ] which we cannot get even tolerable here. The books are wonderful comfort not only to us but to many others, for Mr. Rubidge & Dr. Hutchison have borrowed many from us.

Wed. Feb. 5, ¼ before 12. Tom goes to Cobourg tomorrow & he must have this to put in the post office. I wrote the former part when I was fast asleep. Our winter has on the whole been remarkably fine & mild so far. We have had very cold nights once or twice but till within this week nothing like last winter & we have had a great deal of thawing weather, very unusual here & not so pleasant I think as the clear frosty weather. However I think we shall have some real frosty Canadian weather now, for the ther'r has not been many degrees above zero this week, & is now 16° below zero. But the days are sunny & pleasant & we have fine fires. We have 2 cows going to calve so we shall have a fine store of butter & milk for spring. There is no danger of our being exposed to the miseries described by Capt'n Franklin in this "most deplorable of all climates" as he calls it. I envy you all those interesting books & having time to read them. Oh! I am become a famous Tailor! I have just made up a <u>nice</u> pair of frieze pantaloons for Tom & am to make him a waistcoat of the same materials. I think then he will be a complete Paddy. He is so fond of this frieze that he is determined to have a whole suit of it & it is very comfortable in this climate. I think next year we must get a piece or two out & a pair of good blankets & some linen sheeting, but at present we could not compass it. Good night & may God bless all my dearly loved mama's, pray your own child — F.S.

1825: September 5[65]
To Harriet Beaufort, Ireland
Extracts, bound with ribbon

F.S. to H. Beaufort

Douro Sept 5th 1825

This house has been like a Hotel for sometime past. This you will wonder at in this remote place where I formerly complained of solitude. First about two months ago came a Capt. Stewart from Ireland who brought letters from Mrs. Frood. He and his luggage settled themselves here just before my confinement and here he staid six weeks. I think it was rather inconsiderate of him when he found the situation I was in having my monthly nurse in the house and living in such an unfinished cabin with scarcely accommodation for my own family. However, poor creature, he certainly was not hard to please, but partook of our homely fare and slept in a loft with all sorts of sundries about him and bore it all good humouredly. He was always ill and taking medicine and obliged to be attended like a lying in lady with his bowls of gruel, and toast and tea travelling up stairs. At last he and Tom agreed that farming would never suit him and Tom advised him to try merchandise.

So he and Mr. Bethune have entered into partnership and he is to keep a store just near this at Scott's Mills, which will be a great convenience and advantage to all the back settlers as they can dispose of any thing they wish to sell and procure what they want to buy as Mr. Bethune is to keep it constantly supplied with goods to be sold at the Cobourg prices. He is getting a house built and has taken lodgings in Smithtown about two miles from Scotts as he says our early hours "destroy him" and he wished to go where he could have plenty of milk and whey. He comes every day to take away a few of his things in little bundles.

Mr. Robinson has formed an encampment of Irish Emigrants at Scotts and it is quite a gay place. He is a native of Halifax and is I hear very gentlemanlike. He lives in the midst of his Paddies in a grand tent. They are all in huts round him and every day parties are sent out to their land. Several are placed in this township. They are all from the south of Ireland and have hitherto conducted themselves well. They will be settled five or six miles behind us.

There is a Mr. and Mrs. Armstrong come out. Mr. Robinson mentioned them to Tom as pleasant companionable people, as he termed it. They arrived the other day when Tom was at the camp, wet to the skin and wearied nearly to death. They had no shelter or fire to dry themselves so Tom requested they would come here and he brought them all to remain till their house is ready, which is to be two miles from us. She is an unassuming person who has been in a bettermost style of life; they have four little boys and a baby of 17 months and a servant maid. All have been living here and will probably remain much longer. They do not give much trouble considering all things. The boys are fine manly fellows.

There is a Mr. Smith employed by Government to place the settlers on their land or to locate them as it is termed. He is a surveyor and a very agreeable man. He lives at the camp and has dined and breakfasted here and is one of the most gentlemanlike men I have seen since I left Ireland.

We are soon to have another neighbour, Dr. Read and his family. He has been in this country for some years but went back to Ireland last year and returned with the emigrants. He is appointed by Government to attend those settlers in Douro and is to have a house at Scotts Mills for a year and after that to have land in Douro. Mrs. Armstrong says he is a very nice man and a good physician. I am told he has a very pleasing wife and three children. She is very dressy and Dr. Read has brought quantities of fine clothes for her and his children. I'm sure I don't know what she will do with them here. When I have such gay people around me you may expect to hear that I am become quite a dasher.

Col. Burke is also coming and is to live at Scotts during the winter so we shall have a village there directly and abundance of Society.

There never was so unhealthy a season as this has been and is, scarcely a family without illness in some shape, either ague, dysentery or lake fever. Numbers have died. At Kingston many of the emigrants died. Many now are ill at Cobourg and some are ill in our camp. However, the hot weather is now over and we have had frost for the last four nights which will cool and purify the air, and drive away noxious vapours.

How thankful should we be that we have escaped illness of every kind. Neither the Reids nor we have had the least illness. Our children are very stout, Bessy recovering her [ ], William thriving and growing wonderfully and is a fine stout fellow.

Thank you for the mignotte seeds and all the others. I have great fears about them and the Laurels too.... This year we are annoyed by swarms of fleas such as you couldn't conceive. They crawl on the floors and on the beds, all from the dryness of the season. They are in the woods amongst the dry leaves, earth and dust in great numbers.

My head is quite confused with the bustle we live in after the sameness we had so long. This house is full of comers and goers, chiefly poor settlers. They make much noise and give some trouble occasionally.

1826: May 27[66]
"Extracts"

27th May, [18]26

A very unpleasant accident happened at Mr. Reids last week. John Reid was ferrying over five of the Emigrants, two men and three lads. One of the boys was very obstinate and ignorant and though John told him he would upset the boat he would not mind him but went on to change his place, put his foot on the gunwale. The boat upset and all tumbled into the water in the middle of the rapids. John knew if any of the men could catch hold of him they would, and that if they did they would all perish. So he had presence of mind enough to dive under them so as completely to disengage himself from them. When he rose again he saw one of the men trying to catch at a little branch. He knew it could not bear him and he caught him by his hair and swam with him to the bank. The other man escaped also but the three boys were lost. Three of the little Reids were standing watching the boat coming over and when they saw it go down, screamed out and ran to tell their father and mother who were in the house. They expected Mary and Ellen Reid over and were sure they were in that boat. You may have some idea of the agony they suffered for a few moments. No blame can be attached to poor John for he is as careful as possible in the management of boats and very expert, but it is at this time of year an arduous undertaking to cross in the rapid part of the River. The boat was carried down a little way past this house where it is now sticking among some logs at the side of the River. You will wonder why I have written this letter so badly. I have been interrupted every two minutes, and now whilst I write, Bessy is jumping on the sofa behind me and catching my shoulders and then springing round me on the table. Willy is creeping about my feet and trying to climb up by holding the leg of the table.

Poor Anne McVitie is worse than ever, tho' I have consulted three physicians. She is ill in one room and the boy Delany in another. All last week Ned our other boy was in bed with ague.

I was greatly afraid that Tom was taking it. He was ill and feverish and chilly one day. He looks bilious and thin and complains of headache but he will not yield to my entreaties and take any kind of medicine.

God grant us a continuation of good health he has enjoyed and make me thankful for his mercies. The children are all well and great wild racing creatures. Anna is up to my shoulders, Ellen about a head lower, Bessy very amusing and engaging, Willy a great stout laughing fellow.

Give my love to all dear dear friends including the Meath branch
Ever and ever your own old
F. Stewart

Douro May 27th 1826

I have been in a state of repentance my dearest Harriet ever since my last letter was sent off, for I wrote in rather a disponding humour and am sure you will all be in a state of misery about me thinking that we are very miserable. But I assure my dearly, loved friends that I am not very miserable. I am only sometimes more prone to low spirits than I have been, but I will not yet touch on this subject. I want to express to you how acutely and deeply grateful I feel for all your exertions about the Postmaster Gen'l. Indeed I give you constant trouble and plague, but I hope I shall not do so much longer. I am not at all sanguine about this appointment and have no hope about it for good luck seems to go in particular currents and we are not placed so as to meet any thing which the rapids may carry down the stream. However this does not make me the less sensible of the kindness of those friends who have taken such unwearied means to be useful to us.

31st. I began this on Sunday night but grew sleepy. Well, since I wrote last we have had some variety, Mr. Strickland who is clearing within, or rather less than a mile of us, and Mr. and Mrs. Armour.

On Sunday last I went to Church or rather to Peterborough intending to go to church as we heard that Mr. Armour was to have service in Mr. Robinsons Hall. After being so long, three years and a quarter, without being any place of public worship you may judge of my feelings. So I braved the musquitos which are tremendous this year. When we arrived there, we walked up to the Big house, but behold! we found the doors all shut and locked! We looked in at the windows, but could not see anybody or receive an answer to our repeated knocks. We then went to Mr. Armours and found his house also deserted. But there we learned that old Mr. Thompson had arrived not having known that the Armours had come and he had the service at a house in Smithtown two miles off. So Mr. Armour requested that all the Peterboro' congregation would go to Smithtown, for he thought it right to pay this attention to old Mr. Thompson, and we were left in the lurch.

I was tired and went and sat for an hour with little Dr. Reade who returned last week ill of the ague, and then I came home quite disappointed at having had my walk for nothing. Besides I was affronted at Mr. Robinson who had invited us to go to his house and spend the day and should have waited a little while to accompany us to Smithtown or should have given directions to his Servants to admit me if he could not wait. So you see I was huffed, and so I came home but Tom was

obliged to stay for a meeting about school business. He saw Mr. and
Mrs. Armour and seems to like Mrs. Armour very much. She is, he says,
a very sensible clever woman, middle age and rather plain in appearance with a good countenance and good natured manners. She has no
maid, a very common misfortune in this country and she is obliged to
clean the house, cook, wash, and do everything herself, and she had
seven children. She scours the floors and scrubs away just as all the
people here do. She says she would rather do everything herself than
hire any of the Emigrants for they are not fit for servants, all the best
having lived in the Towns.

I envy people who can do all those things. They are so much better
suited to this country than useless I am. Tom admires that sort of cleverness so much too, and he feels so much my want of it that I sometimes
feel a little melancholy, for I am not half clever enough for a farmers wife,
and he has been so much accustomed to very clever English women that
he is rather hard to please on very [ ]. You know I never saw that mode
of life at all so that I am very ignorant and if we continue to live in this
country I hope I shall improve and shall have now more opportunity of
seeing what others do. For all this time I have been so little from home
that I have only heard and have seen but little of the housekeeping of
this country and hearsay will never teach that art. Indeed latterly I don't
know why I feel great deadness over me, not laziness for I like to exert
myself when I can but a sort of stupidity and compression of mind which
I used not to have at all. Perhaps it is old age coming on for you know
I have just passed my birthday and have crept into another year. I have
many signs of age about me, so I may begin to doat. Mrs. Reid says I am
grown like old Aunt Smyth, and she not but in joke.

June 1st. Yesterday Mr. Armour and Dr. Reade dined here and
indeed I like Mr. Armour very much. When his countenance brightens
he has a look of great benevolence. If I might give an opinion on so slight
an acquaintance I should say that he seems a really religious man. On the
whole I am very agreeably surprised. I have not yet seen Mrs. A., having
no servant. The cares of a family prevent her leaving home. Dr. Reade I
do like. He is so constantly and unremittingly kind and is always on the
watch for any opportunity of obliging us.

I must now tell you about Mr. Strickland. He seems to be twenty three or twenty four. He is an everlasting talker but between times he has some drollery and on the whole is rather pleasant. Tom says he talked very agreeably to Mr. Armour one day. They dined together and [shared] some information. He gave us a description of an evening which he passed at a Tavern or public house in this country where the Master and Mistress wanted to pass themselves off as very fine folk and he acted their manner and changed his voice for the man or woman and made himself very diverting indeed. He is good natured and nurses Willy for me. He has just got his Shanty built and is very busy fitting it up. He sleeps here every night. The mosquitos are so numerous that they make sad havoc when they attack him. He comes here every night swollen and blistered all over. Mosquitos always like strangers best and bite them a great deal more than the old settlers in this country. I think the reason must be that the skin is softer, before it has been weather beaten here, for I never do see here such delicately skinned females as at home. Indeed beauty is very scarce. Mr. Strickland lived in Norfolk and came out last year. I dare say he may get on here as he says he has always been accustomed to hard work but he little knows the work before him. However he has good expectations as to property and hopes to be able in a few years to live at home. I hear of many who say they wish to be at home, but having spent all their capital here either are unable to return or think it better to go on trying a little longer. I do think we are deceived in this country, for one must bear many years of wearying difficulties before they gain comfort or are able to save or make anything. Therefore I am now come to the opinion that people would do better at home, and that we perhaps might have done better at home. Unless they mean to make their children actual labourers I don't think people can make anything by farming. The land will do one no good unless it is cultivated and in order to have it cultivated the land holders must either spend a great deal of money or else work hard and make all his family work hard too. This is what the Reids do, but they neglect everything else, in manners, learning and appearance they are exactly a labouring family. This I cannot bear for my poor dear children.

I have thought a great deal on this lately, but my thoughts have not tended to comfort me much for I cannot decide what is best for us to do.

I have no one to consult, for I am afraid of making Tom unhappy by raising doubts in his mind. I suspect he feels as I do, by little things he sometimes says, but he is frequently tired and bothered and I cannot bear to add to his uneasiness, and if he thought I was unhappy, I know it would make him wretched for he loves me most tenderly. His countenance which used to look so placid has now more of care and anxiety and his manners are not as gentle as they were. These are the effects of the disappointments and vexations he has met with and I must regret it greatly but don't know how to mend the matter. Mr. Reid says he does not think this kind of farming will ever be profitable for Tom as he cannot work nor can his children and that he would do better on a small farm and that he makes no doubt Tom will return home in a few years. I don't like talking of it to anybody but I should like much to have your opinion. My dearest friend and Mammy, I have often intended to write you about this but was prevented by the fear of giving you pain, but I know it will relieve my mind very much for continually thinking and pondering on a subject and having no creature to talk to about it is too much to bear long. If we go on here as we have done, I know we shall live to the extent of our income, without much comfort and seeing our children vulgar and illiterate. If we remove to Peterboro' as every one advices Tom, I don't like that, for we should be in a little gossiping village, and Tom would perhaps sink into indolence or lose his health besides the expense of building and purchasing, &c &c.

In removing to Cobourg I see fresh expenses. The Society would be better and the children would have the advantage of it but there would be a purchase to make and a house to furnish and we would still be as far from all our friends. If we return home we must spend some money for the passage. Our income is small and yet I dare say with good management we might live on a very small scale at least with as many comforts as we have had here, and it would be such a great thing to be near our friends. It would balance many as privations and difficulty. We have the greatest objections in the world to being a burden on the affections of our dear and kind friends and feel this is one reason for not returning home to G't Britain, that from affection our friends would do too much for us. I now wish and so does Tom that we had taken the advice of our friends and not emigrated so hastily but it can't be helped now. I argued and reasoned and entreated Tom as much as I could before we came but his mind was bent on it and nothing would change it and I thought my duty then was to yield. He thought right to come to Canada to try his fortune and he never would have been happy if he had not done so. If we had taken a cleared farm at first we should have got on well and saved an incalculable deal of disappointment and hardship and I should have had the pleasure of seeing the children gentle in their manners and their minds improved. But Tom did not think it right to separate from Mr. Reid's family and for them the woods were the best. But there is no use now in giving way to useless regrets. He did so from kindness of his brothinlaw's family and that was a good motive. I should be sorry to encourage him to go home if I thought he had a prospect of succeeding here, but I see no great prospect of that and I would rather live in a small way near my friends than here where if I want advice I must wait half a year to receive it and in many little dilemmas I could give anything to have a friend like you to consult.

I am always happy when I can write my letters at night for then I am with my friends, but work must be done, torn frocks and worn shirts must be mended.

Now my dearest Harriet I have given you a plain statement of our case. Tom is I am sure tired of the woods. My puzzle is, is it better to persevere or openly encourage him to stop. I hope now my dear friends you will not mistake me and think me discontented or changeable. Let me assure you that I am glad we did come to Canada for Tom thought it right to judge for himself. In all our trials we have been strengthened and supported by the Almighty and I feel perfectly sure and convinced that he never sends us a trial or affliction without good and wise reasons. Therefore I do most humbly resign all to His will.

Will you answer all this fully and in such manner that I can have no hesitation in shewing to my husband. He generally reads your letters before I do or else makes me read them all to him after he has given them a hasty glance. He is warmly attached to you my dearest Mammy and my happiest moments are when I am sitting reading your letters aloud to him.

Capt. Stewart is to set out homewards on the 8th of this month. He has lived almost quite alone till this last month which he has passed at Cobourg. He is remarkably good humoured. I could not help admiring him. When it was the fashion to turn him into ridicule and quiz him, he bore it with such gentlemanlike forbearance and good humour. He has behaved with perfect honor in regard to all money matters. Tell this to Catherine.

Tom has been walking with me to Mr. Stricklands and sitting and talking a great deal with me today. He says that though this place is pretty his heart never warms to it, but that if nothing turns up to add to our income or encourage us to return home, he will go on here, and square his clearing and then stop and go on afterwards on a small scale.

1826: December 10[67]
To Captain Francis Beaufort, Ireland

Douro 10th Dec'r, 1826

My dearest Francis

I think it will give you some pleasure to hear that your kind letter of September 5th has been of unspeakable use to me & has roused me from that despondency which had crept over me so shamefully some time ago. For a month or two back, returning health & strength (of the last of which I was almost totally deprived during our very hot summer) had so far restored my intellects as to make me sensible of the great weakness & folly I had given way to & I have often since regretted most painfully having exposed myself so much to my dear and warmly attached friends & grieved them so much by my dismal representations besides giving them & you my dear & most steady friend reason to suppose that I was ungrateful for the great & active exertions you have taken for our advancement here. I assure you I cannot think of myself with patience & I only wonder how you could treat me with such forbearing gentleness.

But now as ever, I have found, my dear Monitor and Uncle mild but forcible in his advice & admonitions & indeed I am grateful to you for still considering me your child & pupil even tho' an old mama myself & so far from you.

You unmasked very justly that in all my complaints I mentioned my husband very little. It was because I knew very well he would not approve of my writing in that strain & therefore I wrote without consulting him. If I had opened my mind more to him, I should not have been so silly but I did not like to let him know how gloomy I was as I knew it would only add to his pain. His mind was certainly harassed by various disappointments but I never heard him express an idea of "giving up." No indeed he shewed his superior firmness & tho' he could not avoid feeling the sting of disappointment yet he never once expressed any idea like sinking under it. On the contrary, when I at times threw out hints about wishing to return home & when many of his friends proposed to him to try living in some cheap place in England, he always said "No — as I have made this exertion for my family I will give it a longer trial. It is too soon to give up our hopes yet; we must try for seven years before we allow ourselves to be quite [ ]."

I now see very plainly how much better we are off here than we could be at home in these melancholy times. Here we certainly have abundance of all the necessaries of life & escape the misery of seeing our fellow creatures in distress. Of late our prospects have brightened. Our crops have turned out much more abundantly than we could have expected. We have plenty of wheat & potatoes & our cattle so far have gone on well, but winter is a trying time & many people lose almost all their stock in winter from difference causes such as starvation where fodder is not plenty, or perishing from cold or being lost in the woods when they cannot find any food. But we must keep up our hopes & recollect that many many meet with these disappointments in this country who have not the means within their reach of regaining the loss & we, thank God, have, tho on a small scale.

Dear Francis, I cannot tell you how deeply we feel all your active kindness about the Land Company & the other appointments you & kind Maria E. have been endeavouring to procure for Mr. S. He, I assure you, feels it most acutely as well as I do & never [ ] the impression have our hearts let the result be what it may. Of the Military Road app't we have long since lost all hopes as we were told that no one except a military person would be employed. This I mentioned to Harriet as soon as we heard it but I think it must have been in the letter of last Dec'r which was lost. I hope this one may not meet the same fate.

We have just heard of Mr. Galts having arrived in York & Tom has sent to him the letter you so kindly procured from Mr. [Mack-], (the name we could not decipher) but it was certainly a very flattering letter & I hope along with all the other interest may have some good effect. We are anxiously expecting an answer as Tom wrote to Mr. Galt along with it. He thought it better to send the letters as in the present state of the roads travelling is so tedious and arduous that Mr. G. might have left York before he could reach it, but he intends going there as soon as sleighing commences if he finds there is any necessity for doing so.

We thank you most sincerely for recovering the postage of the over-charged packet. I only learned by Harriets last letter that there had been a mistake about the am't & I thought it was for fear of accidents that you had only sent a part of the money at first.

I have participated in the enjoyment our dear Harriet must have had from your short visit to Ireland. How nicely it happened that she could join the wedding party at E'town & that you were there then also. I sincerely wish dear Harriet Butler all the happiness so truly amiable a creature deserves.

Tho' I know you don't admire <u>speech making</u> or sentimentalising, yet I must tell you in plain & simple truth that your letter gave me sincere happiness (tho' not unmixed with pain arising from the consciousness of having deserved the reproof) but it showed me that you still <u>love</u> me & feel the same <u>uncle-like</u> affection for me that you ever did my own dear "Old boy" & I feel tenderly alive to your kindness in giving up so much of your time & attention to me when you might so reasonably & <u>fairly</u> have cast me off as undeserving of your care from my very inexcusable weakness & discontent.

I intended to have written to my dear Alicia but as I could only repeat the substance of this letter, I think I had better defer it till another time & at present commission you to give her my warm love & thanks for her note. The account of all your dear children is most interesting always to one who must ever feel the strongest affection for you and yours, & now believe me to be your grateful niece, pupil & daughter.

Fr. Stewart

1827: August 19[68]
To Honora [Edgeworth], Ireland

Douro 19th August, 1827

My dear Honora

As I learned by Harriets last letter that you were to leave home soon for France, I dare say it may be many months before you receive this. But I was so completely conscience stricken by your letter that I can no longer delay making my confession and acknowledging that I am the negligent and ungrateful person, not so in reality, however, merely in appearance. I did my dear friend receive your long & kind letter last year & I also received that of Feb'y 14th 1827. My not telling you sooner of their arrival & thanking you for them was caused by my feeling that our life so very monotonous could not afford matter to make a long letter interesting & I did not like to return a short one for your charming folios. Now, however, events on your side of the world have caused some change in my plans about long & short letters & you see I am writing a short letter because its contents may be very old & you may have heard a great deal about us from some of your other correspondents before you can read this. I hope you may enjoy your trip to Paris more than you expected. Your reason for fearing to go amused me a little for I can scarcely conceive that you who have always lived so much in literary society & along with people to whom French is as familiar as their native tongue should so much fear visiting a country where everyone goes & which appears now so much in everyones power to visit. But be this as it may I am glad you have gone for I am quite sure you must have found it delightful. I am very sorry that poor Mrs. E. has suffered so very much from illness & hope that Harrowgate may have been of use to her. Pray give my kindest remembrance to her & my affectionate love to my dear Sneyd. Tell him I have read the Life of Monpensier with extreme interest. How very kind of Sneyd to think of his poor old playfellow & how gratifying it is to me to receive so many & such constant proofs of attachment from my dear friends.

I dare say as you passed thro' England you visited Aunt Mary & how much the pleasure of your visit to her must have been encreased by her solitude during the absence of Mr. Mrs. & Miss Sneyd. My dear ever kind & considerate Aunt Mary who has been so to me ever since I was little Fanny Browne, pray give my tender love to her & thank her again & again for her handsome & useful presents. What an admirable bread knife & what a nice butter knife! They are both quite ornamental as well as very useful at our breakfast & tea table. Our home made loaves are a different shape from what you have I dare say seen at home, for we bake in what is here called a Bake kettle or Dutch oven & our loaves are like great huge cakes, more than loaves, so that a strong broad knife for cutting them adds considerably to the ease & expedition with which I may perform that operation, so necessary every morn & evening for a panel of impatient little animals called children.

You my dearest Cricrac Crow friend have also been kindly considerate for our comforts. What a nice large thick hearth-rug! Our sparkling wooden fires made me afraid of its beauty being too soon spoiled as we have not yet had a fender so that I have but seldom used it. However, by Aunt Bess's good nature & generosity we shall enjoy its comfort this winter for I hear she is actually sending out a Fender. The Alphabet is a never ending source of amusement to little Bessy & William, the former particularly, 3½ years old, who knows most of the letters. The Battledores & shuttlecocks were a new & delightful recreation for your young friends Anna & Ellen as well as many older people last winter. Our rooms are much too small & low for playing it within doors but on some of our calm clear days when the snow was so firmly encrusted with ice as to allow people to walk on it without sinking they used to play outside, & as such never had been seen in this part of the world before, many young English children who had left home infants or little children were quite surprised at this new amusement. I cannot tell you with what encreased interest I have lately re-read a great part of Capt'n Halls Journal which you sent me the year before last, for we have really seen & conversed with him & had the pleasure of & honour of having him & Mrs. Hall in this house.

I have so many resources & pleasures now that I am never at a loss for employment & amusement, indeed, that I never was in my life yet & it is a feeling I only can conceive from description. My greatest want

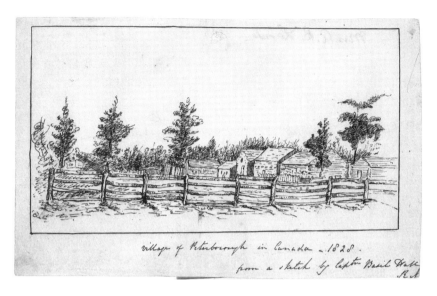

"Village of Peterborough in Canada 1828, from a sketch by Capt'n Basil Hall, R.N."

(Source: Captain Charles Rubidge fonds 83-1022. Courtesy Trent University Archives.)

here is time to indulge myself in any of my favourite pursuits & a lively agreeable ladylike companion to converse with sometimes. These I hope I shall have in time. The first I hope is not far distant for when my nursling little Francis is able to take care of himself & require less watching I shall be able to do much more than I have since his birth, for having no Nursery or Nurse I am I may say at all hours of the day & night engaged a good deal with him. He is, however, one of the most easily managed dear little fat infants I ever saw. He is so good humoured & stout. He has pretty dark eyes & dark hair & when his cap is off is excessively like a person who perhaps you may have seen sometime or other, Mr. Smythe of Benison Lodge. This same man was cousin [ ] to my father & I am in hopes my little Franky may be like his Grandpapa. Here he comes as hungry as can be so I must stop & satisfy his apetite. And now I must end my long Epistle by assuring you my dear Honora that you possess the sincere affection of your old friend & companion,

Fanny Stewart

I send you a few of our wild White Violets in return for your nice nosegay of Violets & Primroses last year. Oh the colour of them was reviving to my eyes but alas! the smell was gone. Our wild Violets smell more like pansies. They are very sweet but not the sweet odour of your purple garden Violets.

1828: June 3[69]
To Mrs. [Mary] Wilson, Maryville, Belfast, Ireland

Douro 3d June 1828

My ever dear Cousin

I don't know how long it is since I last wrote to you but I think it seems a great while. For many many months the Ministerial changes have sadly interfered with my enclosing privileges & have been the cause of my not writing to my dear friends. But my thoughts were still at liberty & I think if possible have been with you oftener than ever for you are connected with every thing that occupies my mind. About six weeks ago your last precious letter reached us, a sad one it was & caused us many tears but my dear dear friends tho we must weep, we also rejoice. That dear Soul has gone to Everlasting Glory. What a scene of trial & affliction has she been taken from. Oh what an inconceivable scene she is now witnessing. What an example she had left!! She has gone to that Saviour who came for her, to that God who gave his beloved Son for her & for us, yes for us, vile & weak & miserable as we are. He died for us & even for me tho I am the most unworthy of all creatures.... Oh may His holy Spirit enter my heart, purify & strengthen it, for without Him what a mass of confusion & wretchedness it contains. Thank God, of late He has given me a much clearer view of the state of my own heart than I ever before had. I always loved or thought I loved Him, but I loved myself too much. I never really felt my total insufficiency till lately. May He still continue to open my eyes, to give me that entire love for him & dependence on Him which will lead me to call upon Him & to pray "without ceasing" & to study His Word.... I could write sheets & volumes, my darling & Beloved friends. I know you feel & understand what I feel & I can write to you with more freedom & tell you the state of my mind better than to almost anyone else.

I owe much to you my best & dearest Mrs. Wilson. The great Director of all things employed you & my own dear Mother Mrs. Stewart as the means of first opening my eyes & directing my thoughts where they ought to be. I was very unhappy & awfully sinful some time ago. I set my heart too much on my friends in this world & pined for them & wickedly thought I never would have enjoyment without their society. How Mercifully He dealt with me in whose hands I am. He gave me his Grace to feel that I valued them too much. I forgot Him, my best friend. He made me to feel the insufficiency of worldly comfort in trials. He did try me & proved to me that His word & grace can alone support & instruct & that friends tho sweet company are but secondary comfort, that their advice sometimes leads one into doubts, but "His help is True." I am here separated from you all & often often have been placed in very trying situations & I found my foolish heart regretting those friends from whom I could procure advice. At last I felt the power of His free Grace & Mercy & flew to Him to shew me my way....

What would I not give to see you & talk to you. If He sees fit He will permit it.... I do hope He may permit us to meet but I don't see that it would at present be our duty to return home. You know Toms affairs have been placed in the care & management of Mr. J. Darling. We cannot see the results it may bring us, an independence & restore our family to some of the property they lost. At present we could not live at home independently. Here we can & have overcome our worst difficulties. We are very comfortable now & have great blessings. Our farm is doing better. Our children are becoming useful & their minds opening. My dear Tom enjoys good health this year. No ague has appeared yet. May the Lord incline the heart of my dear Tom to that Wisdom which never faileth & may He preserve him by being overcome by the thoughts & cares of this life. Your letters do him much good, more than any other persons, for he loves you so dearly. So do we all....

F. Stewart

Tell me something of Betty Taylor. Is she good or bad or at service. We had a letter lately from poor dear John & Anna. I am glad they are improving in health. I say nothing of the Indians as I wrote so much about them to Anna Mathias. You can hear all from her. Forgive this letter all about my own thoughts. You asked me to write my thoughts.

Last Saturday it was 6 years since we saw you at White Abbey.

[1829][70]
To Honora Edgeworth, Edgeworthstown, Ireland

1829

My dearest Honora

When my last letters left this I intended to write in this next packet to you and tho' I had but little hope at that time from Harriet's former account, yet I did not expect the termination would have arrived so soon. It has been mercifully hastened tho' we must all wish to preserve a beloved friend. Yet in this case where hope was nearly gone, how much pain & miserable hopeless watching were you & the dear sufferer himself spared.

Dearest Honora, before you receive this I hope you may in some degree have recovered from the effects of such a loss. It is not at first that we feel most. I am & must for some time be most anxious to hear from you & if you can it would & does at all times give me unspeakable pleasure to receive letters from you, one of my earliest friends.... I will not say any more. I must, however, dear Honora thank you for the pretty seals which are just what I set my wishes on & which I shall love for your sake. I am most anxious to hear how you all have been & how your poor dear Mother is & poor Sophy Fox whose situation was rather critical. In short no creature can wish more or feel or think more about you all than Your ever affectionate old friend

Fanny Stewart

Harriet enclosed me dear kind Aunt Marys note. With my love & warmest thanks will you tell her that the pretty Muffatees shall be distributed exactly as she wished. When I wrote to her I did not know she had sent them & now I cannot write to her but pray will you give her my most grateful love & affection. I think they could not have been better disposed, as suiting each member of our little party.

1829: April 6[71]
To Honora [Edgeworth], Ireland

6th April 1829

My dearest Honora

When I learned that our dear and valuable Aunt Mary had returned to Ireland my first thought was about you for I know how very much it must encrease your happiness to have her once more with you, and I intended then to have written to congratulate you on her being once more with you but various & endless are my obstacles to any employment which requires quietness, and some times I am almost in despair about being able to do any thing but nurse or fuss a little about the children or housekeeping. Then when I have any time I write in such a hurry that I have no comfort. Even now I scribble with John sleeping on my arm & the three next making all sorts of noises in the room as the weather is too wet & cold to dispose of them out of doors. We have had a most unusually long & severe winter. It did not begin till after Christmas for all Nov'r & Dec'r were delightful. But then it became extremely cold & for a month I don't think the ther'r rose above 10, added to which we had high northwest winds & but very few sunny days. Now, tho' we have nearly reached the second week of April, the weather is bitterly cold & blustery, no appearance of Spring anywhere.

How different from Ireland I dare say your Daffodils & Narcissus are, all in high beauty, as well as the other sweet & beautiful flowers which make their appearance at this sweet season, but which with us here don't bloom till June when every thing comes at once, but soon droop & fade from the heat & dryness so that the only time of year we have any pretty flowers in our gardens is between June & September, by which time all are gone to seed & beginning to grow brown & withered. I for this reason am not half so fond of my flower gardens as in days of yore. Indeed all my pursuits are so completely changed that I scarcely can help thinking I have been changed by some Evil Fairy, for no people could be so totally different as Fanny Browne of Dublin & Fanny Stewart of Douro, except that my dear friends are the same & equally fond & tender. Oh this makes me know most exquisitely that I am Fanny Browne still.

But though my employments are of necessity so much changed my tastes are the same & I still enjoy reading, music &c &c as much as I did 20 years ago. In walking I admire just as much as ever the works of Nature, altho I have not much time for walking. I wish much dear Honora to hear from you again. It seems so very long since I have had a letter from you. You may perhaps think that I don't deserve it and I know that I have not written to you for many months, no, not even to thank you for the nice & valuable addition you sent to our Library, which I assure you have contributed very much to our entertainment during the dark days we have had this winter & have helped to keep away low spirits which will sometimes come in spite of all our efforts to keep them at a proper distance. Letters are also delightful restoratives & always have a very instantaneous effect tho' I must say my pleasure is always blinded with a good deal of apprehension on first breaking the seals. I hope soon to see one of your fine folios make its appearance. You have much to tell me about all the different branches into which your family is now divided. So pray indulge me soon. Begin at the root & tell me about <u>home</u> & all its inmates & about all you like to tell me of what you do, say & think, for nothing of that sort can be uninteresting, then about Fanny Wilson, H. Butler, Sophy Fox & her little nice young Foxes, Sneyd and his [ ], my dear William, who I do & always will love with the warmest & steadiest affection, which like every impression imbibed in early life lasts long & increases by age I do think, for I have seen so very little of him since our childhood that my love of him must be just the old love I had for my dear playfellow, strengthened & encreased by years.

It is curious that just as I left Ireland he should be employed on the very spot I may say where we lived & that he sh'd know so many of our friends & acquaintances there.

I cannot tell you any news because I don't know any which can interest you nor have I any anecdotes or adventures to relate, never having passed so tiresome or dull a winter. We have had few visitors & those we had were no way agreeable. Indeed I am rather disgusted with our neighbors than otherwise. However, we have so many resources within ourselves that I find myself independent of society.

Now adieu, with kindest love to my ever loved Aunt Mary, believe
me your ever affectionate friend,
F Stewart

1833: November 16[72]
"Extracts": addressee unknown

Douro Nov. 16, 1833

Our mill is going on prosperously. We are only to have the saw mill now
& the grist mill is to be added & the dam finished in summer when the
water is low. Scott says he will engage them to be the best mills in the
District. The foundation of the Dam is completed which was the heavi-
est work and the carpenters are now preparing wooden patterns of the
wheels which are to be sent to the foundry at Rochester to have metal
castings made from them. There are 2 other carpenters morticing the
great beams for the building & it is to be raised in a few days. We have
a blacksmith at work & it is a source of great pleasure to the young
things to go to the forge. They never saw a Smith at work before & their
delight at seeing a horse shod was amusing to us. The workmen are
quiet civil men. One poor man who had his leg broke some time ago
is very useful to me as he <u>darns</u> stockings & is glad to have something
to do. The wood for the wheels had all to be boiled & dried at a fire to
harden & season it before they began to turn the moddels of the wheels.
Dec'r 20 — The mill is half up. It has been delayed by severe weather &
sickness & accidents among the men but a few hours now will put up
all the frame.

There is an Indian encampment about a mile from us in the woods
near Mr. Reids & we are beginning to get acquainted with them. They
are terribly shy & so much afraid of our Dogs & Turkey Cocks that we
can seldom get them to come near. They go to Mr. Reids frequently &
are much delighted with looking at prints or maps. Every Sunday 7 or
8 Indians & Squaws sit round the parlour table there looking at them. I
went to the Wigwam one day where 4 or 5 Indian families live. The hut
was not more than 10 feet long & about 6 or 7 wide, of an oval shape,

made of poles covered with Bark of Birch. The floor was made merely of branches of white Cedar spread over the ground. Deer skins and blankets were laid over & on them they sit in the day & sleep by night. There was a fire at each end & a pole across from one to the other near the roof where they had bits of inside parts of deer hung up to dry in the smoke. One Squaw who had an infant only a few weeks old was making a very nice little frock of dark cotton for it quite neatly & putting green braid on the little band round the top. She wore a thimble & held her needle quite nicely. Another was preparing a deer skin for moccasins. Another was making a pair, an old Squaw making a Basket. An old Indian whose name is <u>Squire Martin</u> was making a pair of Snow Shoes & his son, a boy of 18 or 19, helping him. The young man (called Jim Bigman) was our interpreter as he spoke English tolerably well. Four Squaws & a boy came to me today with Baskets & sat for a long time at the kitchen fire. I shewed them some Beads I had in ancient days on a gown. The Squaws laughed & seemed much pleased & promised to bring me some more baskets for them. I want to tempt them here. There is one very nice girl among them called Charlotte McCue. Her father is a white man.

I am much better in health than I was for 2 years past. The children all well & improving much tho' sadly uncultivated. Mr. S. is gone for the 1st time to York to take his seat in the Legislative Assembly.

1838: October 5[73]

"Extracts": addressee unknown

After an early breakfast we all proceeded in Mr. Wallis's fine large boat, *The Victoria*, to Sturgeon Point in Sturgeon Lake, six miles from Fenelon Falls and here we were to be stationed to see the Regatta. There were a great many parties of ladies and gentlemen as several had come from Peterboro and other places to see this gay affair and it was really beautiful. The lake is large and surrounded with points and bays and islands. Of course all is forest but here and there relieved by small farms. The day was particularly lovely and everybody looked gay and happy. I think there were about two hundred people assembled, 25 nicely painted boats of different kinds with new flags and 14 bark canoes. There were several matches. The first was most interesting as both the boats belonged to gentlemen of our acquaintance, the *Alice*, a four oared boat of Mr. Langtons and the *Calypso*, a two oared of Mr. Wallis's. Miss Langton joined our party and I could not help feeling most interested for her brothers boat, particularly as the majority of the ladies were on Mr. Wallis's side. The *Calypso* won, poor Miss Langton felt quite nervous and said she could not help feeling more than the thing deserved. But there was perfect good feeling preserved among the gentlemen.

We had refreshments laid out in tents, abundance of cool meat, pastry cakes and fruits as well as wine &c, all provided by the gentlemen of the Fenelon Hunting Club. We sat under the trees watching the different matches between the boats and canoes till near sunset when the business of the day concluded and we all prepared to return to Mr. Wallis's. We sailed part of the way but the wind deserted us and we were obliged to depend upon the oars to take us up the stream so that it was past 8 o'clock when all got back. We then had to dress and refresh and cool ourselves.

The gentlemen all went to dinner but we ladies, namely Mrs. Kirkpatrick, Miss Fisher, Mrs. Hagerman, Miss Woodford, Ellen and myself all preferred having tea, so we put on our dressing gowns and took tea upstairs, in dishabille rested and cooled as well as we could and then dressed in our best and proceeded to the drawing room where we found Mr. Wallis, Mr. T.F.K., Mr. Stewart and Mr. Shaw waiting to escort us to the inn where there was to be a supper given by the gentlemen of the Fenelon hunt. The room soon filled, music and dancing commenced. There were twelve unmarried ladies and two married dancing besides one or two matrons who did not join in the "giddymaze," F.S. amongst the number. There were Beaux in abundance, very fine gentlemanlike young men. At 12 o'clock supper was announced after which dancing was renewed with great spirit. We left it at half past four, but the rest of the party kept it up till six.

1840: December 14[74]
To Harriet Beaufort, Dublin, Ireland

Douro, Monday 14th Dec'r 1840

My dearest Harriet

I have at last the pleasure of telling you that the little box with the Tartan has arrived after all our fears & frights as to its safety. It has been sadly delayed somewhere for Edward saw it in Montreal at the beginning of October & as he was not returning immediately he desired them to send it on under charge of the public forwarders & expected to have heard of it having arrived here long before he did. But it never came till last Thursday. However, it is all safe & dry & in good order & just the thing we wanted & every body likes & admires it & we are up to our chins in work preparing dresses for all our boys. Each of the six are to have little tunics or coats & trowsers with black belts & blue caps & Kate is to have a frock & cloak of it too & Tom says he <u>must</u> have a coat too but it will <u>look</u> horrid & we all want to prevail on him not but he seems determined. Well my dear on Wednesday last a rich post came in & brought a long letter from you & another from Catharine by the new Halifax route. They were dated 3d Nov'r & we got them 8th Dec'r so you see that was very nice. They reached Halifax in 14 days but the tedious part is between that & this.

I am writing with a pen made of one of those nice quills you sent in the box which are, I assure you, treasures but from some cause I can't discover I cannot write at all decently. The pen looks plausible enough and the ink is that which you sent me properly diluted to prevent it from thickening too much, but I cannot write you see so I must try a steel pen but they cramp my hand. However, I will write small & close & give you, I am afraid, a little more trouble to read it. I am so glad that you & Mrs. Flood have met & I hope you may often meet for I think the more you see of her the more you will find in her character that is estimable & valuable. We only knew her well latterly for poor dear little soul, she was always under such restraint before that we could not half know her best qualities, fear of exposing her brute of a husband, & her own sorrows made her so extremely reserved that people considered her quite an oddity. But we had the more reason afterwards to admire her for the very reserve & apparent coldness to many who wished to be her friends. Tom thinks it is better not to have that declaration or certificate drawn up which you mentioned Mrs. Lucas was desirous of having. He does not think it would do any good for of course Mrs. Flood's friends never could or would believe any such fabrications as she thinks he has set afloat & what matter for the opinion of strangers. However, Tom will consult Stafford & Doctor Hutchison & Mr. Sanford who are all her friends & equally acquainted with her & aware of her trials & provocations & if they think it prudent to have such a document written he will have it done. But he thinks it should not be done hastily as, if Mr. Flood heard of it, it might irritate him afresh & do more harm than good. Tell Mrs. Lucas that if we could see the least good likely to arise from it we never would hesitate but we have already done so much & have been blamed so much for interfering between man & wife that we are cautious of doing more.

Wednesday Dec. 16th 12 oclock, day. Just as I had got so far on Monday even'g in came Mr. Haycock & Frederick & as Tom had just gone out I was obliged to sit & do civilities all evening & yesterday being a busy day from beginning to end I never could write till now, so here I am & I must return to Mrs. Flood. I expect to see Dr. Hutchison today & I will speak to him about her & perhaps have some more to say. If I don't see him I will write again. I don't myself see what use it would be. I don't well understand what Mrs. Lucas meant, whether it was the stories Mr. Flood told here before Mrs. Flood left this that she alludes to or whether he has written home stories about her. If she means anything he has said here, no certificate is necessary for not one person of respectability believes anything he says against her. He is disliked so much & if he has been writing home, it seems to me equally useless to contradict stories which of course her own friends would never believe, & does Mrs. Lucas wish to have this certificate sent home to her? for we don't understand exactly you see. I wrote to Mrs. Flood a few days ago but of course did not hint at this at all as I had the message from Mrs. Lucas & not from her. You did not tell me half enough of what she said about us, particularly about Ellen, who was her greatest favourite & who she used to call "her better judgement [ ]" because Ellen used to help her to cut &

make up things & arrange & pack up. She had a fancy to have Ellen married to her brother in law Mr. William Flood but she need never expect that for none of us like the name or connection tho Ellen liked Mr. W.F. very well as an acquaintance.

Here again I have been interrupted by two sleighloads of visitors, Mrs., Miss & Mr. J. Forbes, Mr. Dixie to whom Miss F. is going to be married, Mrs. Tho's Fortye, Mrs. George Hall. Months have passed since we had so many visitors as have come within the last few days. 2 causes have brought them. 1st, sleighing has begun & the roads are in tolerable order now & 2nd, many friends have called to enquire about our poor Edward who lately met with an accident which alarmed us greatly & might have been very serious but most providentially has turned out not so bad. A gun went off accidently and wounded him in his shoulder. He bled most profusely, indeed frightfully, so that he was, as I thought, lifeless when brought home & for some hours we feared he never could live but <u>miraculously</u> the Dr. says no vital part was touched tho' the space was inconceivably small between the wound & a great artery on one side & a muscle on the other which was only grazed but which would have injured the use of his arm. Thank God he has escaped in every way & is now recovering tho still wan & weak & suffering a good deal of pain. But we all have reason to feel thankful that the life of our poor excellent friend has been spared. He is such a useful upright honourable young man so perfectly free from vice of every kind & so attached to Tom & indeed to all our family. He has been so long with us & is so very trustworthy, he is quite like one of our family & is generally supposed by strangers to be my nephew as his name is the same as mine was. Tom is going to give or rather has given him the promise of 100 acres of land which he was to have had two years ago but still Tom has not been able to arrange it. Indeed he is so useful I don't know how in the world we shall do without him. But he is now old enough to feel anxious to settle & I have no doubt he will be one of the most successful settlers here for he is industrious & steady, experienced & is able to do so many different things which will save him laying out money. He is a first rate carpenter as well as farmer & a good enough saddler to be able to make all sorts of harness. Then he is a shoemaker which has saved him a good deal here. He was to have begun to put the frame of our new building together & got all the boards ready to raise & finish it in spring but this wound will I fear put an end to that. We get on very slowly as all poor folks must do. Our labourers who were excavating were obliged to stop to go home & dig their potatoes & a few days after they returned the frost set in so severely as to end their labours for this season as the ground was as hard as iron.

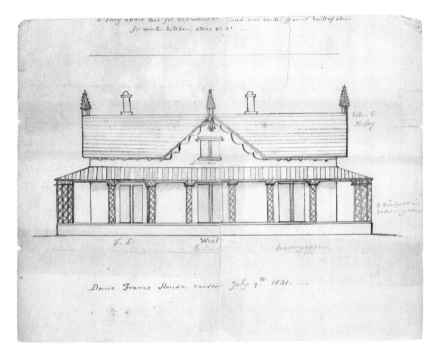

"*Douro Frame House raised July 9th 1841.*" Sketch of the Stewart's frame house, Auburn.

(Source: Frances Stewart fonds 97-023 Folder 5. Courtesy Trent University Archives.)

Thursday 17th. Another interruption came. Up drove the Kirkpatricks & old Mrs. Fortye, then came dressing Edward's arm & then up came another cutter, Mr. & Mrs. Rodger, a nice dear little couple. They paid but a short visit but it was a very pleasant one. They are young people, at least only 4 years married. He is the Presbyterian minister at Peterboro, a well educated & exceedingly pleasing person, very mild & quiet but cheerful & even merry sometimes & one that all who know must <u>love</u>.

Mrs. Rodger is just what a clergyman's wife should be. She too has had a very good education & is rational & pleasing as well as conversable & they seem so happy together that it is delightful to be admitted into their little domestic circle. They are both Scotch & I like their way of speaking too. The Scotch accent is not broad enough to be vulgar as some have it.

This time 24 years [ago] my dear Harriet I was a bride and driving along the road to Drogheda. It is a long time to look back to & good proof I have around me. My ten children all drank our health today & Tom is in better spirits than I have seen him for months. He is enjoying it so much & indeed, though I may have had trials, yet I have had unbounded blessings which more than balance them. I have seen a good deal of life here tho' so secluded & the more I see of others the more reason I have to be thankful for domestic peace & happiness. We are indeed a happy & united family & the only thing that ever clouds it is seeing dear Tom cast down by anxiety & care, & this anxiety & care chiefly on my account. So it is his love for me which causes it. He is going tomorrow to Cobourg for a day with Stafford K. to some meeting about Emigration & I think it will do him good. He has been so very little from home of late. I often wonder how he bears the sameness of the life he leads here, passing months without ever leaving home except to church or seeing anyone except when the Haycocks come.

I was near forgetting to tell you about the Plaister of Paris. It has been found that sprinkling or dusting Plaister of Paris over plants or fields will improve their [ ] & vegetation, not by enriching the ground, but by drawing or causing moisture on the plant. Tom dusted his oats & pease in this way last summer & in all the spots where he used it the luxuriance was visible & remarkable. Also some apple trees. He used the Plaister on one side of some trees & that side was greener & the fruit larger than on the other. There is [a] story told that a gentleman who was bald was dusting a tree in this way & some of the P of P fell on his head & made his hair grow but you may believe it if you can. Another story is of a Yankee woman who had a very old much worn Broom & she told her servant to take some Plaister of Paris & dust it on the Broom to make it grow new!! So much for nonsense.

Ellen is going to send you the rest of her journal in the form of a large letter but at present she is so busy making up the boys clothes she has not a moment as Papa says they must be ready for church on Sunday. My time is divided between attending Edward who is still helpless as his right arm is disabled, dressing his arm 3 times a day, writing & cutting out the work for the girls to do. I am going this evening to walk to drink tea at the Reids. They are just going on as usual, growing old & the young ones growing old too. John is quite grey & a curious little old bachelor. Mr. [ ] has been at Toronto & I suppose will soon pay us another visit. I don't think he is quite as cordial with us as he used for we rather discourage poor Henry's advances. I think they wished for a connection but he has fallen off so much of late years that we could not like it. He is a good young man now but is stupid & dirty & careless in his habits & person & seems to have sunk in the esteem of his friends. But I must always feel a particular interest & affection for all the family of these dear kind friends. I find I must now send this to the post & love to all my own dear friends who are kind enough to care about me, to all my own dear & near relatives & to the dear kind Hamiltons, Lynes & all. I hope you gave my love to poor Catherine Hamilton & do so too to [ ] Wade.

I have never got any letter from Aunt Sutton about money at all. Oh yes pray by Uncle Sutton to pay Mrs. Flood £10 on our acc't & at the Marie Frosberry & the Gerrards, [ ], Thompsons & all. And now my own dear Moome, Adieu — Ever your own child FS.

I wrote to Lou last month & this day month began a letter to you.

1846: December 7[75]
To Maria Waller, Allenstown, Kells, County Meath, Ireland

I can tell you of another family, Scotch people who came three years ago & purchased a farm in Douro from one of those poor south Irish Emigrants who had been twenty years doing nothing. Old Waddell the Scotchman had to pay the purchase money by instalments & the second year he cleared £100 by his wheat! He now has a good farm, plenty of everything, a good pair of horses & waggon & has paid all the instalments. He has two Sons to help him on the farm but he is an old man himself & has had some severe attacks of illness. He has two other sons who live in Peterboro & are going on well & I believe they have helped their father a little. One is a blacksmith & Iron founder & Wheelwright & another a shoe maker. I believe there are three in town but they are prospering. However, I am told they work like <u>Negroes</u>.

Amongst our own tennants we have great prosperity. David Porter who rented our farm for 10 years came here in debt. He owed £7. He had lost his wife of a lingering illness, cancer, which had kept them all back & had caused his debt. His children, six in number, were young & only one, a boy about 14 (his eldest) at all able to help him, the eldest girl only 12 & she had the care of all the rest! Tom charged him no rent the first year & half as he found the farm bad order & had no profit at all the first year. But every year after he paid 7s 6d an acre. He got on by <u>sheer industry</u>, he & his boy alone, for at first he could not afford to hire people to help him & his children at that time could neither save nor earn nor manage for they were very ignorant & idle. But in a little time he hired a good woman as housekeeper who attended to his children & all the domestic affairs & when she left him he married & by the time his term with us was over he was an independent man. He now has a property for which he would not take £1,000. He purchased 100 acres of wild land from Mr. Reid adjoining Edward Browns farm & has all sorts of cattle & sheep & horses & plenty of crops & <u>not one bad potatoe</u> this year. This mans brother William Porter is another of our best tenants. He also came here without any means to begin with & Tom charged him no rent the first six months. Ever since that he has paid regularly at the rate of a dollar & half or 7s/6d per acre. He had about 15 acres & pay his rent in produce, work or firewood as we require. Tom Martin came here so poor that he was obliged to pledge his bedclothes to pay his expenses coming up & Tom was obliged to lend him a few shillings to go & redeem them. He then hired out as often as he could as he had but a small spot of his own to work on having only taken 5 acres. This he cultivated by degrees & raised some potatoes & then wheat & by degrees has got more land. He now has 15 or 16 acres cultivated & cows, oxen, sheep, pigs, a comfortable house, a good garden & his wife makes pickles & preserves every year. They have been here 9 years I think but they are Papists & very bigoted ones too tho' they are from the North. We have another Papist tennant & he is from Tipperary. He has been only a year here & took a cleared farm & he is likely to get on as well as the others. He has a large family of young idle children & an ignorant wife but works hard himself. Tom charges all his tenants the same rent for the land & built houses for some of them. We have now only four tennants of this kind as David Porter left this last winter & our Willy took the farm he had as well as some more & now has about 200 acres in his own hands & under cultivation and I hope & trust the same prosperity may attend our dear boys as has been with David Porter.

Saturday Evening. Yesterday evening I was interrupted in my writing by a visit from dear Ellen who we kept all night & now she is gone to see her Aunt Fowlis & I take advantage of her absence to write a little more. You see I have given all the information I can about settlers as Maria wished to be able to tell anyone that might wish to come out, & as I have no other way of being of use to my poor suffering countrymen and women I will try to let them know something of this fine country, & I do think all these people that I have mentioned have got on so well that it might encourage others. Wherever Protestant settlers are they certainly do thrive best but they must be of sober steady industrious habits or they cannot get on at all. We see too many sad instances of the contrary tho' I am happy to say almost all this part of the country is fortunate in having good settlers now. As for the States I don't know much about them. Mrs. Fowlis lived only in the towns & had no opportunity of knowing much of the poorer settlers & farmers but the Irish were hated in the part where she lived & generally are considered quarrelsome & bad settlers. Here we have a mixture of Scotch, English, & Irish & certainly the Southern Irish Catholics are the worst — everywhere — & often, if they do get on for a time do something dishonest which sends them to jail & so to ruin & destruction. We must all work as hard as we can & spend as little as we can & save & make all we can & by dint of all we can gain independence but nothing can be gained otherwise.

As I am writing to you I think I need not write to dear Aunt Sutton but pray give her my fond love as well as Tom & Bessies. We all thank her for her amusing account of Old Peter, poor old creature. I fear he & Betty will feel a sad change this winter for they had every comfort here & plenty of everything & at Christmas had a good fat Goose & plum pudding & <u>plum cake too</u> in her own house of her own. Can she have that in Ireland? Give my love also to dear Harriet & Louisa & all the dear friends everywhere who you know I love….

I have I fear wearied you saying so much about our poor tennants but it is a subject upon which I feel great interest as I am partial to dear Canada & wish to encourage people to come here but only a particular class of people ever do well here, hardworking, steady managing people, but spendthrifts, drunkards & idlers never succeed. We have plenty of them. Thank you for the fine package of Quinine which was most welcome as we had a few poor lingering invalids longing for its arrival & it has cured them now & they are beginning to look less death like for the Ague is a ghastly looking complaint you know. I hardly expected it so soon. Indeed you were good to send it off so quickly.

Give my best love to dear Rob't & Catharine, James & Julia & to all my old friends in your neighbourhood for I love & think of many. Goodbye my own loved Aunt.

Ever your own child <u>Fan</u>

1847: May 5[76]
To Mrs. Waller, Allenstown, Ireland

Auburn Wednesday Evening
5th May — 6 oclock

My own dear Aunt

Our early tea is over. Bessie has gone to her garden for a little while & I will take the quiet time before all the <u>labourers</u> come in for their supper to tell you that last Friday I had the enjoyment of reading letters from several dear friends dated 1 April…. What dreadful sickness there is now. It seems quite as fatal as the starvation. Oh what a state that poor poor place is in!! I really fear the whole air of the island of Ireland will be polluted by the masses of putrefying bodies animals & also the rotten vegetables. I fear the pestilence may not be confined to those who have suffered from bad food, or <u>no</u> food, but that the very air they breath much be loaded with foulness. I sometimes wish all I love there were safe out here. But then I begin to recollect how very irksome a Canadian life would seem to those who have been accustomed to elegance, ease & refinement. How insupportable it would be to those who have lived in a round of amusement or enjoyed intellectual or scientific society. What a desolate wilderness it would seem to those who have enjoyed the privileges of Christian conversation & intercourse with the Religious part of the society at home, for alas! we have but little of that here. When I think of all these things I begin to find that I am selfish in wishing anyone to come here for few of my friends are not too <u>well off</u> at home not to make the change felt in some of the three ways I have mentioned, & yet does it not seem a contradiction to say that positively & truly I am as happy here as anybody need wish or expect to be in this world. I will even go farther & say that I do think I am much happier than most people I know anywhere. In the first place I never have anything to do that is the least fatiguing for my dear kind thoughtful husband never could bear to see me exert myself & has always endeavoured to save me from the necessity of doing anything that could hurt me & now my dear good children never allow me to do anything but some very trifling part of the household department & needlework or knitting. Not many have such thoughtful affectionate husband & children. As for society or amusement I have lost all relish for parties or anything of that sort & I am never at loss for variety for every hour there is so much going forward that there is constant change & movement going on. As for religious companionship I have dear Mrs. Fowlis who is a treasure to us all & occasionally we have Mr. & Mrs. Rogers & they refresh us delightfully. Then we have all your letters & Mrs. Wilsons & some others which give us a fresh supply of interesting matter every month besides all the books of which we read a small portion every day, sometimes <u>very small</u>. But no day passes without some serious or improving reading. Now have we not every thing to make us happy? & we live so retired that we have nothing to do with politics or Gossip or fashions or <u>keeping up appearances</u> which really in many instances causes much trouble & plague. We always try to dress neatly & <u>to be clean</u> & to have our tables decently & comfortably laid out & generally have a very plentiful supply of plain substantial wholesome food & what more <u>ought</u> we to require. We have now got abundance of oatmeal which for many years we never had at all & till now it was always very difficult to procure. Now there are two good oat mills, one of them on our own property, so we can always have it. We have also plenty of Indian Meal & as both are liked, they use Indian Meal porridge for breakfast & the oatmeal for supper. We have very substantial breakfasts as soon after six oclock as all can be assembled. But as some are attending to horses or cattle or pigs or fowl it is not easy to collect all to a moment. Then Tom reads a portion of scripture & prayers. After that in come the smoking <u>Sepanne</u>, the nice smiling potatoes, <u>cold meat</u>, Eggs, Toast Bread, butter, 2 large jugs of milk besides the tea pot &c & all set to work with much energy according to their taste or fancy. But they don't waste any time after it is over for all set off to their different employments & Bessie & Kate carry out all the things & settle up the room & I sit at my reading or knitting for a little while. The routine of work tho' simple is not at all monotonous now & sometimes I can't help wondering how Tom can go on as he does keeping all going on in so many different departments & thinking of such an extraordinary variety of different matters but he never <u>slackens</u> or tires tho' he often looks weary & anxious. This is an unusually backward season and every thing is some weeks later than it ought to be. The ground was so lately covered with deep snow that ploughing could not be done in low ground at all and consequently we shall have but half the quantity of wheat sown which we otherwise w'd have put in. However, we shall have enough for our own use tho' none to sell I fear, which is a loss as it will probably bring a good price next year having been too low in price for any profit last year.

Thursday morning — 10 oclock. Good morning my dearest Aunty. Here is a most lovely day, warm & bright, the birds & insects & every-thing seeming to rejoice. The vegetation has commenced & is making rapid progress, the lilacs are all bursting into leaf, the grass growing green & the forest trees all changing from the stiff wintry grey to a red-dish tinge which will soon change to green.

We have had great difficulty in getting into Peterboro for some time past. The bridge was <u>ricketty</u> & dangerous all through the winter but at last gave way to the encreasing force of the river which always rises in spring & it was carried off one day. Fortunately no person was on it.

Tho' horses were not able to cross it for a long time, yet people used to walk over. Edward Brown had just come over & was not far on this side when he heard it cracking & going off. There are boats for passengers to get across but they are not well <u>manned</u> & the charge is too high. Our boat here is not in good order so we are obliged to borrow one but these difficulties will soon be over for some means of crossing must be established for the public. Our river has risen unusually high this year & has overflowed the banks to a great distance & has partially injured all the Mill, dams & races so that there is great plague about having flour but it will soon go down & these injuries will be repaired. My own dear Aunt I think you have been much too generous in your contribution this year for our box commissions. I assure you I feel it is wrong where you have so many calls on your purse, so very urgent as they are this miserable year but as it is done I must only try to express my thankfulness to you which indeed I cannot find words for. £10 is quite too much but I am sure Harriet will lay it out to the best of her judgement. Pray tell my dear Maria she need not have said one word about her not sending her usual gift. Oh I am glad she did not for I do feel I am a continual tax & drain on your purse & heart my ever dear & kind friends. Mrs. Hay & Dr. Hays sisters & cousins are sending out a box to Anna. They (like you) seem to be always thinking of <u>useful</u> things to send & it is very delightful to find them all so kind to Anna. The good old lady is I find sending out some books too & desired Anna "to choose out one for each of her six brothers & for little Kate." Is not this very great kindness. She writes beautiful advice to Anna, as a mother, & gives her many good hints about early leading little James to know & love the Lord.

I heard from Mrs. Wilson of Maryville that the two Kirkpatricks had hooping cough very mildly. I hope dear Catharine may not take it. I am not sure whether she ever had it. We shall have another mail in a few days & I hope for good acc'ts of all. Surely we have reason to be thankful for generally having pleasant news of my friends.

I am happy to say all my dear children & grandchildren in both families are well. I have just heard that Anna & the children & the little maid were at the opposite side yesterday trying to get over to us but there was no boat. Little Fanny has just got over the <u>weaning</u> most easily &

prosperously without any trouble or ever being taken from her Mama except for a few nights when she slept with the maid. She is a most sweet dispositioned gentle infant. She has got two teeth. I was amused at your sending the old linen for <u>Baby</u> purposes. Indeed I believe it will all come into requisition towards the end of the year for I am sure poor Anna is in that way & I suspect Ellen is beginning also. They are rather <u>hasty</u> I think but I hope the Lord sends them for blessings as mine are to me. Ellen walked over to see us the day before yesterday. Poor dear her heart seems with us still tho' she has every comfort she can require & the best of husbands & she thinks no one like him. She is very thin but that does not signify. Little Mary is growing more engaging every day & Ellen says "<u>has sense beyond her age</u>!! <u>She thinks & reasons in her mind</u>." We have all had colds. I have had my usual tedious cough & found my [ ] loz-enges a great comfort. Poor Willy has had several attacks of ague but we generally stop it with Quinine, first giving Calomel & sometimes an Emetic. He looks very thin & washy & is very weak. He has just had a pretty smart attack & it disheartens him not to be able to do his share of the work now when so much is to be done & the season so far advanced. They are sowing a good deal of oats & pease & turnips. We will plant a couple acres of potatoes as we have good seed but expect next time will be worse than the last. Will you thank Aunt Sutton for her kind letter & for all her kindness about everything on money matters. Oh she is very very kind to us. I wrote a fortnight ago in a letter Bessie wrote to Mary Rothwell so I will not write to anyone but you dear Aunt.

A few lines I must write to Harriet if you have the goodness to send them on to her. Poor dear she wrote to me but I fear it must have hurt her greatly. There is still a great deal of sickness in the country here, princi-pally ague & bilious fever. All who had it in Autumn have it again now & many people are kept from attending to their Spring work which is a serious loss here where <u>all</u> depends on industry.

We find the supply of Quinine most useful & will probably require a small supply again during the summer. Little Flora Macdougall has got ague again & old Mrs. Reid & James Reid which is a great loss as he is the head worker there. He is terribly reduced. Poor Dr. Hutchison has had another bad attack of apoplexy. I have not heard for some days but

Upper Canada

his life hangs by a <u>cobweb</u> & Dr. Hay attends him. I am sorry poor Mrs. Blakeney's recovery is not so rapid as was at first hoped but at her age it could hardly be expected. Tell me how all the Blakeneys & [Battersbys] out here are going on. We never hear of them at all. They are a long way from us & many like that west country best. Thank you dear Aunt for sending me those nice Sermons. I suppose the Box is now near starting. Poor Harriet must have employed someone to do it for her. I hope she may not have hurt herself for my sake. I am glad she has that nice useful Nanny. My paper says stop & so I must. Give loves in loads to all my dear people beginning at home & extending by Athboy to Rockfield & everywhere. Ever your own fond F. Stewart & grateful child…

147

Part 3

☯

The Final Chapter: Widowed Life in the Developing Nation,
1847–1872

In 1847, Tom Stewart succumbed to typhoid fever. For Frances, this transitional period was marked by heightened anxiety and loneliness. Her husband of thirty-one years, Tom had attended to all their affairs and Frances felt utterly incompetent to make key decisions on her own after he died. A letter to Tom's brother written in the mid 1840s by Stafford Kirkpatrick, a Peterborough lawyer associated with the Stewart family through marriage, corroborates Frances's claims that she had little worldly experience upon which to draw after Tom's death. In the letter, Kirkpatrick mentions with apparent unease that Tom had requested money from Frances's account in Ireland.[1] While there are no surrounding details regarding the circumstances of the request for money, Kirkpatrick's statement is suggestive of the control that Tom had over the couple's finances and the resulting fear of having to depend on others that Frances experienced later on.

Frances, like other pioneer women, had little voice in family decisions, although the circumstances of their migrant lives called for her direct and constant involvement in the activities of the household. Douglas McCalla has ascertained that the complex, self-sustaining economy of nineteenth-century Ontario required the direct involvement of all members of the family.[2] In the case of Frances and her daughters, this meant performing duties that helped to sustain the family's farming operation. A study by Alison Prentice, et al, suggests that the multitude of tasks performed during this period by immigrant women, whether they were "managers, servants, or slaves, mothers, unmarried aunts, or daughters,"[3] invariably supported the occupations of the men who lived in the household. Frances's considerable contributions, regardless of her inexperience and self-proclaimed ineptitude, are at odds with the submissive posture that she was obliged to adopt in the marital relationship.

Fundamental differences in points of view between Frances and Tom may have played a part in the lingering self-doubts that characterized Frances's life after her husband's death. In one letter, she comments that Tom had been unable to bear the thought of his sons leaving home and had tried to arrange farms within close proximity for each son as he reached the age of twenty-one. That Frances was set against this plan is evident: "I am decidedly of opinion that it is better for young men to go a little into the world & feel their way thro' life. It shews them what life is and teaches them how to be independent."[4] Frances resisted, at least through her writings, the standards that prohibited her from having a voice in the family's affairs. Her complaints about her husband, however, were ordinarily carefully guarded or diminutively situated within accounts of his depression brought about by his many trials and worries, although she did once allow that Tom had "ruled most strictly."[5] It may be that the couple did become closer, as Frances was wont to write on the occasion of their nineteenth wedding anniversary that their love had increased with the years.[6]

That Frances was afraid of finding herself in a state of dependency is evident. Knowing that her illnesses placed strain on her family, she laments the burden she had become after Tom's death, especially when suffering with her frequent bouts of asthma. Sally Chivers purports, "The idea that a person may become dependent threatens whatever stability and boundaries one has set up in one's life."[7] Alleging in a letter that "a woman is a very helpless creature in this world,"[8] Frances evocatively commits herself to a category of vulnerable beings lacking the wherewithal to care for their own selves. Such a statement underscores the lack of self-assuredness that she suffered in her later years.

At the time of Tom's death, some of the children had already moved out, including the two boys, Robert and Edward Brown, whom Frances and Tom had raised from childhood. The eldest of the two, Robert, was to marry Kate, Frances's youngest daughter, in 1856, while Edward married Bessie not long after Tom's death, the timing of the wedding having been arranged by Tom from his deathbed. As Frances faced the heavy task of caring for the family homestead, Auburn, she became increasingly anxious with each new problem that arose. She particularly missed Edward, whom she loved as her own son; she had come to count on him for his practical assistance around the house and farm and his common-sense advice concerning all matters, including her problems with her sometimes wayward sons. In 1851, four years after Tom's death, Frances finally relinquished Auburn to her son William, who had been living there with her, together with his new wife. Unfortunately, a few years after William's death in 1864, Auburn passed out of the Stewart family

The Stewart's frame house, Auburn. Reverse side caption:"The House I was Born in near Peterboro Ontario Canada, Mar. 17th 1865.Wm. Stewart." (Frances Stewart's grandson, William Stewart, son of William Stewart and Louisa McNabb, was born on this date.) Photographer and date of photo unknown.

(Source: Jean Shearman fonds 05-013 Box 1 Folder 22. Courtesy Trent University Archives.)

altogether as a result of some undisclosed fraudulent dealings involving close family associates. William's death and the loss of Auburn were to signify the beginning of an especially difficult period for Frances. In December of 1864, Bessie's family home, Goodwood, situated a few kilometres walking distance from Auburn and the location at which Frances had been spending much of her widowed life, was lost to fire. There is speculation that some of Frances's letters were lost in the Goodwood fire.

Except for some concerns about Ellen, Frances's relationships with her daughters seem to have been less fraught with worry than with her sons, who she felt sometimes neglected both her and their duties on the farm. Regardless of the trouble they may have caused her, however, Frances's sons were also a source of personal pride. Having learned that the family name had carried them in good stead in Toronto, she proudly relays the details in a letter: "Even in Toronto George & Charlie seem to inherit the regard & interest of many in the highest classes there who were acquainted with their dear father & who till lately we had little or no idea of recollecting us. They have proved themselves kind friends to the sons of one who possessed their respect & esteem, & where memory is still revered & cherished in their hearts. This is very gratifying to me."[9]

Such a statement, written a good thirty-two years after she immigrated, provides unmistakable evidence of Frances's deep-rooted class-consciousness — and pride. Her daughters, rather than her sons, however, were the ones whom she relied on to care for her as she aged. Anna, the oldest, was considered steadfast and dependable and had assumed responsibility for many household duties, even as a child. Ellen was warm, affectionate, and unselfish, but suffered from unknown illness and depression, and was frequently under the care of a physician. Bessie was the pet, having been born on the heels of baby Bessie's death, and Kate was witty and "always rattling away at some fun or nonsense."[10] Naturally, Frances was attentive to her daughters as they married and began having children of their own. Her comments, in line with conventions of the period, deal little with details of pregnancy, labour, and delivery. In one instance, she writes, "I suppose you have heard of my poor Bessies 3rd disappointment. This was the most severe as all would have been right if the poor infant could have been restored but tho' it did breathe for an hour & half, it was too far gone to recover, some difficulty having delayed it in its Birth," and later in the same letter, "I am every day expecting to hear of Anna Hay having an addition to her flock. I saw her yesterday looking well, her three children all well & full of heart & glee & making tremendous noise racing & laughing."[11] Intriguingly, the silences and omissions in such discussions weigh heavily in their absences.

Stewart family composite: (seated, left to right) Bessie, Anna Maria, Ellen, Kate (daughters of Tom and Frances Stewart); (standing) Charles Dunlop (husband of Ellen), circa 1880s. Photo credit: Sproule, Peterboro, Ontario.

(Source: Jean Shearman fonds 05-013 Box 1 Folder 17. Courtesy Trent University Archives.)

Frances lived to know the love and admiration of many of her grandchildren. Using many of the approaches in her letters to them that her own adoptive mother, Harriet, had taken, she discusses aspects of mathematics, nature, and religion, and indicates her clear expectations of receiving their informed responses in return. Her letters time and again convey her grandmotherly curiosity about their activities and interests and suggest deep affection in the relationships. An apt exemplar, the following passage written to a granddaughter on Christmas Day 1869 movingly positions Frances in the role of an old and loving "Grandma":

I have been some weeks intending to write to you so that you should have my good wishes and loving remembrance on this day but I have not been very well for sometime nor in very good spirits and you know people cannot write cheerful or pleasant letters unless they feel quite well and happy. One cause of my feeling dull was having been disappointed in my wish to send you, all my very dear little Grandchildren, some little presents but I found I could not manage it.... though I have not been able to send you presents or to prove the truth of my words I am always your very loving Grandma.[12]

This passage is testimony to the easy relationship that Frances had with one of her granddaughters and is symbolic of her humble deportment as she struggled to maintain and nurture her relationships through the medium of letters. Although combatting physical ailments — nosebleeds, rheumatism, weakness, and deafness — in addition to her lifelong asthmatic condition, Frances kept contact with her loved ones through letters to the final year of her life. Conceding the chore this had become over time, however, she states, "I am grown so stupid & slow both in thinking and acting that letter writing is now quite a task for me."[13]

Throughout her immigrant life, Frances was sustained by her belief in a divine being, a factor that contributed to her ability to cope. Having experienced a religious conversion a few years after settling in Upper Canada, she drew solace from her Christian understanding that God would support her through all her tribulations. The following passage is a clear indication of the comfort that her faith afforded her: "When we feel ourselves alone & obliged to think & act without the friend to think & act for or with us, when we look around & see all others happy & gay & that each possesses some one friend who makes them their first object & that all have some tie, then we who are widows do feel our desolation. We then feel ourselves drawn closer to The One Friend whose love never fails ... whose love is more lasting than any Earthly friend."[14]

Although strictly raised in Church of England doctrine, Frances became noticeably non-denominational as she aged, unbound by a formalized canon. The trigger for digressing may have been a misunderstanding that occurred between the Stewarts and Reverend Robert J.C. Taylor of Peterborough's St. John's Anglican Church at the time of Tom's death. Frances wrote a letter of apology to Taylor a few months after Tom died explaining that the visit to her husband's deathbed by his friend, the Reverend J.M. Roger, a Presbyterian minister at St. Andrew's Church, was by no means meant to slight Taylor, and that "it never occurred to us that you could feel hurt at any of us for receiving a visit so kindly paid & so kindly meant & at such a time."[15] Both the visit by Roger, and Frances's comments in her letter of appeasement to Taylor, suggest that the family was in the process of making a break from the Church of England. Writing in a conciliatory tone to Taylor, Frances reasoned, "[Tom] admired Mr. Rogers as a Christian & for this reason he bespoke a pew in addition lately made to the Scotch Church but he never intended to leave our own church where he found its devotions as he said, those of the Catholic Christian Church of England."[16]

Selena Crosson pinpoints the family's increasing unease with Anglicanism in the era of the Family Compact, writing "The Stewarts had gained much in Canada from their Anglican connections but disdained the political churchmanship that characterized the era of the Family Compact, where membership in the Anglican Church was a minimum requirement for advancement."[17] Over the decades that followed her husband's death, Frances displayed affiliations with the Anglican, Presbyterian, and Baptist churches, a factor that Joyce Lewis considered unusually "broad-minded" in an "age of sectarian intolerance."[18] Frances's daughter, Bessie, asserts that her mother "made no show of her religion … bearing up under all trials & difficulties to the last day of her life."[19] Bessie's summation is particularly astute, fittingly capturing the essence of her mother's life in one brief statement.

THE LETTERS

1847: September 20[20]
To Reverend Robert J.C. Taylor, Peterborough, Ontario

My dear Mr. Taylor

I am so desirous & impatient to remove from your mind an impression which has caused me much sorrow & weighed on my mind so heavily that I can no longer defer writing you a few lines of explanation in hopes of proving to you that you were misinformed on some points & I am deeply grieved ~~to find~~ you could allowed your ~~mind~~ self to be so ~~much~~ thus ~~influenced~~ misled by a report or misrepresentation.

On your last visit to my lamented husband on the Friday evening your agitated manner & some expressions you made use of about "intruding" puzzled us all & grieved & vexed the dear invalid deeply. He could not understand how the visit of a clergyman at such a time or at any time could be considered an intrusion but he was too weak then to seek an explanation & you made your visit in so hurried a manner there was no time for it. A few days after your note to me confirmed me in the most painful certainty that you considered you had been slighted by us & some other clergyman preferred and summoned to attend the death bed of our venerable & beloved friend.

Dear Mr. Taylor, do believe me this was not the case. On the contrary it was always the nearest wish of his heart to consider & to find you, our Spiritual pastor, advisor and friend, and his, in truth, greatest & constant source of regret was that you never ~~came to~~ visited us in this character.

On the Sunday afternoon when you came here along with Mr. Ferguson you saw how very ill he was. He was then under the influence of fever, restless & uneasy in body & confused in mind. Still to his latest hour here below his most earnest & first concern was for the Salvation of his immortal Soul & the Souls of all Mankind. His earnest desire & prayer to God was indeed that all might be saved & his ~~anxiety~~ sincere & fervent prayers were also most particularly offered for you my valued friend as our clergyman & as a minister of the Gospel of Christ our Saviour.

You said in your note to me that another clergyman had notice of his illness or had offered assistance and you hinted that advice & assistance had been sought for from some other clergyman. This was not the case. You were the first who heard of his illness & came to his bedside & he felt happy at seeing you & he & all of us would have been grateful if you could have come more frequently & given him the comforts of Prayer, Scripture reading or Serious conversation which he constantly & urgently <u>cried</u> for during the two or three last days of his life.

Mr. Rogers was not in Peterboro till a few days before his death. When Anne Reid called in & asked her uncle if he would like to see him he answered, "Oh yes!' — surely." He always had a sincere regard for Mr. Rogers as a Christian minister & friend & enjoyed his society & conversation most particularly as it generally turned upon serious subjects which for the last year interested him more than any other. Mr. Rogers did come on Thursday I think but the dear subject of this letter was so restless & ill that he could not benefit much by his visit. These are times when the heart seems open to receive the only true & solid consolation that can be given & naturally withdrawn as much as possible from the trifling vexations of life & believe me my ever dear friend that it never occurred to us that you could feel hurt at any of us for receiving a visit so kindly paid & so kindly meant & at such a time.

You were well acquainted with the universal benevolence of his heart & his wish to promote union & unity amongst <u>Christians</u> of all denominations. He admired Mr. Rogers as a Christian & for this reason he bespoke a pew in addition lately made to the Scotch Church but he never intended to leave our own church where he found its devotions as he said, those of <u>the Catholic Christian Church of England</u>. I think he said this to you about the last time he spoke distinctly to you just as you left his bedside. He called it out loud.

Forgive me my dear Mr. Taylor if I have encroached too far on your time or attention but it was a subject too near my heart to be touched upon lightly.

I regret to hear that you are suffering so much from hurting your leg & that your family are like my own, still afflicted with this tedious &

obstinate fever. We have now four invalids though none of them are <u>very</u>
seriously ill & I hope all in both houses may soon be quite well.

I shall be sincerely happy to see you or my dear Mrs. Taylor whenever you can come up but I know how difficult it is for either her or you
to leave home.

With every feeling of sincere regard & affection for you & dear Mrs.
Taylor & your family, Believe me dear Mr. Taylor

Ever Gratefully

Yours F. Stewart

1847: September 21[21]
To [Harriet Beaufort], Ireland

To Miss B.

Sep. 21st 1847

I am sure my dearly loved & loving friends will be anxious ab't me & I
must not let this mail go without bearing some intelligence of your poor
desolate & afflicted child, tho' I am wrong in using that first term. My
heart must be desolate & lonely but I cannot be so in <u>reality</u> when I am
surrounded by my dear children all trying who can show me most tender love, consolation & attention & when every one who ever knew us
write in showing kindness, but afflicted I must be for no one can know
how severe our loss. Thank God I have been & am supported & can see
such unbounded love & mercy mixed in the bitter cup that it would be
profane & rebellious indeed to allow any repinings to arise in my breast
& the height of selfishness to sorrow without rejoicing, for we must all
feel certain that his soul which had been ripening for a long time past
has now attained the Haven where all troubles cease & where sighing &
sorrow are unknown. That he is now enjoying a peace which passeth all
understanding & oh what a change from the years of anguish & misery
he has had!! & probably would have had for some time to come. I have
long prayed that his poor tortured mind should be relieved but oh how
little did I forsee the full & complete relief & release that was so near, or
the depth of misery left for us here, but still I feel the hand of the Lord

has smitten us & <u>all</u> is well, <u>all</u> is mercy & we must now look forward & <u>press</u> forward to the mark set before us of the high calling of God in C.J.

At 1st his illness was intermittent fever which, however, <u>this</u> year has been much more formidable than any other. About the 5th day it became steady fever. He had no head ache or pain in back or limbs, indeed he never had the slightest pain, but after Thursday the fever encreased & his tongue showed it was a worse kind, his mind in general perfectly clear & calm tho' his body was restless & sickness of the stomach most exhausting. All usual remedies were tried & next week he appeared better, the brown crust peeling off his tongue, but on the 2d Wednesday it began to return & the thirst terrible. Towards days break Thursday he grew restless sick & chilly. I sent for the Dr. who had only left us a few hours. Twitching came on in his limbs. Dr. Hay was very anxious & sent for another Dr. who did not think the symptoms so bad, ordered Calomel & [ ] &c but he grew worse. He plainly knew <u>then</u> he was leaving us & looked often at me saying I am happy! happy! Anna & Ellen came & Dr. Hay only left us when obliged. Friday he spoke much to us all when able but his throat & tongue were so dry he hardly could & we could only hear by putting our heads close to him but every word was precious for all breathed the most perfect resignation under suffering & joy & earnest desire for the safety of the Souls of all round him. He spoke separately to each calling for any absent & did not omit one. He made us read & pray with & for him. He constantly prayed & called for [ ] & enjoyed extempore [ ] most as it was the utterance of the heart at the time. Mr. Taylor came twice & Mr. Rogers & Mr. Benson. He could not keep his attention fixed for more than a few minutes, but joined his voice in the [ ] when it applied to <u>himself</u> or any one for whom he felt particular interest. Friday night he gave Wm. & John advice & instruction & placed them under Ed. Browns care & asked him to be a friend & advisor to his boys which poor dear Ed. promised with tears & the dear one added "I mean religious as well as moral." Many wonderful impressions & touching expressions did we hear. The dear one seemed hovering on the brink of Eternity from Thursday till 9 oC. Monday 6th Sep'r when the Sp't [spirit] fled. They were days never to be forgotten. Never did any of us witness such scenes. They are awful, for the Sp't [spirit] seemed <u>more</u> in Heaven than on Earth but glorious & rejoicing too. I have often heard & read of Triumphant Deaths & read of such scenes but this was indeed <u>victorious</u>. Death had no sting to him. During these 3 days his breath often stopped so long we thought all was over, but there was no struggle or sign of suffering. His tongue was quite black. He made Ellen, Bessy & Edw'd sing hymns & psalms frequently & took more pleasure in it than anything. He also had psalms, &c read. Mr. Reid & Jas. often prayed at his bedside & read to him. On Sat'y night he spoke to Dr. Hay & Ed. of many matters, gave solemn directions as to many subjects, his funeral &c & made Dr. Hay write it down, signed & had it witnessed. He could not bear Ed. a moment out of his sight & sent for Rob't & spoke affectionately to him.

All belonging to this world seemed as nothing during this time when we were watching his soul passing into Eternity. We were elevated above this life. Sunday morning he was quite exhausted & the restlessness of <u>body</u> continued. He asked the 3 "to sing his Soul to Heaven." He slept heavily for some hours then & I sat & held one hand which was cold & blue. Some flies were about the bed & I touched his hand in trying to wave them off which roused him. A rush of heat came on & he seemed to revive. His voice became stronger & clearer & he again said how happy he was & repeated his entire trust was in his Sav'rs atonement & he longed to be with him & then added & to join my dear sister. He was able to swallow better & spoke to <u>all</u>, gave Ed. a Bible Bessy had given her Papa the year before & begged him to read it frequently in private as well as in family reading, asked him to kiss him & showed such love to all as I never saw him show before. Mr. Benson came & talked & prayed &c but hearing hymns sung was his greatest pleasure. In this way he passed his last Sab'th on Earth. Dr. Hay, Ch. Dunlop & Rob't Brown sat up that night & all made me lie down as I was worn out not having lain down for a fortnight, at first from asthma & then I could not leave him. I slept so sound I did not hear Ellen get up at 2 & she shut the door & I never wakened till 4. I then ran to the head of the stairs & heard Dr. Hay praying. I dressed quickly & as I went down I heard <u>his</u> voice unusually loud & clear calling out "Oh my Sav'r, come for me." This was the last I heard him say. Bessy forced me into the parlour to take a cup of coffee & when I came out he was sleeping & never awoke. He had some pain in the night but not severe. He opened his eyes once, turned himself & looked at me, but the eyes were dim & a strange look in them, but he soon slept again. He breathed on quite regularly till it just stopped. I have been quite well except asthma.

1848: May 31[22]
To Catherine Kirkpatrick, Ireland

Auburn 31st May 1848

My dearest Catharine,

Last week I had a great part of a letter written to you but from low spirits & one cause or another I could not manage to finish it in time for Saturdays Mail & so I have just thrown it into the fire and have taken a fresh sheet to make, if possible, a better attempt. You will be alarmed at my being in such low spirits & will naturally fear I have met with some new affliction or got into some fresh trouble but tho' I have met with a very great loss, it is not so bad as to amount to an affliction. I have lost three members of my family! — my darling Bessie & the two Browns who have been 15 years as my own sons & under my care! And on Wednesday night, or rather on Thursday morning last, Edward carried my sweet Bee off & neither of them can or will ever be in exactly the same position again in my family circle, tho' they will I am sure never change in affectionate & tender fondness for the poor old Mother they have been with heretofore. On Friday Robert Brown (who remained here after the wedding) drove me over to pay them a visit & they kept me till the next day & I did enjoy the 24 hours most exceedingly. However, I must go back & "begin at the beginning" as the children say. They both wished to be married on my birthday & so on Wednesday last, the 24th, the ceremony was performed in our drawing room by Rev'd Mr. Taylor, our clergyman. We had merely our own family & some of our nearest connections here as we wished it to be very quiet, for at best it must be a melancholy business under my present circumstances & of course missing the presence of the beloved & tender parent who had given away our two elder daughters & who had always given the bride the first tender embrace!!

But tho' not with us in body, I trust his blessed Spirit watched over us & witnessed the ceremony he had himself directed should be performed in a reasonable time "after," when he so solemnly joined their hands & gave her to him last September. Dr. Hay performed the part of a father on the occasion & gave my dear child away. Our party consisted of Mr. & Mrs. Taylor, Dr. Hay & Anna, Ellen & Charles Dunlop, Edward Brown & his two brothers Templeton & Robert, Anna Falkner who came some days before to spend some time here & Fanny & Kitty Reid & our own family circle, all except poor William who was confined to bed with intermitting fever. The ceremony was performed about six o'clock in the evening as we thought having tea soon <u>after</u> would give us some occupation & take off the <u>silence</u> & formality. The little Bride looked simple, innocent & composed & behaved with more self possession than I expected, for I knew she was "<u>heart full</u>." She was dressed in a neat simple manner. The dress was a pale colour, more blue than Lavender, & more Lavender than blue, if you can understand what that can be like. It was very pretty & cool looking. I don't remember the name of the material. It was very soft & nice looking. The body was made with bias folds round the bosom & sleeves & buttons all down the front. On her shoulders she wore a very handsome blond scarf which poor Anna Stewart sent out to Anna Hay, her hair hung in ringlets round her face & neck having been cut sometime ago, as it came out so much after the Ague. Everyone seems to feel interested about both Edward & Bessie for both are much liked & loved by all who know them.

Then came tea. Anna & Ellen presided at the tea table at one end of the room & poured out tea & coffee which the boys handed about as the party sat in groups in different parts of the room. In the middle was a table with bread & butter, buttered buns, plum cake, little Shrewsbury cakes & some other kind, all made by Bee, Anna Hay & Anna Falkner. The Brides cake was cut up. It too was <u>home made</u> & excellent & nicely iced & ornamented with coloured comfits. It was made by Anna Hay & Bessie & just as good & rich looking as any bought plum cake. All this kept us busy till candle light & at [9] oclock we had some nice singing & playing as both Mr. & Mrs. Taylor are very musical. It was the first time I had heard any music except hymns or psalms which were sung here on

Sunday evenings for above a year & it seemed strange to my ears & melancholy at first but it soon went off & I enjoyed it very much.

Templeton Brown has a beautiful voice & he & Edward sung together. Poor Robert was not able to join having had Ague that morning. These three brothers sing nicely together. Mrs. Taylor played on the piano, which is the wonder of everybody. It sounds so well & everyone likes the tone of it so much better than many of the modern ones. Poor dear old thing, it goes in & out of tune of its own accord for I never allow any of the common travelling tuners who often come round here to touch it for fear of spoiling it as they do sometimes & it has not been tuned for six years! It sometimes gets a little asthmatic like myself in damp weather but recovers when the air is dry & sounds quite well again but it is always very low, below concert pitch. However, I suppose you don't understand or care much about that. At 11 we had a little supper, cold fowl & lamb & ham & salad & some tarts & Raisins, Almonds & Apples, &c & &c & the Bride and Bridegrooms health were drank, & we left the gentlemen after which we heard great cheering and hurrahing. When the gentlemen had chatted some time over their glasses Edward went to change his dress & put on a warmer & commoner suit & then went off to get his Waggon ready & we all went to [ ] up the darling bride & pack up her trunks & parcels. So it was near one oclock before they started & a lovely night, the moon just above the trees. I never wished more to do anything than I did to go with them but I thought they would excuse my company just then & I said nothing. No one went with them except old Anne McIntosh an old servant who lived with me many years ago when they were all children & tho' she lives 18 miles off she always expects to be invited to the weddings & to attend the Bride. She always stays ten days or so & goes home with the Noveaux Mariées. She has been at Annas, Ellens & Bessies weddings. Bessie has a nice little maid, a young girl of 16 who came from Ireland last year from near Ballymacash & whose mother died soon after they came to Peterboro. She is a nice good little girl & I hope may answer very well for Bessie. On Friday morning about 10 oclock I reached Goodwood which is nearly 3 miles from this & there my own dear children met me with smiles & a hearty welcome. It was a happy meeting to us all & I rejoiced to see so much comfort &

prosperity in every part of the premises. The clover looks so beautiful & green & luxuriant & also the wheat & the woods are so verdant & fresh & lovely, the house so clean & airy & comfortable, so much neatness & convenience in the arrangement of everything & the laying out of the house & rooms, that it plainly shewed the young proprietor thought much of the wee wee wifey when he was planning it all. They would not let me return home till the next morning as the day was warm & the rough road & jolting had given me a little headache.

You may suppose how very lonely I felt after I came home. Dear Ellen had staid with me for some days before & after the wedding to keep me company & also to remain here when I went to pay my first visit to those dear ones, but she has her own establishment to take care of & it was necessary she should go home on Saturday morning, & just as I returned she was setting off home so that I was only in time to say goodbye.

Then indeed the house did seem empty & forsaken. Bessies room looked like a deserted birds nest with fragments scattered about, ragged, & everything out of its place. The boys rooms too were changed for both the Browns had kept their clothes here till now, as they had no servant to wash or take care of them or any safe place to keep them till now that they have got all complete. I have always attended to their clothes & had their washing & sewing done here ever since they have been with us, so that when their trunks, boxes, boots, brushes &c &c were all taken away it seems a complete emptying of the rooms upstairs. On Sunday too I missed my three dear children terribly for they were my constant companions in any leisure hours & were fonder of being with me than any of my own sons. We used to walk & talk & sit together, Bessie, <u>Ted</u>, <u>Bob</u> & I, & were more like brothers & sisters than Mother & children. All last winter I used to long for Wednesdays & Saturdays as on those evenings Edw'd always came & he & Bee & I had such sociable evenings & when I was overcome with low spirits he used always advise & sooth & comfort me, or if I was in any dilemma about the farm or the boys he always put things right & I felt sure that if he saw anything going wrong or neglected about the place he w'd see that & put it right. Indeed I have always had a feeling of safety & <u>security</u> whenever Edward was with us for many years back. Now of course I must relinquish much of this, for having an establishment of his own he cannot be so often here & not having his little <u>Sweet heart</u> to come to, he will not be so anxious to come over & having her <u>there</u>, I cannot think of his leaving her. My dear William is exceedingly careful & really shews much discretion & judgement in attending to everything so that <u>in fact</u> we do not require Edward so much in that way, but not one of my boys are <u>companions</u> so much to my fancy as dear Bessie, Edward & Robert. I think Robert will sometimes come & keep me company. Poor fellow, he is now very ill with Ague & much reduced. So is my poor William. His fever has turned into Ague which is not so bad. I am always afraid now of intermitting fever ending in Typhus. It is so weakening, but Ague is not so bad. Quinine seems to have no effect now in stopping Ague & it is in every house in the country & you go no where without seeing two or three miserable yellow emaciated creatures crawling about. Williams illness has come at a busy time & we are obliged to hire people to plough & plant potatoes which is very expensive. Frank cannot settle his mind to work <u>at home</u> & is trying to push himself forward on his own farm. I cannot blame him as he is 21 & he wants to be independent. He is a fine active pleasant fellow, very much like his dear Papa in his character & ways. Johnny is a steady hard working lad but having had Ague for two months & being naturally of a delicate frame his strength is not equal to much exertion. He has many good points but is awfully <u>selfish</u> & old <u>batchelorish</u> in his ways & particularities. Frank is the pleasantest companion of any of the boys but he scarcely ever is at home & never seems to care for any of his own family. He is now staying at the Browns. We are obliged to keep Charlie from school which will be a terrible loss to him as we require him to help on the farm. He too is but weakly as he has had Ague & is growing very fast. You see now my dear why I have been low spirited since I lost those three who were <u>everything</u> to me. I have not yet got a housekeeper but am in hopes of soon having <u>Ellen Duffield</u> & she will be a treasure to me as she is a most excellent housekeeper in every way & knows <u>practically</u> all that is to be done in a country house like this where economy is necessary. She is active & healthy which is another requisite as I am not myself quite so well able to <u>run about</u> as I once was. We have known the Duffields for many years so she is no stranger.

June 1. There was a terrible frost last night which has killed all our Indian corn, pumpkins, squashes & all the plumbs of which there was an immense quantity. Today we have good fires on, it is so cold. This day 26 years ago we sailed from Ireland.

1848: July 29[23]
To [Harriet Beaufort], Ireland

Auburn Thursday 29th July 1848

My own darling H. Good news! good pens! new paper! new Ink, new ink bottle, & many other nice things! I have the pleasure of telling you that my Box arrived here in safety on Tuesday evening & all its contents have been examined & admired. And now I must try and express to you & my other dear friends how truly & heartily grateful I am to all who contributed to the valuable contents of that same box, but all I can say seems to come far short of what I wish to say. All seems too cold, for my heart is full of love & thankfulness. I have also many messages from those who were so kindly thought of in this most acceptable & well chosen collection of useful & pretty things! — but all seem to centre in my breast because it is for my sake that you all shew such kindness to my children.

As usual the Box was tedious in its passage from Montreal where it arrived on the 16th of June, but having been detained above ten days at Port Hope (only a days journey from this) it did not reach me till 25th July. I had almost given up hopes of having it even so soon as the steamboat from Peterboro & Rice Lake had met with an accident. William had gone into Peterboro Tuesday & fortunately took the waggon. Just as he was leaving town he heard the steamboat bell & thought of going to see if it was there.

At the landing place he met Charles Dunlop who did not know that Willy was in town & was just coming here with my box. Was he not kind.

So Willy soon got it on board his waggon & drove off. Edward also had gone to Peterboro that evening & had left Bessie here till he came back. So it happened nicely that she could see the box opened & take her own share of the goods home with her.

Well, about 8 oclock in the evening, Bessie, Ellen Duffield & I were sitting at work at the drawing room window when we heard wonderful shouting & cheering on the road & presently saw two waggons coming along at a <u>tearing</u> rate. I knew the hindmost was Edward's. He & George had gone together & both were dressed in dark clothes. But the foremost waggon had 3 men in it, all without their coats, & one had his hat off & roared & cheered loudest of all.

The horses were galloping at a furious rate & I concluded they were some of our neighbours who too often return from town drunk & very noisy. But these people turned in & galloped straight up to the yard gate.

Henry & Kate ran to open the gate for they saw before I did who they were & what the cause of the noise was. They flung open all the gates & cried out The Box! The Box! & the first waggon galloped round the house & stopped at the veranda opposite the little parlour window. Then I discovered the reason but I was nearly breathless with fright for I was sure some accident would happen. I found the three men were Will'm, Mr. Fowlis & Frank whom they had picked up on the road & he had jumped up on the box wh' made him higher than the rest. The heat & excitement had made them throw off their coats. The poor horses too were equally excited & tried to run off before they had the box out of the waggon but no one was hurt fortunately. No time was lost in removing the tarpaulin covering but we did not take off the lid till W'm & Edward had put their horses, as every man is his own groom here, & till John & Charley had come in from the hay field where they were still working. In about 20 minutes all were collected & the box was brought into the parlour & put by the window. W'm opened it & handed out the contents. Many ready hands were stretched to receive each article & lay it on the table where Bessie & I were standing to receive them.

Shirts, sheets, shoes, parcels, bundles, boxes — all were laid on the table, but not in silence I assure you. You never heard such gabbling & exclaiming, such running & tramping backwards & forwards. But in the midst of all, we all & each felt bitterly the blank there was! the loss of one who was ever foremost in the pleasure of opening the Dublin box! We could not help feeling a pang in the midst of our joy.

Anna & Ellen too & their husbands were always here before but this time we could not manage to have them as it is now quite a piece of [business] to fetch Anna & her 3 chicks & their maid all up & she cannot leave them at home and as Ellen has no servant at present she could not come. Bessie, however, was on this occasion the person most concerned having so large a share in the property. So we decided to proceed without delay.

Bessie's sheets, shifts &c were laid on one end of the sofa & mine on the other & all the parcels on the table to be opened. Bessie & Ed'd were of course much delighted & overpowered with admiration & gratitude. Indeed they w'd be heartless creatures if they were not but they have hearts that can feel & appreciate the kindness of such friends. Everything was so nice, good & beautiful & handsome, useful & substantial of their respective kind.

It was late as you may suppose when all were taken out & opened but the Browns were obliged to go home, late as it was, as Edward was to be out at his hay field at five in the morning. So we put back the nice bonnet & black silk & scarves & shawl & all the small things of Bee's into the tin box & put it & the larger articles into the large box. Edward fastened the lid & put it into his waggon. He next put in his little wifey & then drove off. There was so much hurry I only had a <u>sight</u> of Bessie's nice things but they have invited me to go as soon as I can to spend days with them & look over everything quietly.

The beautiful writing case was a most unexpected present & a most useful one indeed. It is a very handsome one & just what they particularly wanted as neither of them had any desk or box to keep papers or writing materials in & this [answers] for both so well. It was indeed very kind of dear Louisa to think of it. I am sure Bessie will write her own thanks for every thing better than I can. I have not seen any of the things which were inside of it yet. Thank dear Lou too for the [B-] dress. It is exceedingly pretty & cool & light for summer.

The bonnet fits Bessie very well. She says it is the most comfortable fit she ever had. It looks nice & the ribbon is very handsome. Thank you my dear for that & the other pretty things, the [ ] shirt &c &c. But I have only seen them as yet by candlelight.

The Black silk seems very nice & a very good one & I think the material for my dress beautiful. It is so soft & fine. I must have it made by a dress maker to do it justice. Was the beautiful Shetland scarf for Bessie — it is not on the list.

W'm is greatly pleased with his knife & [ ] which he says are <u>capital</u> & he is truly thankful for them.

George has been in quite a fever of expectation about his treasures & you never saw a boy so delighted as he is. The beautiful box of instruments & the books too! the exact kind he wanted! He says he is quite made up now. From the time his books & box were taken out he had no eyes, ears or interest for anything else. He sat looking at them & the books & I could hardly get him to bed at half past twelve oclock.

I must now come to my own share & thank you dearest for the Books. The numbers of *Chambers Miscellany* are a delightful addition to our own stock. We have now twenty volumes complete, a nice library. I gave them to Willy as a Birthday present each year as they came. Kate has been busy reading *Uncle Sam's money box* & Henry has taken a fancy to Orlandino so I think I must give it to him for he is a very good little fellow & deserves a little present now & then. They all seem to prize any thing sent from home as peculiar <u>treasures</u>. I have not had time to look into any of them yet.

You asked if you had sent me Sir Walter Raleighs life but it has never come. Thanks for the black stockings. The cotton ones are very nice & the silk ones <u>quite a luxury</u>. We can't get any such things here unless we pay extravagantly for them & even then so bad, mere cobwebs. We can only get worsted which are too warm for summer so those are most acceptable & so are the black gloves & thank you for this nice paper, wafers, envelopes & the lozenges & the brown stick which I am sure is good for coughs. It is so like old [Danesous] lozenges.

Thanks thanks thanks to all dear friends for all & to Maria Noble too for the nice little pen knife which I was really in want of. It is hard to meet with good cutlery here. I think I could fill sheet after sheet in thanking my kind friends & saying how much pleased I am with every thing but I must write my thanks separately to my other friends another day. This is Friday 28th.

Yesterday I was annoyed at being interrupted in this letter but it was very well for I had your letter in the evening of the 7th of July, only 20 days from the date.

I have been very comfortable for some time past as Ellen Duffield saves me all trouble in household affairs & I have more time for quiet enjoyment. She is no needle worker so she does not assist me in that way but I have very little work now compared to former times. Alas! the numbers of those I worked for are much decreased & the quantities of made up things sent out the last two years from home have helped me unspeakably.

1849: November 2[24]
To Mary [Wilson], Ireland

Auburn 2d Nov'r 1849

My beloved Mary

I have been for some weeks past thinking of you almost constantly & longing to know something of you & still intending to write to you but waiting from week to week, still hoping to hear from some person who could give me any satisfactory account of you but I have waited to no purpose. So I will write, but what can I say? How can I express to you what I feel, how deeply I feel for your loss, for I fear the report is but too true.... I am more anxious than I can tell you to have every <u>particular</u> & <u>circumstance</u> connected with the <u>whole</u> of your blessed Mothers illness & departure & your own mind & your plans & prospects....

I am vexed that my sister has never written to me to tell me of you for she knows how closely attached we have been since I have been acquainted with you, my own darling friend & cousin.

I am sure Eliza Frood will write to you. She has been waiting for me to write some time. Dear Eliza, she is a fine & valuable girl & I love her more & more every day & am most thankful that I have them with me. They are pleasant in the house as companions for my young people & are exceedingly useful too & most anxious & ready to do anything for me & very kind & thoughtful. The only thing that I regret is that they don't seem yet to feel the Spirituality of Religion in their hearts but I think the great change in their habits & ways of living has unsettled their minds....

Now my dearest Cousin, Adieu. May every Spiritual & temporal Blessing & Comfort be yours, in & through Christ our Lord. Your affect' cousin

F. Stewart....

1850: May 27²⁵
To Sandford Fleming, [Toronto, Ontario]

Auburn, Peterborough
27th May 1850

My dear Sir

I hope you will forgive me for again encroaching on your time & attention, as well as your kindness in this way but I am tempted to do so by having heard a message you sent to my son George by Dr. McNabb, advising him to try & get some means of improving himself by going to Toronto.

This he has been long wishing much to do & could he hear of any employment or situation to enable him to pay the expenses attendant on living there, & afford him an opportunity of learning and advancing in the branches of Science and Art necessary to the Professions he has chosen, he is most ready to accept of it.

If you know of any place of this kind or could without inconvenience to yourself make some enquiries to seek one for him, he & I shall both feel deeply indebted to you.

He writes a tolerably fair hand & understands accounts & Bookkeeping & would be most thankful if you will have the goodness to let him know as his great wish is to do what he can & to feel that he is doing <u>some thing</u> or <u>any thing</u> to improve himself & to be independent. He would devote his spare hours to improvement in different branches of Science if he could procure employment in some Store or office & a moderate salary to enable him to live.

I remain dear Mr. Flemming
Your sincere friend,
Frances Stewart

1850: November 15[26]
To "Aunt Mother," Ireland

Auburn 15 Nov'r 1850

My dearly loved Aunt Mother

About ten days ago I received your letters, always welcome, & most thankful am I to find a continuation of pleasing accounts of your health & happiness.... How perceptibly I have felt the comfort of this since my dear sons have been separated from me. When their dear Papa was here he never could bear the thought of their leaving home & he arranged so that each should have a farm ready & near this where each sh'd commence for themselves at 21. But his plans all ended with his life, and I am decidedly of opinion that it is better for young men to go a little into the world & <u>feel</u> their way thro' life. It shews them <u>what life is</u> and teaches them how to be independent.

My dear boys had never been from home till last summer & I trust it has not injured them. Poor dear Frank has not succeeded so prosperously as John. He took a wrong direction at first & went to some people merely to see them "en passant" but they advised him to stay there instead of going nearer to where John was & he found they were not his best advisers. He has been now more than two months out of employment, not earning anything & forced into some expense by illness. He had a tedious & debilitating complaint, a sort of aguish fever & when I heard last he was weak & had caught a bad cold which gave him a cough & pain in his chest. But as he has always been very healthy I hope with common care & prudence he may soon be well. He had some prospect of employment as teacher in a school which he seemed inclined to take up whenever his health should permit. He was offered £6-5-0 per month which w'd be £75 a year but he w'd only take it for the winter months, I suppose as he w'd like some more active employment for a permanent occupation. I wrote to beg he would come home for the winter but he could not. He is determined not to come till he has some money to begin in earnest at his own farm. He seems a good deal cast down by his illness & idleness but I hope he is by this time better in every way.

George has completed the job in which he was engaged & has got safe back to Toronto for which I am most thankful as I was excessively uneasy at his having the dangerous voyage on Lake Huron to undertake at this tempestuous time of year. However, in this Providence guided them for the wind proved contrary & the danger was so evident that the party determined to travel by land tho' a most fatiguing & difficult matter & they walked through the woods for four days & carried all their luggage on their backs to Goderich & there took waggons to Hamilton. I heard very seldom from my loved boy for the last two months. It was so difficult to have letters conveyed & the last interval was so long that I became very uneasy. However, at last came a hurried & short letter from Toronto saying he had at last reached it in safety tho' much wearied & all his clothes worn to rags. I have not heard since but he had some thoughts of remaining in Toronto for the winter & pursuing his studies under his friend Flemings direction as he has now opened an office there & will take pupils. This will I trust prove advantageous to George but he had not made any agreement with Fleming so I don't know anything of terms &c &c or how he is to earn enough to support him there but I expect another letter soon & thank God I shall now be able to assist him myself if he requires it.

I wish to help on all my sons as long as I am permitted to be with them & give them every advantage that I can in education. How thankful I am that I shall I hope have the means in my power if I live a few years longer. Oh yes I have much to be thankful for tho' I do sometimes give way to weakness when perplexities overcome me. For a woman is a very helpless creature in this world & I have been so completely unaccustomed to acting for myself in any way or degree for the last 34 years of my life & particularly after I became subject to asthma that now I really am ignorant of everything & become bewildered & constantly forget things which ought to be done, always having had those with me who could think & act for me much better than I could for myself & now I miss the assistance of my children so much tho' indeed they are always helping me as much as they can.... And now my dearest Aunt, with love to every member of your family absent & present, I am your ever affect' child

F. Stewart

forgive great haste

[The following text is located on one sheet loosely inserted in the above letter]

Thank you my dear & loved Aunt for getting me the little books & Tracts you said you were going to send me in the Box. I do give many of those you send & lend many. I have let Hugh Whites sermons to several & Stevensons on the 22d Psalm.

I wish very much to have all the works of Rev'd H. Blunt. Aunt Sutton sent me his lectures on Abraham & I have his lectures on the [ ]. I should like his lectures on St. Paul & St. Peter & the life of Christ if you could get them cheap second hand & pay for them out of my money dear Aunt. I have no time as I have had 50 interruptions.

I would write the remainder of my Cobourg visit if I had time but I forget where I stopped. I am ashamed to send such a useless uninteresting scrawl, indeed my own Aunt you must employ Maria to read this to you for it is not fit for your eyes.

Give my love to dear kind James & to my Athboy brother & sister & to all my Rockfield darlings & all old friends who remember or care for me.

Ever your affect' child

FS

[1851][27]
To Louisa McNabb, Peterborough, Ontario

My dear Louisa

Willy told me you were going to town this evening and as I may not see you before you go I will leave a few lines as I want to beg of you to get me some of the thin muslin at Snyders for Joan's dress & also some of the kind you got for lining & any thing else you think she may require. I will enclose an order for the muslin & for the lining & you can put in the number of yards in the blank I leave.

I am going to Goodwood but shall be home in a little time. When are you coming up again. As you will have a better chance of seeing Kate Brown than I shall, you had better make up the parcel, or if you like to send it to me I will put my letter in. I suppose Kate will be here or at the Reid's before she goes.

I am writing in such hurry I scarcely know what I am doing, but hope you will be able to make out what I mean.

With love to your Father & Mother. Believe me dear Lou. Your affec't Mother

F. Stewart

Wednesday night

1851: June 6[28]
To Betty Taylor, Ireland

Auburn

Douro

Peterboro, 6 June 1851

My dear Betty

I received your letter a few days ago & am very happy to find you are well. I am thankful to say I and my family are all well at present. I have often enquired about you and was truly very sorry to hear of poor Peters death and that you had been in distress but hearing you had left Ireland and gone to Scotland, I had no way of writing to you or sending you any help.

Mr. William Stewart is now the head of this family and he is soon going to be married to a very nice young lady, a Miss McNabb, daughter to Doctor McNabb of Peterborough. Mr. William says he will give you a place here & keep you in the house to look after the chickens & children if he has any and I will give you a note to Mr. Rothwell near Kells, the same gentleman Peter went to before, and he will give you £5-0-0 which will, I am sure, pay your expenses out here and I hope you may get on safe.

I never had any letter from you or could hear anything about you, but that you had gone to Glasgow. I was in Rochester last September and I went to see Ally McCabe. Felix keeps a Huxter shop and a Boarding and lodging house. They are getting on middling well. I did not see little Mary Jane. She was at school & so was James but I saw four other fine children. They went over to the States two years ago and have lived in Rochester ever since. And Ally says she likes it very well.

This place is a changed place since you were here and never will be the same again. I feel very lonely as you may suppose for nothing will ever in this life restore me the loss I have had. But I have a great deal to make me happy. My children are all round me & all good to me and I have every comfort. The people all live round here but we never had anyone to keep the little gatehouse or the garden as nice as poor Peter did. Mrs. Hay & Dr. Hay & the children are all well. They have three children & one dead. Mr. & Mrs. Dunlop have lost 3 children but little Mary is alive and a fine little girl she is.

Miss Bessy was married three years ago to Mr. Edward Brown and has a very nice place but no family as she lost two. Mr. Robert is well & doing well. He has not married yet. Mr. Templeton Brown is married to a niece of mine who lived with me, a Miss Frood. David Porter & family is all doing well & live in Douro near Mr. Browns. William Porter & his family are still in the same place. They have lost two children & now the youngest living is very ill. His oldest girl lives with Mrs. Hay always. Tom Martin & Mary are well but had much sickness & Mary was near to death last year but has got well again. Neddy was laid down all winter with rheumatic fever but got better. He is not strong yet. They have had great trouble, poor people. We have several new people about here but you will I hope know all when you come.

Mr. Frank & Mr. John went to the States last year & are coming home next October please God. George lives in Toronto. He is a surveyor. Charles is at school & grown quite a man & so is Henry. Miss Kate is quite a young woman & is a first rate housekeeper.

I think I have told you all about your friends now Betty, so hoping to hear from you & then to see you I remain

Your very sincere friend,

Frances Stewart

Please to write as soon as you get this to let me know if you are coming this year.

I think it better not to send the letter to Mr. Rothwell in this but I will write <u>by Post</u> & tell him to send it to you as this letter might be lost.

Miss Haycock was married three years ago to a Mr. Williams. She is living a long way from this. Old Mr. & Mrs. Haycock are both dead. Mrs. Strickland died last year & left a large young family.

Mary Devine is married & doing well. She lives in the Scotch Village. I think I don't know any more to tell you about your friends. Nobody knows anything of your sister Charlotte. I believe Ellen is married in the States. She did <u>not</u> marry Mr. Spalding.

1851: July 18[29]
To Mary Wilson, Ireland

Another marriage is likely soon to take place more immediately in my own family. My eldest son William has been fortunate enough to succeed in making himself agreeable to Louisa McNabb. She is stepdaughter to Eliza Reid who married a physician Dr. McNabb about 2 ½ years ago. Louisa is a very amiable affectionate girl & I hope will make a good & prudent wife for dear William. They are to be married in about a fortnight and when she is established here I intend to leave the new married pair to themselves for a little while & pay visits to my daughters. Bessie is to be confined next month & I must be with her at that time.

My family is now much scattered & by that means very much reduced. Frank & John, the two next to William, are still in the States but hope to return home in October. George is studying engineering in Toronto. Charles is boarding with Mr. Taylor our clergyman & preparing for college so that I have at present only Henry & Kate with me and of course William who always lives here. Henry is learning farming and is to go to work with Edward & Robert Brown next winter as I think he will learn a better method from them than he would by remaining here with Wm. & I will keep Kate with me or with one of her sisters. This marriage will make a change in my situation tho' not very materially at first. This house is my own for my life but it is on a very large & expensive scale & the whole establishment is too large for a single female so that I am rejoiced to give up the management & profits of the whole place to William & let him & Louisa have the use of the house & I will give up the housekeeping to her, reserving my own rooms for my own use & the liberty of coming & going as I feel agreeable or convenient, at least till I see how all goes on.

I have taken up too much of your precious time dearest Mary but I hope you will forgive me & write to me very soon. See how my letter has been blotted here and in another place on the first sheet. I have a pet kitten & whenever I am writing it makes a practise of coming up & lying down on my paper & sometimes I am obliged to take another piece of paper.

When you write pray dear like a good kind friend tell me all you know of that precious & beautiful Saint, Mrs. Morrison, if still living. It is a long time since her nephews have heard from her. The letters of even those dear old Aunts are prized above gold & looked for as treasures. They are beautiful specimens indeed of Christian piety & humble submission. It is quite a high privilege to have such relations & correspondents. The Browns only regret deeply that their own circumstances do not allow them to send more assistance to these dear afflicted relations. By steady and most unflinching industry these dear young men are becoming independent. They keep themselves above want and out of debt. James is working hard & living very steadily & has a most valuable wife. He has a farm about half a mile from Edward. Edward works as hard as any man can for you know none of them have anything but their own industry to depend on. They both have good farms. Edward's is his own. James rents his but wishes to purchase it if he can. Templeton has a farm just between Edward's & James's but he lives at present in Peterboro as his farm is not yet under cultivation nor is his house built yet. He & Eliza are longing to get out there but must wait patiently a year or two longer. Robert has a good piece of land, 157 acres, joining Edward's on the other side but there is no house there yet & he is not quite ready to begin for himself as he wants to assist Templeton first. They are all so united & attached to each other. They set a good example to all brothers.

This has been a wonderfully wet season. The crops did look beautiful but fears are now arising about so much wet & there is great difficulty in saving the hay.

I have been writing in the greatest haste as this letter must be in the post office tonight. So my own dear Mary pray give my best & kindest love to your home circle first & then to the outside circles all round. I mean those who care for me, of course....

Dear Mary write to me soon & <u>fully</u> & Believe me to be as ever your attached & affect'e cousin, F. Stewart

"Part of the Township of Douro," circa 1851. Transcription of legend:
References
[double lines] All double lines are for roads
[grey] Clergy Reserve
[pink] Crown Reserve
xiii, xii &c are Concessions
1.2.3.4. &c are the Lots
R's are Rob Reids Lots
S's are T.A. Stewarts Lots
7, 132, 99, 158, 34, 170, 183, 17, 196 are the number of acres in those Lots.
The other Lots that are not broken by the River contain 200 acres each.

(Source: Frances Stewart fonds 97-023 Folder 4. Courtesy Trent University Archives.)

1851: August 25[30]
To Maria [ ], Ireland

Goodwood — Monday
25 Aug't 1851

My own dear Maria

I have now come to this sweet place where all is peace & comfort so very
much to my taste & I have longed for this rest after some months of busy-
ness, much more than I have had for above 20 years! How true it is that
strength is always given for the situation we are placed in & the duties
we have set before us. How much this must encrease our confidence in
Gods many and loving kindness which indeed in my case & all through
my life has been so peculiarly shewn. I often wonder why? But certain
it is that from my birth on, through a life of some vicissitude & trial, the
Lord has sustained me & been with me in a way so plain that my eyes
must have been covered [ ] with scales not to perceive it. Oh — may He
increase my love and keep me closer to Him in Spirit!...

I have had many letters lately from my own loved friends at home
all giving me useful & judicious advice as to my arrangements as to my
future residence & these are all helps & in many aspects are quite in uni-
son with my own sentiments....

You all know that for some years back I have felt the responsibility
and expense of keeping up such an establishment as ours was, far beyond
my powers. And I have long wished for some way of making a change.
This has been brought on at length by Williams marriage. Some new
arrangement must take place. I have always observed that it never does
well for two families to live together & therefore I had made up my mind
to make a separation but as I could not see how it was to be done I came
to the resolution of spending some time with my daughters & as Bessie
requires me now it answered best for all parties and as this place seems
best suited to me in every way dear Edward & Bee begged I would return
here after visiting Anna & Ellen & spend the winter here or live here
with them as long as I wished. This was great temptation and I selfishly
thought it was all right & I had consented & I thought I would retain my

right of being Mistress of Auburn & return there as my home whenever I liked or let it be a home for sons as long as they were unmarried keeping Kate always along with myself wherever I was. Dear William & Louisa would not hear of my having any other home & Louisa always treated me as the Mistress & head of the establishment & never seemed to wish or think of placing herself forward in the smallest degree. Indeed she is a very amiable sweet creature & I thought we should all do nicely but my mind has been changed since by considering every side of the question & now conscience tells me that selfishness guided me too much in that plan for I did not consider my dear boys. Frank & John are coming home in Autumn. Frank has his own house to go to but of course it is not just in a proper state for him to return to nor has he any provisions or furniture to begin with so he must have "a home" to come to. So must John & I feel that they cannot make Auburn their home when I am not there. If my home & Kates is really at Goodwood & only <u>nominally</u> at Auburn I fear my sons could never feel really comfortable nor could I at all conveniently manage about their washing & mending of clothes, &c &c even tho' I paid Wm. & Louisa a sum annually to entitle them to it. So now I have been thinking & weighing the business in every way & I believe my wisest plan is to have a house of my own for my children to be with me till they all have homes of their own. I have some idea next month of giving up Auburn to the young couple & taking for myself & my own little flock a very nice cottage adjoining the Auburn property. It is hardly a mile from the house & very near Johns farm & as near to Franks as it is to Williams place. The house is new but [ ] & pleasantly situated and I believe conveniently laid out there on 10 acres of land with it, which would enable me to keep a cow & have potatoes & other little matters. George will be his own master next June & I think he would like to have a quiet home to return to so that I do think it is my best plan to take that place for two or three years or from year to year as life is uncertain & my boys will either settle or disperse in the course of some years. But in the meantime it would be exceedingly inconvenient to me to have my party divided between Auburn & Goodwood and would I think make the young men feel uncomfortable & be almost an unreasonable addition to Louisa's cares & labours. I think with Kate & a servant I can attend to all

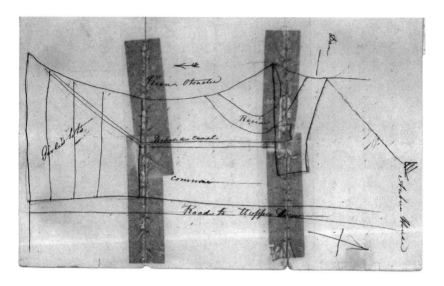

The Stewart [and Reid] "mill properties," 1851. A map by George Stewart depicting "Girls lots" [the properties belonging to George's sisters], "River Otonabee," "Ravine," "Dam," "Road to Upper Douro," and "Auburn House." This map is located in a letter dated August 18, 1851, from George to his mother, Frances Stewart. George writes, "I send you a sketch of the mill properties which if Charley [Stewart] would take to John Reid and get him to put in the lengths and courses of each line, which he will get from the leases..."

(Source: Frances Stewart fonds 97-023 Folder 4. Courtesy Trent University Archives.)

the housekeeping of my small establishment & I shall find it much less expensive. And I think when the Auburn party is so reduced William will find it much easier to keep the place in good order & it will no longer be the Hotel d'Amitie it always has been too much.

There is quite furniture enough in the house to make a division and I think reducing the <u>beds</u> when the family is reduced will be favourable to them as there will not be so many then for "droppers in."

I shall not have very much to buy and now I hope this plan may meet with the approbation of all my dear people at Allenstown & Rockfield. I am sure Catharine will like it when she hears it too & I hope Harriet & Lou may also when they consider that I found it too arduous a task to keep up the great establishment at Auburn. A large house in Canada is different from home for the ladies must be their own housemaids here <u>generally</u> & all <u>suitable</u> furniture to make such a house bear a consistent appearance would be expensive, then the offices, stalling & sheds & houses for cattle for such a farm! & for Willeys Lime & Quarry establishment also! & then the keeping the garden & ground in proper order, it would require an active & systematic <u>master</u> as well as an active & prudent & <u>wealthy</u> mistress. As long as I resided at Auburn & kept the name of mistress I know Willey would take no interest or care of the place. He has good taste & cleverness enough but he is indolent in some things & likes to attend to the quarry better than the farm. I wanted him to give me up the farm & keep the quarry himself but he said he must have the land to keep his horses & people. So I thought my best plan to give all up to him & let him make the most of it & have the benefit of it to himself.

And I think the small house & garden & a few fields will give me employment & occupation without the onerous task & struggle to <u>keep up</u> a large place. It is too much for a female unless she can arrange it for her own convenience which I could not do without casting my dear William out of his own rights or making some uncomfortable impressions arise in his mind.

I wrote to Aunt Sutton & Richard last week & mentioned my new plan to them so perhaps you have heard of it already. The more I think of it the more I feel convinced that it is the best thing I can do & most for the comfort & happiness of my sons which must be my leading object & impulse.

I have had these matters pressing on my mind for some weeks past and I could think of nothing else night or day almost. It is difficult to know how to steer amidst so many interests & drawings of heart.

Your visit to Mrs. Nicholson at Rostrevor must have been very pleasant. It is very useful to the mind to move about & change the Society we live in. It opens new views & ideas and refreshes the mind. I see the bad effects of the want of some change of that sort very evident in many people here who never can leave their own homes. I remember Rostrevor perfectly well as it was 41 years ago. The village & the country around must be much improved since then but the natural beauties of the place must be much the same. I spent five months there in 1809 & went along the coast to Newcastle & Tollymore Park. I remember it as well as if it has been only a few years ago.

I think I never have written since the arrival of my precious cargo nor thanked you & our beloved Mother for your kindness in contributing so much to the contents of the Box. Harriet mentioned you had sent her some money to add to the stock I had of my own & indeed you were very very kind. I never can say half what I wish to express but I am sure you know I am deeply sensible of your kindness & grateful for it. I don't know who sent those five strong blue shirts. They are most acceptable & came in very good time to meet my boys who I expect home in Autumn tho' I have some of the former set still untouched but all these nice new ones will save me a great deal of sewing. Thanks also for all the books & Tracts which are a most valuable part of the gifts. I have not yet had time to look into many, for weddings and Bazaar & then arrangements about new plans &c & being as much as possible with poor Anna Hay has broken up my quietness of mind & time & I have not been able to read. You have divided the little books so nicely amongst us that I shall have some of them wherever I go & those little tracts & small books are so convenient. One can take them up in little "gussets of time" & are a nice size for putting into a pocket. Pray give my kindest thanks to dear Mrs. Blakeney for her very valuable present which I prize most highly & which I am sure will do good.

The Bazaar succeeded very well beyond our expectations & we hope to be in our own church in November. Nearly £230 was cleared after paying all expenses. The pretty articles contributed by the Rothwells were greatly admired and added considerably to my share.

What a nice contrivance that Hydraulic Dam must be. It is such a comfort to have water convenient.

I see my Charlie coming along & I have some thoughts of going to Auburn this evening & returning here tomorrow evening as Bessie has her nurse now staying here. She is I am happy to say very well & quite active & alert & not tensed with head aches as she used to be. I hope & trust all may go on prosperously & that in a little time hence I may have some good news to give. I hardly think she will be confined for ten days or a fortnight yet but it might come sooner & as this place is 5 miles from a Doctor we think it safest to have the nurse here beforehand. I have had some asthma but that I must expect. We have had a great deal of hot damp weather but the harvest is plentiful & good; all crops are excellent except potatoes which in most places about here seem bad. The leaves are all black & shrivelled & no roots.

Dear little Tom Hay has had a most tedious & dangerous illness but after all hopes were gone he rallied & has been recovering the last week. Poor Anna has gone through much fatigue but I hope may not suffer. She is very anxious always about her children....

Your ever affect' sister love

F. Stewart

2 oclock Monday — 25th August

1851: October 7[31]
To "Aunt," Ireland

Goodwood 7th Oct'r 1851

My ever dear Aunt

Here I am still at Goodwood. I am not sure if I was here when I wrote to Maria but I think not. However, I brought Marias letter to Bessie when I came here and we both enjoyed the pleasure together. I had yours to me & she had Marias to her & then we exchanged. What a happiness it is to hear so regularly & constantly & to have such dear friends to write. You can hardly form an idea how I long for letters & enjoy when they come, for you have never been so far away from so many dear to you. Anna Hay has sent me a little letter to enclose & therefore I can not put in so much myself. I suppose you have heard of my poor Bessies 3rd disappointment. This was the most severe as all would have been right if the poor infant could have been restored but tho' it did breathe for an hour & half, it was too far gone to recover, some difficulty having delayed it in its Birth. However, she is now reconciled to the loss & sees it in a proper view. Poor dear it was a great trial to her & to poor Edward & it was such a lovely fine child & unusually large, <u>20 inches long</u>, & 8 inches across the chest & shoulders & fair & lovely more like a child 2 months old than a newborn one.

But it is better it sh'd be taken then than if its life had been spared for any time & He who gave it or I should say lent it, knows best. His will be done. I am sorry to say Bessie did not recover so rapidly as we at first expected. But as soon as she could bear the drive she went to Auburn for a week & returned on Sunday evening much better. Louisa is cheerful & very warm hearted & kind and paid her every attention & so did William and Louisa drive her out every day in my little poney carriage which was useful & pleasant as the weather is delightful now and the country beautiful. Today Bessie is gone away again to stay a few days with her cousin & sister in law Mrs. Templeton Brown while he is gone to Montreal and I have promised to stay here & attend to the affairs for her. I think it is good for her to be from home till she is quite well & able to employ herself actively here or her spirits could sink. I am every day expecting to hear of Anna Hay having an addition to her flock. I saw her yesterday looking well, her three children all well & full of heart & glee & making tremendous noise racing & laughing. Tommy is quite well again. He is a dear infant. Indeed they are all fine children....

I believe it is very difficult to provide for young men now. Even here it is so, for this country seems overstocked with young men and <u>all</u> cannot be farmers. Tho' it is a very <u>independent</u> business yet it cannot be called <u>profitable</u> & requires such drudgery & unremitting labour that people must have a decided taste & <u>character</u> to bear it at all. This year the grain crops have all turned out well but the prices are so low. Nothing can be made by them & it causes a great deal of trouble & distress. The potatoes are wet & small & scanty but not much of the disease tho' the leaves blackened & people were afraid of it but they are not good in general. William Stewart is quite active now & looks after things more than he did. Has got a Scotch man now to work for him who bears a good character for industry & knowledge. Robert Brown has now begun to help his brother Templeton to cultivate a new farm just adjoining this place & we can see him at work every day from the windows. Templeton lives in Peterboro at present till his farm is ready & a house built....

I am expecting Frank & John home soon & hope poor Frank may settle in time & marry. He has been very unfortunate in the States & when he had made a little sum & was going to place it in the Saving Bank he was robbed! This has discouraged him & he will have a great deal to do when he returns & every thing new to buy, cattle & horses & implements

& every thing as he had sold off all when he went. But we all intend to join what we can & push him on & try & get his place ready for a wife as soon as we can. John has had a tedious rheumatic fever which has kept him back a little but he is not badly off. Poor George is working away at Toronto but earning nothing & it grieves him so much being any expense to me that he denies himself every thing & scarcely will even allow himself good clothes. Charles is very busy studying & trying to be ready to stand his Examinations for a Scholarship in College next August. It will keep him busy. Oh I am come to the end of my paper. With best love to all in which Bessie & Kate join. Ever Believe me your own child FS

I never have room to say anything about these wonderful times or the Papers which we [receive] very regularly & are most interesting. We get the Achill paper very regularly & all the others & now & then a Belfast one from Catharine. She never writes now, at least very seldom but don't say anything to her.

Love to James & children

Today the thermometer is at 70 in the shade. 7th Oct.

1852: January 3[32]
To Mary [ ], Ireland

Auburn — 3rd Jan'y 1852

Peterboro, Canada West

My dearly loved Mary

A new year has begun & it makes me feel grateful to our Heavenly Father & preserves for all the Mercies & blessings we enjoy from day to day, month to month & year to year....

I shall be rejoiced to have a letter from dear Mrs. Black & shall indeed prize it for it is many years since I have had that enjoyment before & all my old friends are as dear to me as ever & their kind love to me as fresh & warm in my heart as if I had only left them 4 or 5 years ago instead of nearly 30. What a large portion of life has passed since we parted & what changes have taken place.

I am always pleased to hear of your sister Emily going to see my sister who is so fond of her but who so seldom has the pleasure of seeing any friends. I wish you & she could be more together & also that you were better acquainted with the Rothwells whose father I know you have sometimes seen on his visits to Mr. Thomson. I think since I wrote last to you Maria Frood & James Reid were married. They live with the old people who are very fond of Maria & she seems as happy as possible & I am sure must be a great comfort to them. Both Maria & Robert Reid are wonderfully well but we see very little of them as none of us go out very often. I have been confined almost entirely to the house this winter & during three months of the summer I staid with Bessie Brown.... Bessie Brown has had rather a severe trial in losing another Baby but she is one who tries to see the hand of the Lord in everything & to throw herself more on His unfailing Mercy & loving kindness & to know more of Spiritual things & seek for comfort from them in all her trials & afflictions. I think you would love these dear children of mine if you knew them. Anna Hay too & Ellen I have reason to hope all are inclined to turn their hopes & views Heavenward.

My son Wm. was married last July about a fortnight after Maria Frood. Louisa my new daughter is a sweet tempered amiable young creature & one who I am sure will be a good wife. She is very young, only 18, & has been always much indulged & admired from her infancy & yet really has not been spoilt by it. But of course she has much to learn & I hope her heart may in time be changed as well as my dear William. All my dear boys are constantly the subject of many prayers. My poor Frank is still far away in Pennsylvania struggling to make some money but having met with many disappointments & some illnesses which have kept him back. I have been expecting him home some time. My other sons are all trying to push themselves on in life & I hope are free from vice & all well disposed & amiable & great comforts to me. George is still in Toronto learning Engineering. He is most like his dear father in face & Frank in some points of character & manner. He is light hearted & gay & a favorite with all who know him. I have had a severe attack lately, which required care & I felt the affection & kindness of my dear children...

1853: December 23[33]
To Aunt [ ], Ireland

My own loved Aunt,

I cannot send my letter to dear Bessy without adding a few lines to thank you for your dear affectionate letter which I received some weeks back. I am not nearly so quick in mind or body as I was before my last illness so that I don't get through half of my daily course of work or business, & now darkness is coming on rapidly while I am hurrying to be able to send this to the post tonight. How very kind you were to write to Charlie. I sent your letter to him. He prizes any letters from his kind Irish relations more than I can tell you & both he & George are always wishing for some reasonable excuse for writing to you in hopes of receiving an answer. Charles has the most wonderful love for his Fatherland & for his kindred there & lives in hopes of accompanying George sometime or other across the Atlantic to visit their relatives & see some of the wonders of the Old World. I am happy to say they are both well & as busy as possible.

George seems to have his time fully occupied & fears he cannot join our home circle on Christmas day. I am now on the fidgets in expectation of having my poor wandering son Frank home tonight or tomorrow, as John started off just a month ago & found him at Xenia in Illinois, just the same warm hearted good natured fellow he ever was, but looking very thin, having but just recovered from a tedious illness. He was obliged to wait some days to settle up his accounts with his employer & I have not heard since but I am sure they will try to be home before Christmas day & if possible will try to bring George along with them.

Poor Charlie will be the only absent one & he will I am sure feel it, but as he paid us a visit so lately he could not ask leave of absence again so soon. He is wonderfully anxious to know anything he can about my Father & has requested me to write & ask you & Aunt Waller to tell me everything you can, all particulars of his life & death, his college life & his age when he died, & if he had been promised a Bishoprick or not. I don't know why Charlie wants all this. He has repeatedly asked me as a great favour to procure for him any of my father's papers, sermons or manuscripts which were to be had. But I never liked to ask for them.

I suppose Catharine has them as I think Aunt Susan had them but of course Catharine would not like to part with them & much as I would value them I could hardly ask her for them but will be very thankful for any particulars you can give me about my father of whom I have always been too much in the dark.

Many thanks dearest Aunt for the *Sentinel* which I receive pretty <u>regularly</u>, but not weekly. No numbers have missed tho' they come slowly. It is a very good paper & I like it very much. It is pleasant to have an Irish paper as now it is the only one I have except the *Christian Examiner* & *Layman* which both came from you, I believe, my own kind Aunt. Indeed it is too much for you to subscribe to the *Sentinel* on purpose for me. I think it w'd be better if you w'd allow James to give you the subscription from my money which I could afford now I am sure. But indeed I am most grateful to you for this & all you are always doing for me. I have a great deal more to say but can't try your eyes by crossing, so much cut short the thread of this hurried scratch. I hope soon to hear. I am always longing for letters but now am particularly anxious about dear Emma. So with every kind wish for a happy Christmas & New Year to you my own Aunty & all whom you & I both love. Believe me to remain your ever affect'e child & niece,

F. Stewart

All here write in kind love to all their cousins & Aunts.

23rd Dec'r 1853. Auburn.

1854: April 11[34]
To Maria [Noble], Ireland

Goodwood, Tuesday
11th April 1854

My dearest Maria,

I am sure I need not tell you how I have longed for home letters since I received your last dated 2 March & which reached me the 23d, but none have come since except one from Catharine to Ellen in which there was no mention at all of your dear Aunt's illness. In the very letter I had before that from our dear Mamma she mentioned her own declining years & requested me not to be shocked or to grieve for her if it should be the Lords will to call her to Himself. We cannot help grieving at losing even for a time the social connection with members of our own family whom we have ever loved & revered from our earliest years....

I feel deep sorrow for poor dear Bessy Rothwell. She has been wonderfully supported but I know that the time which immediately follows a bereavement like hers is not the worst. At first one feels a necessity for exertion which keeps one up & there is always so much to be done & arranged & ones situation altogether seems so changed that there is an excitement which actually keeps one from feeling so deeply. But when we feel ourselves alone & obliged to think & act without the friend to think & act for or with us, when we look around & see all others happy & gay & that each possesses some one friend who makes them their first object & that all have some tie, then we who are widows do feel our desolation. We then feel ourselves drawn closer to The One Friend whose love never fails, who we can never lose unless by our own forgetfulness. Oh what should we do if we had not this Friend to fly to who is closer & whose love is more lasting than any Earthly friend.

I can't help seeing a great similarity between Bessy's situation & my own for indeed my ever dear husband was all to me that hers was to her. He was the centre point of the whole circle to whom all turned & all looked for guidance & I may say, for happiness. Rich & poor alike looked up to him & always found him a ready friend & councillor. He was the life & spirit of every company & yet his influence ruled & regulated the whole country around us. In our own family & associates he ruled most strictly but at the same time so judiciously that he never gave offence & seldom appeared harsh till the last year or two when the state of his affairs evidently affected his own stretched & over wrought mind & feelings & actually his brain. But this was "The hand of the Lord." His heart was always inclined to religion & his adversity seemed to draw him closer to God & induced him to study the Holy Scriptures for edification and light. And he did receive light & shewed it & tried to lead others by it & to it....

All this winter I have been very idle about letter writing. I have not been as well as usual & never have been good in spirits & I felt that if I wrote it could only be in either a restrained way or else a history of my own little troubles so I just wrote as little as I could. Now I am better & hope my mind will return by degrees to its own tone. I have been staying with darling Bessie & Edward for the last four weeks & enjoy myself greatly. I feel here as if care & sorrow were left behind for this is a happy little place & I have not seen Bessie so well & so like herself as she is now. Her eyes are bright & her heart seems light & her health is good & tho' her little twins & her little adopted daughter, Mary Brown, add to her cares & very much to her <u>trouble</u> & work, yet she manages them all wonderfully & never is in a fuss or out of patience or temper. The children are very healthy & very interesting of course as all little children are to their parents & Grand mammas but I don't think either Bee or Edward make too much fuss about them or think them anything <u>wonderful</u> as many mothers I know do.

I have not been able to get out for three weeks, I mean to see anybody, for I walk everyday, but the roads are nearly impassable for any conveyance that ladies could join. So we must wait for some time longer tho' I am longing to get down to see Anna & Ellen & Kate & Louisa & all my friends. Frank is living at his farm & working steadily making preparations for adding to his house as he hopes to have his little wife in some months from this. I am truly rejoiced to say her father is now on the best & pleasantest terms with Frank & I hope all may go on smoothly & happily. John is to be married very soon as he has fitted up a loghouse for the present, & as he must study economy more than indulgence he wishes to settle down at once as he finds it "does not pay" to go every week or ten days to Grafton 25 miles off to see Anna & besides it will be much more agreeable & better economy to have a housekeeper for good & as her parents have consented I believe they think of concluding all matters on my Birthday, the remembrance of which will be preserved by several weddings.

John is a very industrious steady fellow but he has nothing to depend on but the work of his hands. Anna has no fortune but she is very prudent & a good manager & is active & industrious. If they have health I have no fears. Frank's wife is also a very good manager but is rather [*incomplete*]

Pray give my love to James & all your little flock & the Rockfields & Athboys and to any of my old friends who care for me or that you think I love. Goodbye dear.

Your ever Affect'

Fanny S.

1854: August 1[35]

To [ ], Ireland

Goodwood 1st Aug. Tuesday 1854

I believe I never answered your last yet I think I could not have delayed so long thanking for all your tender prayers & wishes on the anniversary of my birthday, only think, 3 score years.

It seems strange that I have been allowed so long a portion of time & so large a portion of happiness when I am so useless & unworthy but it ought to rouse me, though late to redeem the time, & try to do more good. I have so many blessings & sources of happiness & indeed my heart is most thankful for them. I don't know any person who has such great & numerous blessings & mercies as I have. Health, one of the greatest, has been much better this summer than at any time last year. Asthma comes occasionally but is not so very over-powering as it was last year nor so constant. My mind is much more at ease than for many years back, as I am free from the responsibility & exertion of managing the establishment at Auburn to which I was quite unequal.

My dear Frank, who was far far away from me last year & about whom I was in ignorance then is now settled down into a steady respectable member of society and established in his proper place & grade of our society. I am thankful to say that there is a respectability which seems to attend on & belong to our family which all my sons are likely to keep up. Even in Toronto George & Charlie seem to inherit the regard & interest of many in the highest classes there who were acquainted with their dear father & who till lately we had little or no idea of recollecting us. They have proved themselves kind friends to the sons of one who possessed their respect & esteem, & where memory is still revered & cherished in their hearts. This is very gratifying to me.

My leaving Auburn has been advantageous to Willy as he now does more there than he would while I remained. He is doing a great deal now & the fields & every thing look more thriving & promising than for many years back. I go there very often. I love Louise & Wm. very much & they both always seem to wish to make me comfortable.

Malone has been very full but now they are alone again & dear Ellen is looking much better & growing fat again. She is too apt to forget herself & do too much when she feels well & then she [ ] back pains & swellings & other ailments which require care & active remedies to set all right again. I spent 3 days with her last week as George came to spend a week or ten days with us & he made Malone his head quarters. He has now returned to Toronto but there is a prospect of his coming to reside in Peterboro & opening an office there as Engineer. There are some new arrangements making but of course he will be guided by the advice of his friends, & by circumstances.

His leaving Toronto would be a great sorrow to Charlie who has a year & ¾ still of his time to serve with Mr. Tully. Mr. T. seems to have the highest opinion of Charlie & places the greatest confidence in him leaving all in his charge when he goes from home.

It is expensive to push young men forward but it fully repays one to find them so deserving of all that one can do to help them. You may laugh at me for praising my children but I just write my thoughts as they arise.

This has been the hottest summer I have felt for above 25 years. We are all nearly stewed to jelly. The Therm'r has been up to 96°–98° & one day 106° in the shade.

That very day poor Charlie had a slight sun stroke I think. He had been allowed a holiday & went early in the morning to spend the day with Mrs. Turner, mother of a fellow pupil. They were hay making. He joined them but was overcome by the heat & not sensible of any thing more till he found [himself] on the sofa in Mrs. T's drawing room & all the family anxiously watching him & bathing his head with cooling applications w'h they had been doing for 5 hours!! However, in the evening he was able to go home but had a Dr. to attend him & every day at the same hour for several days, severe head ache & high fever came on. He was quite well, however, when George left him & I hear from him every week. Cholera has been very bad in Montreal & Quebec but there have been only a few cases in Toronto & Peterboro.

Anna's little flock are quite well, Barbara a nice fat smiling dark eyed thing. They all say she is ridiculously like me. They are all fine healthy children.

Mary Dunlop is very tall & looks much healthier & better than she did when she first came back but she has lately had a pain in her right side. It comes & goes & is worst at night when lying down. Ellen thinks it is from her liver. She is a fine little girl & wonderfully little spoilt, considering.

Bessy & her little boys are very well. They are very healthy & run about & are in all sorts of mischief. Bessie has a great deal to do but is never in a fuss & just goes on through her course of daily work & duties like a little Steam Engine & it is wonderful what a great deal she gets done in the day & yet never seems in a hurry or disheartened.

My little Emily is a good child & her arm is rather stronger but I fear will never be of use. She has to dress herself.

I think I have given you a family history but I have not done yet for I must tell you about my new daughters. I told somebody that Frank & Joanne had removed to a temporary dwelling at their own place. We all went to spend an ev'g there while George was with us. They have a nice little parlour, small but neat & snug, a sofa, & Rocking chair (an American comfort which [ ] but Americans enjoy). It looks really comfortable & was nice & cool. It opens into the new house. Their bedroom is next the parlour & at the back is the nicest little kitchen you ever saw, like a kitchen in a child's baby house, floor, table & shelves are all so clean, all the shelves filled with [ ] & the walls hung with Tin utensils all bright & a nice little stove in proportion to the size of the house. Several people came in unexpectedly so that in a little while we were quite a large party, all connexions. Oh! what do you think, Frank & [Joanne] have just come to spend the day & have interrupted me. Good bye, I had much more to say.

Love love to all dear friends

F.S.

A long & violent thunderstorm all yesterday from 11 a.m. to 11 p.m. I hope this dreadful heat is over.

1856: July 31[36]
To William Stewart, Peterborough, Ontario

31st July 1856

Many happy returns of this day to you my dearest William & may each returning one find you better & happier & prospering in all worldly comforts, still remembering that there is a better life to look forward to where we may hope for greater happiness than we can conceive here, where no sorrow or pain can ever come & rejoicing & joy is Eternal, never failing.

I wish my darling Willy I had a good sum of money to send you as a Birthday gift which I know would be the most acceptable at present, but I fear it is out of my power now more than ever. I seem always to have new calls on my means. The poor Hays require all I can spare now, to say nothing of poor George who has not been able to earn anything for many months back & seems as far as ever, poor fellow, from being able to follow his business. These are dark prospects which cast a shade over us, but if it is the Lord's will, perhaps we may yet see better times & if not, we must look to Him who alone can give us strength to bear all He sees right to send. Dear William I hope you may not be ill from fatigue sitting up so much at night & this time of year always makes you ill. Do take care of <u>night chills</u> after the heat of the day & put on a coat in time before you feel the dew or chill of evening.

I wish you knew how dearly & truly I love you dear Willy, or that I had it in my power to relieve your mind of some of the weights which I fear oppress you at times but you have a good deal in your power now & I hope you will have more & with prudence you will get on well.

Good bye. I have written in great haste, as time is passing too quick.

Your own affect'e

Mother F. Stewart

This time 31 years ago I thought no small [B-] of my Son & I think just as much of him now & more too!

1856: November 10[37]
To Mrs. Sutton, Ireland
Fragment

"Nov. 10 1856; to Mrs. Sutton" [*date and name written in another hand*]

I must now tell you something of our wedding. It went off in "first rate" style I assure you. We had a party in the evening of a good many of our relations & connexions & some of Kates young companions. Several sent apologies & even so I think there were between 60 & up people collected together besides a good many of my Grandchildren & a great many old servants & tennants who were invited to a kitchen party & to witness "Miss Kates wedding" as she has been a favorite with all who have ever known her. I must say she looked very nice & behaved with the greatest self possession during the ceremony which was performed read by Mr. Warren an English Clergyman who is stationed at Lakefield in this township, a large settlement about 6 miles north of this place & which belongs to Mr. Strickland. Mr. Warren is a pleasing man. He seems not to be at all a Puseyite which is a great comfort. He is a very liberal churchman tho' not at all careless or slack in attending to his Duties as far as I know. He has not been in Canada much above a year but I rather like his manner of reading the Service. I have been at his church two or three times. His preaching is nothing very <u>lively</u> or deep but I think very much to be preferred to our Peterboro clergyman, Mr. Burnham, so that we requested him to officiate at Robert & Kates wedding & indeed he did read it remarkably well & I was quite glad we had one who read it so impressively. He is a sort of connexion of our family as his wife's brother is married to my Great niece Emma, a daughter of Mr. Stricklands. Only think of my having had two Grand nieces at Auburn that night, both married women & mothers which makes me a Great Grand Aunt!!! But I have digressed sadly.

After the ceremony was over we had tea & then dancing & some good singing & then supper which looked very nice as there were two long tables

& a handsome 3 storied cake on each table. These cakes were placed in the middle & then there were all sorts of jellies & custard, Russian [ ] Trifle, tarts & pies &c, besides turkeys & fowls, tongues, ducks, &c &c. Every one said it was excellent & plentiful & everyone seemed pleased & satisfied with the whole proceedings of the evening which was extremely gratifying to me.

We were all greatly disappointed that Johnny Noble could not come. He told Kate to let him know whenever she was going to be married & that he would come if he could. So I wrote to tell him as soon as the day was fixed and hoped he would have come, but he could not leave as one of the salesmen was absent & there was so much to be attended to that he could not leave & we were all very sorry. Four of the young Kirkpatricks (Staffords) were there. They are very nice young people & I was very glad to see them but Mrs. S.K. never goes to parties & Stafford having suffered so much from Rheumatism was afraid of the night air. So Anne, Helen, Katharine & William came. They are nice unaffected merry girls. I am sorry this place is so far from them, for which reason we seldom can meet.

Tuesday night was miserably wet & stormy & dark so that all the people were obliged to stay for daylight & the young folks seemed to have no objection to keep up the dancing till 6 oclock but some of the elders grew very sleepy & some lay down on beds & others nodded in armchairs. We remained till about 8 & had some breakfast with Louisa & then came home. The ground was very hard frozen the first time this winter & when we came to Auburn the evening before it was muddy & sloppy. We have had frost & some snow ever since & I suppose we may soon expect winter with all its rigours. You never saw a nicer little dwelling for its sire than Roberts is. Of course all the outside part is rough & there are still piles of mortar & lime & bricks & timber all round the house. But the inside is very comfortable & Kate seems as happy as can be. Indeed she could not help it for she has a most affectionate & indulgent husband who is perfectly devoted to her.

Here (at Goodwood) we are now quite a reduced party. Robert is a great loss to our family circle & indeed so is Kate who was always rattling away at some fun or nonsense. She has a few constant flow of spirits not boisterous, but steady & "comes out" with very amusing remarks sometimes which used to make us laugh & kept us alive.

Henry who has lived here for the last three years I think has now begun to build on his own farm & is very busy preparing for independence which he seems in a fair way to reach in some not very distant time. He has a nice farm close to Auburn & has a very pretty situation for his house. He is a steady sensible straightforward lad & I hope may succeed well.

It is time to say something now of the poor Hays. The Doctor seems to revive a little. He is in much better spirits than he was sometime ago, but he is still very helpless. Dear Anna is very delicate & far from strong enough for the performance of her heavy duties. I have not been much with her lately & have not seen her for ten days but I know she is not gaining strength as she ought. Poor soul, I fear the exertion is too much for her & we cannot get any nurse to hire for any wages that could assist her in her charge. She looks dreadfully ill at times & is very pale now. The little baby is going on nicely & is a very pretty fair little creature. He is called John Patrick.

Ellen Dunlop is only pretty well. She has almost constantly some pain or ailment which shews there is still something wrong. She looks thin but not at all ill & she is wonderfully strong & able to go through all her housekeeping in a very active way & to walk to see Anna very often. Dear little Mary is a charming girl. I never saw such a warm hearted affectionate creature as she is & she is improving greatly in looks as well as in every other way. Ellen & Charles have every comfort about them. They have a sweet pretty place & a most convenient and comfortable house just as much land as affords him occupation & amusement & supplies them with many of the necessaries of life & enough of money to keep them quite independent. Ellen is always complaining of her poverty & of the difficulty in making "both ends meet" but still I never find any want of every comfort & even luxuries & tho' their income is nominally only £50 a year yet they have other helps which make it out a very good one. Mrs. Dunlop sends out handsome gifts constantly & valuable boxes of clothing every two or three years so that they hardly ever have to lay out anything on clothing & Ellen is an excellent manager & delights in economising. She makes a good deal by her poultry & dairy too & having no great family they don't require to spend much. She is very like her Aunt Kirkpatrick in many ways & I often tell her so. She is also like her in having a warm affectionate heart & being perfectly free from Selfishness.

I am sorry to say my dear daughter Joan is in very poor health. She seems never to have recovered the death of her little infant & she has had a great deal of trouble about the little boy Willy who is delicate. He is a very pretty little fellow but she looks very ill indeed & is far from well. I have spun out my letter to an unconscionable length & I fear worn out your patience but I know how kindly interested you always are about me & mine…

[1858]: January 27[38]
To Frances Brown (Fan), [Peterborough, Ontario]

Thursday Jan'y 27

My dearest Fan

I think I must try to write to you today to thank you for your nice long letter & that very pretty poem about the old man & his sleeping child, or grandchild I mean, for of course it was one. I am glad you like Poetry & have good taste so as to know the difference between really pretty poetry & only rhymes for there are many pieces of poetry that are just rhymes, without sense & no pretty ideas in them. You know those nice allusions to flowers or other objects give so much beauty to Poetry. This is called Metaphor. If you look for it in the Dictionary you can understand it better. It is different from Allegory which is a story made from some imaginary objects & is something like a sister or cousin to Metaphor. So you see I am writing figuratively now & giving you so many long words that you will be out of patience before you are half through this long letter. I am sorry I have [ ] poetry or anecdote to give you [today]. [ ] stupid & tired & I cannot write decently my hand is so weak. I think it is the change of weather that makes me feel so weak. You have so many friends to write to that you must be kept pretty busy. I had a very nice letter from Edward last week. He is very good about writing. I think you had a pleasant surprise in seeing Lizzie the other day. I am glad she is going to Aunt Dunlop. I hope she will stay there a good while. I think it is dinnertime. So I must shut up & say *à Dieu ma chere grandfille, toujours à vous.*
F. Stewart

1859: April 4[39]
To Aunt [ ], Ireland

Douro — Monday 4th April 1859.

My own darling Aunty

I have just been reading over for the third time your kind & precious letters of 26th Feb'y which I received on the 25th March along with one from my dear Charlie. I do indeed feel deeply thankful for your great kindness in writing to me so regularly & telling me so much that is so interesting. I often think I don't know any person in Canada amongst the hundreds who have left their homes & friends who is so fortunate as I am in hearing so constantly from those dear ones who I left so many many years ago who still retain me in their home circle by constant intercourse on paper & communicating those <u>small</u> incidents which keep up our <u>close union</u> so much more than the mere mentioning of subjects which perhaps might be of more importance in the opinion of many but to me the small ones are most precious & which I think may be considered the "pith & marrow" of love & friendship between members of one family and which take away much of the pang of feeling separated from those we love best. It always seems so lonely to think, "If I were now at home I should hear & know all the little things going on," but I have seldom felt this for any length of time. Soon nice letters come from different quarters, each conveying <u>news</u> of the nearest & dearest interest from the different parts of the country so that by degrees I know more than could almost be expected of all my darlings beyond the Atlantic.

Our winter has been like yours, very mild, & our spring is unusually early, so much so that ploughing was commenced about the 20th March in this neighborhood which is some weeks earlier than usual & the buds of currants, Lilacs & other shrubs are actually bursting open & the tops of the trees in the woods have lost the <u>hard</u> grey appearance they have in winter & now look quite a reddish green from the swelling of buds, but alas! all this fine mild weather has its own disadvantages. These sweet buds now encouraged to open will I fear be nipped by the frosty nights we may expect to have between this time and the middle of May which is the most trying season in the year to vegetation as well as health.

There has been much illness this winter. Influenza of a new <u>species</u> has come in fatal force into many families attacking the head & brain & swelling the ears & neck most painfully. Thank God none of my family have had it in that form. None of my numerous offsets have had more than bad coughs & common feverish colds, but poor Bessie for about two months had dreadful agony from neuralgia in her head & face which latterly extended to her neck & throat but I am thankful to say took its departure there & has not returned for nearly a fortnight. So I am in hopes it has gone for this year at all events. She is beginning to look more like her bright little self again....

I grieve to say we have had no tidings of my dear Frank since the wretched letter of last July written in the depth of despair. His truly admirable little wife is still with her parents who are aged & not well & require her care. The eldest boy little Willie has always been delicate. But little Alex'r the Baby now 20 months old is a fine child. I earnestly hope they may prove comforts to their dear Mother. Your favourite, George, was staying with Ellen & for some days with John lately. He was employed in Surveying that neighborhood. He suffered a good deal from walking so much & had a great deal of pain in the front of his ankle near the instep which I am inclined to think must be from rheumatism. He was greatly tired every evening after his days work as it is so disagreeable walking in deep wet snow. I wish dear George had not taken his <u>marrying fit</u> so early but had spent a year then visiting the auld country & married afterwards. He often regrets he cannot now hope ever to be able to see the wonders of Art & Nature with which Charles letters are filled as well as to become acquainted with the many relations & friends who have given his brother such a kind reception.

Dear George would I am sure make as many friends as Charlie has done tho' he is more <u>reserved</u> and of a more thinking disposition than Charles. Kate had a very pleasant letter from dear Charlie yesterday dated the 11th March. He was still at Leicester where he had been detained by the illness of his Uncle who had been in France & requested Charlie to stay with his Aunt till his return. He finds is quite a difficulty to get away.

His Aunts heart seems to have opened & bestowed on him all the love she has for years back withheld from all her own relations. It seems very strange that this poor wanderer from the backwoods of Canada should be the only one of her nephews she has ever seen. I don't understand where she kept her heart. He was to go to London the next week & on to Bristol & accross from that to Cork!! We have had terrible high winds & the papers filled with disasters at sea which make my heart beat when I think of his going that apparently tedious route.

But I suppose he does [ ] some advice or instructions from the Hoare family as their relations are Cork people & friends of the Cork Beauforts & I am glad Charlie will be able to see them as well as the southern parts of Ireland. He has travelled over a large part of G't Britain in a short time. I don't know how he will reconcile himself to our homely ways but I know he is my own dear old Charlie still in heart.

I have not seen Anna Hay for a long time as I have been shut up from bad roads. She is very well as I hear constantly of & from both her & Ellen. The latter walked here one day about ten days ago, 3 good miles! & home again after early tea so you may conclude she is well. Anna has taken a small house in Peterboro as she is now quite strong & able to undertake the management of her own affairs & family & I think will be much happier living independently as long as her health continues good which I trust may be for many years yet.

I had a very kind letter from Allenstown on Saturday. James sent me his half yearly account & notice of having sent the draft for my money to Thos. Kirkpatrick from whom I hope to have it soon & when I do I will write to James to tell him of its safe arrival. I also had a charming letter from Anna Waller who is so kind in writing to me as if we had been cousins & well acquainted all our lives. You don't know how I delight in these proofs of kindness. Dear good Mary also wrote me a very nice letter some time ago which I have not answered. This winter has been a time of so much care & anxiety to me from many causes, that I sometimes cannot rouse myself for writing to anyone.

I have had rheumatism all over me constantly for many weeks & today it is in my right arm so much that at times I can scarcely guide my pen as you probably have observed by my rambling writing.

But I find I am drawing near the end of my 2d sheet & must "curb my genius." Indeed it is time I should release you from this weary job. Bessie unites with me in [kindest] love to you & Bessy & all your dear surroundings, and believe me

    my ever loved Aunt
    Your grateful & attached
    niece & child, F. Stewart

[1859: July 18][40]
(Fragment): Addressee unknown, Ireland

My dear Son has returned to us very happy to see all his own kin again & very ready to tell me all he can about so many I so dearly love. He expresses regret at not having been able to see more of his Meath friends but having treated poor Harriet so unceremoniously on her first kind invitation, he could not hurry away from her sooner than was absolutely necessary. I suppose you have heard of the cause of his prolonged visit at Southwold where at first he only intended spending a few days, but Master Cupid flew in & cast a net over him which detained him & I suppose will draw him there again as soon as he can make arrangements for settling down as a married man, & the prospect of visiting Europe next year (DV) gives him hopes of seeing many friends who he could not go in the meantime. I have heard a great deal about Miss Ellis from some of her friends who are in this country & are greatly attached to her. And I can only feel astonished at Charles's extraordinary good fortune in having gained the affection so soon of a person of truly excellent sound sense & prudence. I can only account for its having proceeded from her discernment in judging of his character from his countenance & his quiet unpressuring manner which I rejoice to find is perfectly unchanged, notwithstanding the very partial & distinguished attention paid him everywhere & by all he met & especially his relations & connexions as well as some perfect strangers. I was afraid he w'd have been a little <u>elevated</u> in his own estimation but I must say he is exactly the same dear old 'Charlie' except he is grown stouter & broader in his <u>shoulders</u> than he was & looks quite a year older.

[1860: August]⁴¹
To Aunt [ ], Ireland

How very kind you had been my own dear Aunt to write me such a delightful letter which made me truly happy giving such pleasant accounts of
yourself & my other dear friends & relations & telling me so much about
dear Charles & Charlotte who I am sincerely happy to find you like so
much. I am sure if one quarter of what I have heard of her from all sides
is true she will indeed be a blessing & comfort to me & to all her connexions. It is most amazing to me how Charlie contrived to gain her affections so soon & so completely. But he has been equally fortunate in all he
has undertaken for he has now got Auburn, a very pretty place & a very
excellent house & a fine valuable property without the smallest trouble or
difficulty on his part. I have had the whole house painted & papered & I
think it will look "first rate" for them when they come.

Oh may they be preserved in the dangers of the voyage and may we
all meet at my own dear Auburn in safety & thankfulness next week.

I shall look out for them about Thursday next the 25th. They might
come sooner. I can't help feeling anxious but I know they are under the
care of Him who holds our lives in His hands & knows the time & the
way to call us hence. Many are preserved in apparent danger & taken at
an unlooked for moment. All are in His hands & we know His Power
& His Mercy & His Love which is boundless. Oh may I in this trial &
all others place all I hold most dear in His care who is our best Father
Guardian & Protector.

1861: June 15⁴²
To Mary [Wilson], Ireland

Douro, 15th June 1861

My very dear Mary

I have been some time past intending to write to you but always some
hindrance came in my way. I think my last letter to you was written in
March soon after poor Maria Reids release and I have never heard from

you since so I don't know if you have received that letter but I am sure you heard most of the details it contained from my sister as I told her to let you know in case I might not be able to write myself. I little thought then that in my next letter I should have another death to mention! One least to be expected indeed according to our own limited knowledge of what is to come. "It is well" we do not for how wretched we should be anticipating every sorrow.... Perhaps you have already heard that by the unsearchable but no doubt wise & merciful Will of the Lord our dear Edward has been removed from this life to a joyful & glorious Eternity, I may say in the prime of life with all appearance of health and life till the attack came on which was caused by taking cold but it became an extreme case of inflammation of the lungs which reduced his strength with the most extraordinary rapidity and in a fortnight & two days terminated his valuable existence amongst us. Oh you can't think how we feel his loss. He was so truly excellent in every way as a father, a husband, a son (which he was to me even before his marriage) for indeed I loved him as a son & he returned it.

From early in his illness he gave up hopes of recovery before we came to believe there was really danger & before our Dr. could see any decided danger, but he himself said, "I shall not be long with you." He seemed to be completely loosened from this life for he seemed to take no interest in anything that was going on but said frequently he rested on his Saviour & his Hope was in Christ. He had so much difficulty in speaking that he said but little but when asked any question he always gave a clear & satisfactory answer. He had several conversations with Mr. Rogers our Minister who often visited him, which he always enjoyed & looked for eagerly. All this is our greatest consolation. I am happy to say dear Bessie is wonderfully supported for which we are most thankful & she has a kind & most faithful & judicious friend in her brother in law Robert Brown who assists her in the management of the farm & her four fine boys who have a good guardian & an excellent example in their good Uncle Robert. May the Lord direct all for their happiness & safety in their journey through this life & their security of peace & joy in that which is to come.

I think Charlotte has written to you lately so you have probably heard of us before from her. Oh what a fortunate man my dear Charlie is. What a prize he has gained! Dear Charlotte is a treasure to us all & is making herself loved and valued by all who know her. She has a Sunday school in her own hall every Sabbath afternoon and a prayer meeting every Thursday evening & she goes about amongst the people visiting them & reading to them & trying to improve them. I have not yet been able to join in the meetings but hope (DV) to do so soon. She is now trying to have a Church established in their own neighbourhood with a good Missionary appointed but the funds must be raised to enable the church to be built or the Missionary to be supported & for this purpose they are trying to raise subscriptions & have given me some papers to send home so I send you one in case you may meet with some person who may help us.

Now my own darling Mary my paper & time are both used up so I must only request my love to dear Emily, 1 & 2 & all my other dear cousins & friends. I am as Ever Your affect'ly attached old Coz,

Fanny Stewart

1861: August 6[43]
To Louisa Beaufort, Ireland

Tuesday Night 12 oclock
6 Aug't 1861

My dearest Louisa

Though so late I must add a few lines to tell you a little incident which took place lately. Kate who is passionately fond of flowers & gardening took me one evening last month to a nursery near Peterboro to see the varieties of Roses & Peonies &c all in bloom. So we walked and wandered about to our hearts content & examined all the Fuschias & other plants in the houses & were just coming away when the old gardener said, Oh Mrs. Brown, come here & I will give you a nice flower that smells delightful. So he took us to a little bushy shrub & plucked off some dark colored flowers which certainly did smell "delightful" & I saw it was the old Pimento or allspice tree you used to have at Collon & I had never seen one since those dear old days. So I said I had not seen one of them for 50 years nearly!! &

that I saw it in Ireland. And were you ever in Ireland? said he. I said yes, I had been. Did you ever know a place called Dundalk, said he? Oh yes, said I, did you ever hear of a place called <u>Collon</u> for it was there I last saw the Allspice shrub. Well now, said the old cooney, sure, thats where I lived! & served my time in Lord Oriel's gardens under one John Rourke! Did you ever hear of Lord Oriel? Oh yes, said I, I once knew him & have often been in his gardens & have seen Rourke too. So the poor old man seemed quite astonished that I had seen or heard of "John Rourke" and no doubt I do remember him well & you may suppose how many old recollections came to my mind from the poor old Allspice tree & old Rourke. But I must go to bed. It has struck One & I am nearly blind. My pen is bad & my hand painful from rheumatism but my heart love with you dear Louisa.

Your affect' old F. Stewart

1862: November 9[44]
To Louisa (McNabb) Stewart, Peterborough, Ontario

Douro — 9th Nov'r 1862

Please give the enclosed to William [*enclosure missing*]

My dearest Lou

You don't know how glad I was to see Mary McMullen coming just to hear how you were all coming on. Indeed there are not many half hours in the day that I am not <u>busy</u> thinking of you all & wishing I knew more about you. You may say "Why don't you come then & see us" but indeed I have not been out very much till just lately. I was so long kept in by the cough & weakness but that nice mild weather brought a change over me & I have been <u>quite well</u> the last few weeks & more like myself than for nearly a year. But I seldom can get out. Both Bee & Kate have their hands too full & I just get down to town when they have something to go for & have not even been inside of Anna's or any other house. The short days gives us no time to stop when we do go as the roads have been awfully bad out here & Dolly is [lazier] than ever poor old critter. I only passed you <u>once</u> & met Tommy near the gate. The [ ] road is now so bad we always go the other side. Indeed we often <u>talk</u> of going to <u>see you</u> but cannot stop you know, for night comes on before we know where we are. I saw Dr. one day last week. He said you were all getting on well but how very ill he looks! Poor dear, I am afraid he is not well. He looks very miserable. Does he go often to you? I think it would do him good....

You see dear I have but little to say & the children are all sitting round the table shaking & gabbing & my head is <u>dinned</u>. No matter dear Lou. Excuse scrawls & blots & blunders & love me as I love you & I could not ask more. Your affec't Mother,

F. Stewart

[1866: May]⁴⁵
To Catharine Parr Traill, Lakefield, Ontario

Monday Morning

My ever dearest Friend

I cannot tell you how [ ] for your dear children. I heard of [ ] dear Atwoods dreadful calamity by [ ] note from Joan yesterday & hope [ ] there was some mistake but [ ] in the evening I received dear Kate [ ] letter & have thought of little [besides] since I read it. Kate mentioned also that you had hurt your fingers badly. I trust it may not prove tedious or very severe pain. Indeed these do seem most wretched times in many ways. I grieve my dear dear friend to find you have had so much trouble, but I trust whatever it may be that the worst may have passed over by this time. I have much to say but my time is short as the Buggie is at the door, but as Kate said you had a great deal of sewing on hand, both [ ] Walter & Annie, & I wish you would send a bundle of it down to us. I am myself always wanting some work & I am sure Bee & Kate will join me in any spare moment.... Kates note said [ ] might be a probability of Annie being with you. I am not sure if she is still at the Paiges, therefore my dear Mrs. Traill I will enclose to you $20 for her. It is but a mite but I hope I may have it in my power to contribute a little more sometimes hence as my means will I trust be improved, but just now I send what I can, hoping it may help. You were I think intending to get some clothing for them in Peterboro [ ] you can make use of part if you think it required & give the rest to dear Annie with my fondest love....

Dear friend, time passes quickly & I must make up & send this sad scrawl such as it is.

With fondest love from Bee & Kate & myself to you & dear Kate & Walter who I trust may get on happily. Believe me as ever your sincere & faithfully attached friend,

Fr. Stewart.

Pray thank dear Kate for her letter & for the seeds.

1866: May 20[46]
To Annie Atwood, Gore's Landing, Ontario

Tuesday night
20th May 1866

My dearest Annie

I have just heard the dreadful news of your great misfortune, but no particulars. I know too well how great a loss it is to you & dear Clinton. Indeed I have not thought of any thing else since I read a note from Joan this afternoon which was the first report which came to me, & I hoped there was some mistake or exaggeration in what she had heard. But this evening I had a letter from your sister, Kate, who mentioned having heard from you, and that indeed it was too true. You cannot doubt my dear child how deeply I feel for you both. I fear also the effect on you & your dear little children & Mr. Atwood, tho' last, not the less in my mind. Oh, I long to know more about you all. Kate said your letter was short & did not enter into particulars. So that all I know is that it happened on Sunday night & that nothing was saved but lives, & that you had no clothes but your night things! Oh, how you must have suffered, where did you go to! & how did you manage. Is not Mr. Paiges a good distance from you, some miles. Last Sunday night here it rained, but I don't think the wind was so high as it has been lately. But I have great fear you may have caught cold. Kate said Mr. Atwood was ill. I trust he may not be seriously ill or injured in any way.

I feel for your dear Mother too. I am glad to hear her health has been better this spring than usual, tho' she wrote in very low spirits & mentioned having been much troubled lately in mind & seemed indeed to have some heavy accumulation of trial, but did not enter into any particulars. They are busy now preparing poor Walters outfit for the <u>Nor' West</u>. This must also be a great trial to your poor Mother, though it can hardly be so bad as parting with Willie, who I am sincerely happy to hear is getting on so well, and not yet disgusted with that sort of life. I hope Walter may get on as well, poor fellow. I am sure it would now be a great comfort to your Mamma to have you with her for some time, & also be pleasant for you till you have some house to live in. Your Mother or rather Kate mentioned that they were going to make up some things for you. I wish dearest Annie to send you a mite towards providing, but as I don't know where you may be now and expecting you will be with her, I think I had better send it to your Mother for you & if you are not with her she can send it to you.

Kates letter this evening was full of bad news. She also mentioned the death of Mrs. Ellis, Charlotte Stewarts Mother. This was the first intimation I had of it, & both together have given me quite a shock, & I feel my senses quite confused. Poor Mrs. Ellis's death was very shocking. In some kind of fit, she fell down stairs & was killed!! Is not that dreadful. I am very very anxious about Charlotte who can ill bear such a shock as that. So dear Annie I hope you will make allowance for this very <u>incoherent</u> sort of epistle, which I fear you will find almost illegible, but I wish not to lose a day in sending you my best love & sympathy, & hoping you or the other dear children may not have suffered from the exposure, & that I shall soon hear some tidings of you.

I was just intending to write to dear Jane Bird this evening as Kate mentioned that [Pet] was soon to be married, but all this sad sad news has put all my ideas into fire, smoke & death, but I hope to be in a more settled state in a few days. Bee & Kate join with me in most sincere sympathy & sorrow, & desire their fond love to you & Mr. Atwood.

With your ever affect' Mamma Stewart.

Oh, I wish I had enough to send you what w'd <u>really</u> help you.

1866: August 25[47]
To Annie Atwood, Gore's Landing, Ontario

Saturday 25th Aug't 1866

My very dear Annie

I hope to see Mary today and to be able to send you a few lines by her if she goes to Rice Lake, of which I am at present quite uncertain, as I have not yet seen her. I have been & still am in a very anxious state about your dear Mamma, who though she was better when I last heard, was still very weak, & in a very uncertain state, and the complaint is of such a nature that one is liable to a return of it soon again. Your dear Mother has other complaints likewise which may increase the danger, so that I feel more anxious & uneasy about her than I should about any other person, independent of the warm & sincere affection I feel for her, which causes me to bear her continually in my mind & very close to my heart. I most earnestly hope & pray that she may speedily recover & be yet spared to her dear family & to all her friends by whom she is so loved for some years longer, if it is His Will — (in whom we live & [ ] & have our Bessy) to grant her better health & the full power & use of her faculties. Without these blessings, who could wish for long life. I am much grieved that I have not been able to see her yet, but for the last two weeks I have been poorly & out of breath if I move so that I should not be at all fit for visiting an invalid, for this asthma increases my deafness so much that I feel myself quite a tax on the kindness & patience of my friends to talk to me. But I hope in a little time when your dear Mother is better able to talk, that I shall be able to spend a part of a day with her & as you seem to think of being with her next month I shall have the additional pleasure of meeting you there. This is pleasant to look forward to, & I at present have hopes of being able to accomplish my part in the performance of it. I had the great pleasure of reading your nice letter to your sisters which Mary kindly lent me, & which I most thoroughly enjoyed. I am always so much interested in all your home details, my own dear Annie. I hope your dear little children are now quite recovered from the feverish colds they had when you wrote. This weather is most trying for anyone who is not in <u>robust</u> health or with a good water rain proof roof over their heads, which by all accounts your present abode is not. But as I hope & expect you have got some <u>money</u> from your English relations I hope your house may soon be made more comfortable in every way & that you have got a good supply of <u>warm</u> clothing for yourself & the little ones. How delightful it is to have Boxes from home! when they have been filled by friends who know what is required & useful for country life....

I hope you find your girl comfortable and not dishonest which you seemed to have some fears of. If she is I fear you have a bad chance, as I suppose you have not any safe lock up places for keeping your things. How has your harvest turned out. Here poor Robert has not such good wheat as usual, all his fall wheat having failed, & the spring wheat had to be sowed a second time, & the crop he says is the worst he ever had. Bessie has some good Fall wheat. The grasshoppers have done great damage & have eaten up all the grass in the pasture fields which is very miserable, as poor Kate depends so much on her dairy.

You can perceive by my writing how I am shaken. This cold showery weather keeps our young fry in the house, & having but one sitting room they are continually in & out & running past my table, as well as (or I might better say as <u>ill</u> as) making such a noise that my poor ears ring with it. They all have shrill loud voices. Baby is very good now & sits on the floor for hours amusing herself with any thing we can supply for her to play with. She is a dear darling child & is learning many endearing & amusing ways. But she is very shy, & very petted, & has an <u>awful</u> way of screaming when vexed, or if her Mamma leaves her, but these fits of temper don't come very often. I think your boy is two or three months older. She will be 8 months old on the 1st Sept'r. Kate looked very well for a little while after her return from Grafton, but this last week she has grown thinner than ever & has not felt very well. She has a great deal to do as you may suppose, with such a houseful as we make with the addition of the two men, Archy & John Hudson who are Bessies & Roberts men. We have a very active girl & one who is very good natured & patient with the children. There are 8 cows to milk, but Stewart helps to milk his Mothers share. The churning, washing, ironing & baking is no trifle for two such families. We sit down 15 to every meal when Arthur Mathias is at home, which he is now, & there are always two or three in the kitchen besides. Bessie & Mary help a good deal, chiefly in nursing, but Bee has a great deal of sewing always doing, & she makes up all her own Butter.

Monday 27th Aug't 1866

You see my dearest Annie I have not dispatched my letter yet & was greatly disappointed on Saturday at not finding Mary at Malone. I fear now I have no chance of seeing her so I must send this by Post. Indeed it is not worth sending, for I am so stupid. A bad Bilious [headache] makes me almost blind & the noise of the children is wearisome when we want to write....

So ever believe me as of old,
Your loving
Mamma Stewart

1866: September 11[48]
To Harriet Stewart [Acton, Ontario]

11th. Sept. 1866

My very dear Harriette

I wish to show you that I think of you today and one of the best means of doing so is to write you a letter. I very constantly think of you and of Lena and little baby who I suppose is now quite a large baby but I hardly know what name she goes by as I only mentioned Nora by way of a joke. I know Mamma intended to call her Eleanor which is a very pretty name. I hope in some time you will be able to write to me.

I thought of you dear Harriette early this morning & remembered that it is your Birthday and I hope you have been very happy today & that you may have a great many happy Birthdays increasing each year in wisdom [&] knowledge of the best kind as well as in health & strength of body. I am sorry that I have no nice present to send you but at this distance it is difficult to send parcels to our friends & besides I am sure you have all sorts of nice things, much nicer & better than anything I could buy in Peterboro. But my dear child I have a large portion of love in my heart to send you if you could only see it or feel it as

I feel it, but this is one of much that we must believe without seeing or feeling, as I dare say your dear Mamma has explained to you already & she will explain this to you in the same way if you don't understand it. I have not been very well lately & my hand is weak & shakes very much so that I cannot write as neatly as I should like to do when I write to you but I cannot help it & so dear child you must Believe me to be your Ever affectionate Grandmamma

F. Stewart

Kiss Mamma & Papa & your sisters for me & ask Mamma to give you a warm embrace & a good kiss for me.

1866: October 9[49]
To Annie Atwood, Gore's Landing, Ontario

Douro Tuesday
9th Oct'r 1866

My dearest Annie,

Your letter gave me a very pleasant surprise as I had no idea you had come up to Lakefield much less that you had been so long there without my having heard of it. This gave me some pain, which has decidedly been increasing ever since from each day passing without any of our party being able to go over to see you. Kate Brown had arranged with Annie Stewart to go to spend a good afternoon with your dear Mother before you had come, & since that they have had different days named for going, but always one thing or another came in the way. You who have only two children & a very small establishment know some of the difficulties of leaving home even for a few hours, but you can hardly imagine how almost impossible it is for either Bessie or Kate to leave such a tribe of young things together, 7 of them <u>under 9</u> years old & 4 older but not wiser, & myself requiring care & assistance, I am sorry to say unable to help even in nursing now as I have constant asthma if I exert myself in the least, & then the housekeeping is double & everything is so crowded up that much more care is required. But dearest Annie I do thank you for your letter & I do indeed grieve that so much of your visit has passed on without our meeting. Our last meeting was so very uncomfortable too, now nearly two years ago, at least it will be in a few months. At Goodwood we had more possibility of seeing you <u>on your way</u>, as you could make it a resting stage. But I do hope I may live (DV) to see you & Clinton & your dear little ones at Goodwood once more. If you come up again in winter, or even next summer though I can hardly venture to look forward so far. I knew you were to be in Douro in Sept'r & we were talking of you that very day & saying we wondered if Mr. A. had got his crops in, &c, when in the evening your letter was brought to me & we were all so vexed to find you had been there so long & now a fortnight has gone over & none of us have yet been able to get over to see you. Believe me it is not want of inclination dearest Annie. I hope nothing may again prevent Kate from going tomorrow. She has had many days settled but always some hindrance came in the way. I hope your little cottage may be made quite air tight & comfortable for you & that it may be quite dry before you venture to return. Our new home is not ready for us yet which is a great disappointment to us all. We have been <u>ten months</u> living here crowding up dear Kate, but they are so kind they never let us feel that we are in their way.…

Bessie desired me to tell you that she did not expect you to write to her. We all know by <u>experience</u> how one feels after having been burnt out & being unsettled for months after. I have not been quite well today and felt very dull & uncomfortable with asthma & now I find it was caused by this change in the weather. I have excellent health for which I am indeed most thankful. Asthma is my only ailment but it don't seem to affect my general health tho' it exhausts & wearies me & makes me <u>awfully</u> sleepy so that I can sleep at any time of the day if I sit down quietly for a few minutes. This & being deaf makes me very stupid. And now dear Annie as I begin to grow sleepy I must conclude. Wishing much that I could give you a loving embrace & kiss, ever your affect' Grannie,

F. Stewart

Love & kiss to dear Kate & Mr. A. when you can give it.

1866: November 22[50]
To Louisa (McNabb) Stewart

Monday
22nd Nov'r 1866

My own dear Lou

I was rejoiced to see Mack's honest face for everybody seems to be kept prisoners by hard work & bad weather.

Kate said yesterday "I wish I could get over to see Lou & Annie. I am just longing to have a good chat with them." But indeed you would see how impossible it is for her to leave in these <u>horrid</u> times! Horrid to look out at but as the roads are pretty dry now she & Rob't say <u>maybe</u> you could run over here <u>today</u> or tomorrow morning as Robert says he would try to see what can be done about your unfortunate business.

I am out of all patience, indeed fairly <u>disgusted</u> with your brothers treatment of you my poor dear Lou. I see plainly he wants to force me to pay Anna for you but he has no right to shove it over on you & at any rate I have actually not the means to pay the half of what I am at present engaged to pay. My rents are but a small help as they never are fully paid there are so many charges coming on them before I get my share. But even if I had means I could not & would not do it because <u>he is the one</u> that should do it. Robert says just what he said before, that the only way is to let <u>the whole</u> property (down there at your place) be sold, yours & Roberts <u>both</u>, & then you can claim your own but that Robert must give <u>some proof</u> that he has any right to shove it over on you when he got the farm on those terms <u>that he should pay Anna & Mr. Conway</u> & <u>I can</u> take my oath of that.

Robert Brown says he can talk it over again if you can come but he can say nothing else as far as he can see. I wish I had a big boot & strong leg & I would give that little chap a good <u>Kicking</u> or <u>Licking</u> if I could (Pardon the language).

So dear Lou there is my sympathy which indeed comes warm from my heart.

Bee moved down last Friday & I have never been there yet nor have I since the Christening! The weather & my old asthma & &c have kept me close. My breast got into a regular <u>sore</u> after the mustard I had on it for the pain in my side. It is still sore all along the lower part & discharging all the time. It has quite relieved the old pain but has been an unexpected remedy & wonderfully little <u>pain</u> considering, I mean from the sore itself. It was an ugly looking thing and still looks sore & nasty. Kate has had a busy week as her girl has been away all this fussy time. She had great cleaning up & settling to do after Bees things were taken but at last got Jane Hudson to help. Then the churning has bothered her wonderfully. She can't get the butter to come at all.

I was glad to hear some tidings of Georgina as I have not heard a word since last Sunday week & did not know that George & Henry had gone away. I seldom hear any news from that as Ellen seldom writes & never comes. Her <u>wee chap</u> Cecil having the hooping cough keeps him from us.

So we are totally separated at present. I cannot get a pen that will write & I am ashamed of this scrawl. I am now head nurse & it is almost too much sometimes but still I am able for it & glad I can do anything to help Kitty.

We have been too busy to feel small but the evenings seem long & we all grow sleepy. We miss the boys very much. They hardly care now to come here they are all so happy at home, poor bodies....

Your ever affect' Mother,

FS

I wonder can you read all this.

1866: December 19[51]
To Annie Atwood, Gore's Landing, Ontario

Tuesday night or
19th Dec'r 1866, Wednesday morn'g
I think an hour <u>past</u> midnight

My dearest Annie

I am vexed at having been so long delayed in answering you about the Bricks. The reason was that Robert could not see the people he wanted to ask about them & it was only today he could learn anything at all.

There is a man named Curtis who lives near Auburn who makes bricks but Robert could not learn if he has any now. There is such a demand for them but there is another person in <u>Otonobee</u> about four miles from Peterboro which would be nearer to you. His name is Welsh & he makes very good bricks. We got some from him for Goodwood. The price depends very much on the demand being pressing, which raises the price. The usual price is $4 & 1/2 a thousand, but the best are four dollars & three quarters or five dollars a thousand. If Robert can find out anything more satisfactory he will let you know and & I will write again if I have any message to give but I don't like to delay longer now in answering you. As far as we have been able to learn, Mr. Wood, also who lives at Charles Dunlops old place in Otonobee, has sometimes Bricks to sell, but Rob't could not find out if he has any now or his price.

I had a letter from your dear Mamma some time ago. She was much better then but had been suffering from pain in her arm & she wrote rather in low spirits about your poor Uncle. It must be very trying to her & dear Mrs. Strickland seeing him declining & suffering without being able to relieve him or even to venture to give him food to nourish or strengthen him. I must try & see them if possible when we have sleighing....

I find my hand shaking for I was startled a little ago by imagining I heard some one rapping at the door or window but it was some dog I think as I could see nobody but it made me shake all over, & so dear goodbye.

[affect' old friend] [ ]

1867: February 13[52]
To Annie Atwood and Kate Traill, Gores Landing, Ontario

Douro 13th Feb'y 1867

My dearest Annie & Kate

I cannot send a letter to Mrs. Bird without squeezing in a few lines to thank you my dear Annie for your kind letter which I had the pleasure of reading!... I am now enjoying the great happiness of having your dear Mamma with me for some time & I never saw her looking so well & so handsome. She is in very good spirits too considering the sad trial she has so recently gone through, but she & dear Mrs. Strickland can feel great comfort in thinking of the happiness & "Rest" from all pain & trouble the dear object of their tender care & watching is now enjoying. Your Mamma says dear Mrs. S. is of course very low & likes being alone in her sorrow but comes to join the family at meals.

The Roberts S.'s have moved to the Homestead, but I suppose you know this as your Mother says she wrote to you lately & therefore will not put in any contribution to my packet except her love & she is very much better than she was when she wrote. She desires me to tell you to be sure & lose no time in having dear little Clinton vaccinated as the Smallpox is spreading rapidly though the country. Some man who returned from the Shanty brought the infection to this neighbourhood & he & two of his children have died of it within a few miles of us in Douro. Your Mamma is very anxious that little Clinton should be vaccinated without delay. Your dear Mamma is busy writing just beside me. I am so glad to have her here & to have a comfortable quiet room for her to sit in as well as to sleep in & I trust she may keep as well as she was & not become weary of our monotonous life here. Our lives & society here altogether are so different from Lakefield.

Kate Brown is very well but very thin, always our bright sunbeam. Our weather has been very changeable, sometimes extremely cold & the snow drifting in every direction, at other times so mild that it is like spring. Today is thawing rapidly after a night of rain which makes every place look dirty & wet in holes but the snow [is] deep enough yet for good sleighing only too soft at present. It is not wholesome weather. Mr. Percy is better & was out airing one day but not quite so well after it. Joss Collins not much better either, Tom Hay very poorly indeed, & almost every family with some illness in the house. I have very little news that can interest you. Indeed my pens & ink are both very unfit for nice writing & I am very sleepy tho' it is not dinner time quite yet but I was not in bed till near 2 this morning and up at 6 so I can hardly keep awake, but am as ever your sincerely loving old Mamma Stewart. Love to Mrs. Atwood & accept the same from Bessie & me. I hope all the colds are well now....

[1867]: March 25[53]
To Annie Atwood, Gore's Landing, Ontario

Monday 25th March

My dearest Annie

Though you have probably heard from your Mamma or Kate since their arrival at Belleville yet I think you may like to hear the latest accounts I have had which reached me on Saturday night & were posted at Belleville I think either on Thursday or Friday last. I would send you the letter but as it is on thick paper I should fear additional weight with these few lines as my envelopes are also thick, but I can copy what she says:

"You will be glad to learn that my dear son is better than when I just came down. He had been alarmingly ill on the Sunday & Monday previous to my reaching Belleville but though extremely weak, he was quite composed on Tuesday evening & has since been improving, tho' slowly. Dr. Hope tells me that there is now no <u>immediate</u> danger unless the Diarrhea returns in excess. He still suffers from it but not so as to prostrate him entirely. The cough which was so bad last week is somewhat better too. He is able to be dressed and to lie on the sofa or to sit up in the rocking chair. I attend entirely to him myself, so that he is [never suffered] to be alone or to want for anything & this is a great comfort to me & also to him as his wife is more at liberty to attend to other matters.

I no longer grieve or mourn over my beloved one. We hold sweet counsel together, nor does he fear to think of the certainty of death which he knows is but a question of time. As he says, it may be soon or it may be later, but Gods will is best, whichever way it is. I am in the hands of my Saviour, and blessed be the Lord that his faith grows every day and day by day stronger & it is founded on the best of all foundations, the Word of God which becomes more precious, so that whether he live or die, I trust it will be well with him.

My dear Mary was confined on the 16th of a very lovely little girl. It is the prettiest little thing I ever saw, a perfect picture, not very large but as fat and fair & a dear little face like a wax doll & it is very good beside. As to Kate, she looks upon it as a prodigy of goodness & baby beauty. I do

not think my dear girl as well as I could wish to see her. She has had fever
& chills alternately & much pain especially in that hip that she hurt when
she fell before baby was born. I have just returned from seeing her this
evening & nurse thinks she is better & only wants a good sleep which as
yet she has not had since before the little one was born. I trust to see her
better tomorrow morning. I was afraid of [milk-] only that baby keeps
down the milk very diligently.

I was not with Mary but Kate was & she had a good nurse & skilful Dr."

I think dear Annie this is most of the first part of your dear mothers
letter, but afterwards she added a few lines more, which I will give you
on the other side.

Some days later date but not dated:

"I missed the post more than once having been much occupied &
leaving my letter to others, it was forgotten. This is nearly a week since
my first date. James is not so well as he was & my dear Mary is making
slow progress."

This dear Annie is the last part of the letter & I am sorry it gives no
better acc't of both poor James & Mary, I feel very very anxious & I do
hope the next accounts may be better.

I was just going to write to you on Saturday evening when her letter
came & I determined to write to you as yesterday (Sunday) but some
visitors came in & prevented me. And now I am so sleepy I fear you will
be shocked at this scribble. My pen is not a pleasant one to write with.
My ink has thickened in the tube so I must bid you goodnight ...

Tuesday Morning 26th March

My dearest Annie

I am ashamed to send the other blotted scribble but were I to wait to
write it better, I might miss the chance of sending it and in these times
opportunities to town are rare as the roads are now in a bad state for
either sleighs or wheels. You see, my pen is not improved by a nights
rest, nor can I get any that will write well. My ink also is bad as you may
perceive. I long to hear more from Belleville. Still I cannot expect your
dear Mother or Kate to write as both must be fully occupied. I hope dear
Mary may soon be well again & able to nurse & that the little daughter
may thrive & do well.

Our dear boy Stewart has been very ill for some days with pain in his side and high fever. We sent for Dr. McNabb & heard he had gone to <u>Belleville</u> on some Court business as a witness, so perhaps if he has time he may call to see your Mother. But I am sure he will not delay an hour longer than necessary as poor Capt. Rubidge has had an attack of paralysis & he has many other patients awaiting his return. This has been a very sickly season. We have all had colds here & Bee now has an obstinate cough but I have [ ] off with a very slight share which I am surprised at as I generally have a severe cold at this time of year. Dearest Annie, excuse this horrid letter, bad in every way you can take it, but bears sincere love to you & yours in which Bessie unites with your Ever affect' Old friend & Mamma,

F. Stewart

Kind love & remembrance to dear Mrs. Bird & all her belongings. No time for more at present.

[1867] May 2[54]

To Annie Atwood, Gore's Landing, Ontario

2 May, Friday no Thursday

My dearest Annie

I heard in a round about way at first of your dear brothers release which can only be viewed in one light, a Glorious & happy change!! But I feel anxious about your dear Mother & Kate. I had a long letter from Mary begun just before the Event & finished afterwards & she said <u>they</u> intended to return to their own house as soon as possible, so I have waited to hear of their arrival, & since I heard from Miss Caddy that they had returned & were at their own Cottage, I have not been able to write. I have such a cough that it overpowers me completely after one of those long choking fits to which I am always liable & which has prevented me from doing anything till today.…

Kate has been very poorly lately but I hope is gradually gaining a little strength. She is now able to be up for breakfast & to walk from her room to the parlour which she could not do two days ago. Faintness comes on if she walks or stands & pains & weakness in her limbs, but I hope she is now getting better. Mary Dunlop has gone to Toronto to stay some time with Mrs. Rolleston. I am sure she will be very happy & I think the change will benefit her health. She has had a bad cough all winter. How are your Lambs & calves getting on. Poor Robert has lost several Lambs. He is out of patience about his spring work getting [ ] & our veranda is not to be done till Autumn as he has not time to draw the stones &c which he could not get at till the snow went quite off as they were along the fences where the snow remained till too late. We shall feel the heat of summer very much without a veranda.

I must stop for I am quite tired but I know dear Annie you will excuse me & with kindest remembrance to Mr. A. & your own dear self in both which Bee joins, & Kate would if <u>she knew</u>. You must ever believe me, Your Affect' old Grannie. FS

1867: July 17[55]
To Annie Atwood, Gore's Landing, Ontario

17 July 1867

My dearest Annie

I was delighted last evening to see dear Mrs. Bird walking up to Roberts where we had been spending the evening as she had a childrens Picnic & Jane will tell you something of the noise they all made playing different games & galloping about in all directions. There were 24 children altogether so you may have some idea of the <u>row</u> they all made after tea running about the field & orchard playing hide & seek, ball & many other games of which I forget the names....

Your dear Mother was staying at the Dunlops for a few days the week before last but unfortunately I never heard of it till the day she was leaving. I was in hopes she might have passed this way & that we might have had a call on her way home but she went by the stage from Peterboro. That day I sat at my window all day watching in hopes of seeing her coming....

Whenever I hear from you or Mary I generally write to tell your Mama all the news about you. I had a few lines from her on Sunday last.

She said she had not been very well since her return home but Ellen said she was remarkably well & in wonderful spirits when there. She did not mention having got £40 for the Crusoe's but she told Ellen she had got a small present of some money from her sister Agnes.

I think Mrs. Fitzgibbon is treating her very shabbily in only allowing her £50. If she gets a thousand copies of the Flower Book sold, a thousand copies will fetch £1250 & surely dear Mrs. Traill had the half of the work I think but I believe Mrs. Fitzg. has had some expense with it.

You will say "this is none of my business"! but indeed I always feel anything in which your dear mother or any of the family are concerned is very near to my heart.

Dear Jane has been twice sitting talking to me since I have been writing & I feel as her visit is so short I ought to give more time to her. So dearest Annie forgive this hasty scribble & with kind love to Mr. Atwood & kisses to the chicks.

Believe me dearest
Your loving old friend,
F. Stewart

1868: January 2[56]
To Annie Atwood, Gore's Landing, Ontario

Douro, 2d Jan'y 1868

My dearest Annie

My first letter dated in the New Year to you! I hope it may find you better & more comfortable than you have been for a long time as I heard you had got into a part of your house. A part of a good house is better than the whole of an uncomfortably small one. I have often thought of you my dear friends and only regretted I had not in my power to send you some useful little present as a help towards the new furniture & a proof of love and remembrance at this season. But alas dearest Annie, I believe I must deny myself much pleasure in that way. I need not [enter] into particulars for I am sure you know how many members of my family are so reduced by adversity & loss of property from different causes, so that any money I have seems to melt like the snow in sunshine & slides away in small divisions.

You may always be sure I regret it has been out of my power to prove my sympathy & sincere affection both for you & my dear Mary under such trying circumstances in any way more substantial & effective than mere words & professions. But I still hope if I am spared a little longer that times may mend & no more fires or storms come to destroy property to the degree we have felt during the last year or two. But I feel how very wrong it is to allow my complaints to rise when I can see so much mercy & so many great blessings as we possess still. But I am making this letter too gloomy & serious & forgetting what I should have said first of all, my hopes & wishes that you have had a pleasant & cheerful Christmas & a happy New Year, making a better beginning of 1868 than on former seasons & that it may be the beginning of many years of health, prosperity, comfort & domestic happiness to you & your dear husband & children.

I long to hear how dear Kate got down. I was sorry I did not see her before she left Peterboro but she had been gone two days before I heard she had been there. Since that, your Mamma & Mary were at Annas for a part of a day. Ellen Dunlop met them & said your Mother looked very well & seemed in tolerable spirits which I was very happy to hear. I am sure you are enjoying having your own Kate with you. She is such a pleasant companion & a kind & considerate assistant. I am also <u>very</u> much rejoiced to find you will have your Mother with you in Spring when you will have such great comfort in her tender care & experience.

Your dear kind letter gave me great pleasure & tho' so long delayed I hope you will accept my sincere thanks for it. Indeed <u>dear</u> Annie I always do enjoy hearing from you. I feel a warm interest in all your <u>home</u> pursuits & arrangements & all the little domestic details of your household & children....

I wish I was near enough to you to help you with your sewing and knitting but I know dear Kate is excellent in that way & quicker than I am now for I have become very slow in performing every way. I am often in want of work as I have little or nothing to do for myself, & Kate & Bee use the sewing machine so much that they have nothing that I can do. I often grow tired reading & writing, my sight not being very good now. I have a constant [inundation] of books coming to me as some of my good friends <u>at home</u> often send me books by post & our little Reading Society goes on prosperously by which we have a regular course of books coming round monthly. And the newspapers are interesting, not from the [ ] which I never read, but the state of affairs all over the world. I suppose you know the Lakefield news better than I do, & of Peterboro I know very little. The last news I heard was the death of Caisse, the Hotel keeper.

I must write a few lines to dear Kate. Bee joins me in kind love to you & kisses to the children, & with every kind wish of the season to you & Mr. Atwood. Ever dear Annie, your own old Mamma Stewart.…

[1868: February][57]
To Catharine Parr Traill, Lakefield, Ontario

Wednesday night

My dearest friend

I have had from your dear Mary the pleasant tidings of dear Annies addition to her little family, with good acc'ts of both Mother & babe. I long for some further intelligence & hope the favorable accounts may continue & that I shall hear that all has gone on progressively and prosperously since, as well as that you have not taken cold or suffered in any way from the anxiety & loss of rest such events must always cause. I hope dear good Katie has been free from neuralgia & able to act her part <u>as nurse</u> on the occasion. I hope she will be able to give me the pleasure of hearing all particulars, if you have not time dear Mrs. Traill to do so yourself as I dare say your hands are busy enough & probably you have more writing than is either good or pleasant for you.

I hope you have not felt any remains of ill effects from your fall or the sprain you had before leaving Peterboro.…

What desperate weather we have had lately & what dreadful shipwrecks & loss of life & property by the storms in all points in England & what dreadful outrages the Fenians have been committing in England & what a state the whole world seems to be in, all working in a tremendous fermentation, which no doubt will cause some great commotion or explosion in time. We cannot say when, but it seems advancing rapidly.

We are at present very quiet here & seem out of the reach of harm, tho' surrounded by Roman Catholics, who are doing every thing they can to take <u>the lead</u> & have the upper hand in every public establishment & no doubt are all Fenians, but I hope may be kept down quietly.

We are now nearly shut up by snow. The roads have been impassable for sleighs for some days but today we have opened some roads through the clearing. Yesterday the sleigh & horses were just <u>one hour</u> opening a passage between this & Robert Browns!, whose children as well as two of Louisas (who came here to school on Monday) were detained till a road was opened for them to get home last evening.

Dear Anna spent a day & night with Kate & us the week before last & she has had several very gratifying & satisfactory letters from her dear boy James, who at last reached Boston safely after a most awful passage accross from Liverpool. For 30 days they had no hope of being able to ever reach land. They were <u>63</u> days altogether on the Ocean & in such gales all the time that they never had time to change their clothes or were ever <u>dry</u> & with little or no rest night or day.… He seems not the least discouraged by all the dangers & hardships of sea life, but quite the reverse.…

Dear Mrs. Traill, I have written this sad scribble late at night & with not very good light, as in consequence of the difficulty of communication with [ ] our stores of oil, &c as well as in other commodities are rather in a low state. So this must be my excuse for such scribbling, & it was late in the evening when I heard that Archy was to go early to town, so I hastened to my desk to prepare my dispatches. I sh'd have written some days sooner had I been able to send my letter to town. I have not seen any one from Lakefield nor has Bee yet been able to call on any of the Brides. Between the weather & having no servant for the last two months, both Bee & Kate seldom can leave home. She (Bee) unites with me in kindest love to dear Annie & Kate & tho' last not least, your own sincerely loved self & Mr. Atwood.

Forgive this hasty & rambling letter full of errors & blunders, from your ever affect' & faithful friend

F. Stewart…

[1868: March or April]⁵⁸
To Annie Atwood, Gore's Landing, Ontario

My dear Annie

I have been long intending to write to you to congratulate you on the addition of a little companion for your Dot, or Emily, I suppose she is called now as she is an older sister. I hope you are by this time relieved of all your sad suffering from the gathering of your breast and that your strength is returning.... Dearest Annie you were very very kind to think of joining my name with your dear Mothers for your little daughter....

I suppose Mrs. Traill has gone to Toronto by this time. This cold weather will be very trying to her I am afraid. I shall be very anxious to hear of her. I wonder if my last letter reached her before she left you. It contained $6 which was sent for Dr. Marshalls subscriptions to the Book of Canadian Flowers which I hope will soon now make its appearance. $6, 25 cts. was what Mr. Carnegie gave me for the exchange of the cheque on the Toronto Bank for £1-5 <u>Sterl</u>. The weather last week made us all <u>think</u> of gardening but alas we are far from the practical part now. Robert began his spring work last Monday & sowed his wheat & I think some oats but I am not sure of the latter. All the <u>lawn</u> or fields near this house is green now with fall wheat. Robert has above 40 acres of fall wheat & will have 30 acres of Spring wheat. So you see if all turn out well it will help him on but, if a failure terrible will be the loss, for he has laid out a great deal on the land which is in beautiful order. He is badly off this year as to horses. The poor old Chestnuts are gone. One was long nearly useless from some injury in his leg & was shot lately and the other one is doomed to the same fate. As he is so lame we seldom can use him & the others are not in good order at all. They have had short [commissions] this winter in consequence of the total failure of oats, carrots, &c last year & the scarcity & price for them this winter.

Our Stock is very much fallen off in every way — quality & number — in consequence of want of turnips & almost all winter food. Our fowl too have been reduced by wolverines who have been doing great mischief

amongst the poultry in this neighbourhood. We all go on as usual. Bessie
& Kate have both done without any servant since Christmas & find it
quite a relief....

I am dearest Annie

Your sincere & faithful old friend, F. Stewart.

1868: March 25[59]
To Harriet Stewart, [Acton, Ontario]

Douro 25th. March 1868

My dearest Harriet

I liked your letter very much and I hope you will write to me again. I
have letters very often from my other Grandchildren and now I send
you one from your cousin Herbert. I asked your cousin Harriet to write
to you but she has not one ready but she writes very nicely. I think
you would be very fond of her. She is a very nice little girl and always
merry. She sings very nicely and sings a great many hymns and songs
too. If you ever come back to Canada you will be surprised to see Aunt
Carolines new house. I have not seen it but I hear it is a very pretty
house and I should like to see it and Aunt and Uncle Strickland and
Charlie and Agnes and Arthur.

We have had too much snow and could not go out for a long time.
I have not seen any of your Aunts or cousins except the Browns who
live very near and Aunt Louisa's family. We have no flowers yet but I
suppose you have Violets now and crocuses. Have you a garden? We
sometimes hear a little bird who comes to a tree near the house and
sings in the morning and we hear the crows cawing & see lots of wild
Pigeons. Some beasts called Wolverines have been here this winter and
have killed our hens and amongst them a dear little black hen with a
large topping of black and white feathers. She was so tame she came to
me whenever she saw me and [would] eat bread out of my hand. I was
very sorry. These Wolverines cry at night like some person screaming.
They are like a very large cat. Oh! dear Harrie how much I should like
to kiss you again.

Poor old Betty sometimes comes to see us and she often talks of your Papa. She often nursed him when he was a little boy about as old as Nora. I should like to see you all my dear little children for you are all warmly loved by

Your own fond Grandma

F: Stewart

Give my love to Lina and Nora and Henry. Is he to be Henry or Elliott.

1868: December 15[60]
To Harriet Stewart, Acton, Ontario

15th Dec'r 1868

My dear Harriet

Dear Harriet, I have sent out a little money to Mama to buy some thing for each of you, my four dear Grandchildren, as Christmas presents. I am going to give some little gift to every one of my Grandchildren. There are 38 besides your four. So you may suppose I have to think a great deal about you all but I thought it best to send some money to Mama though it is but a small sum to send so far but when each of the 42 have a little it all makes a large sum. I suppose you have a slate to do sums on so you can see it. And now I hope you may have a merry Christmas and a happy new year. Kiss your sisters and little Henry & love

Your affectionate

Grandma,

F. Stewart

1869: February 10[61]
To Annie Atwood, Gore's Landing, Ontario

Wednesday 10th Feb'y 1869

My dearest Annie

I wish we were nearer each other but there is no use in wishing for what cannot be. But it can be & may be perhaps probable that you will come to visit your northern <u>Mammas</u> this winter. So I often look out when bells are heard & I say perhaps they are the Atwoods bells. Every year we seem to have less intercourse with our friends. It seems as if people were afraid of us! so few ever come to see us now.

Do you know your dear Mamma has been here only once & that for less than one hour since this time two years [ago] when she spent a few days here soon after we were settled in this house! & I don't think you have been <u>here</u> at all. Your last visit was when we were staying at Robert Browns. So my dear just think upon this & <u>act</u> upon it too.

I hope you & Mr. A. & your little ones are well & have not had any of the dangerous illnesses now so prevalent. Scarlet fever has taken off several children in Peterboro but happily none of my Grandchildren. Influenza has also been travelling into every family & in some cases very dangerous, often ending in Typhoid fever. Quinsy & Bronchitis too have been very severe. The season has been too mild & damp to be healthy. I have not heard from dear Mrs. Traill for some weeks. She is troubled very much with rheumatism & also has a great deal of care on her in [diverse] ways. I met Mary one day at Annas & I have been looking out for a visit from Katie who was staying at George Stewarts in town last week & I heard was coming to spend some time here. But yesterday I heard she had returned home which is a great disappointment to me but I hope she will make it up to us soon. We have been so plagued about horses that Bessie don't ask your dear Mother to come. There is so much difficulty of getting out, as you may suppose when Bessie is going today <u>on a load of hay</u> part of the way to town, as she means [to] <u>walk</u> when she is near the town & return with Robert when he is coming back....

Ever your own old
Mamma Stewart

1869: March 18[62]
To Annie Atwood, Gore's Landing, Ontario

Douro, 18th March 1869

My dearest Annie

We are always most happy to see you & Mr. Atwood & <u>all</u> your small appendages whenever an opportunity comes. But as it has turned out in the present instance I fear had you come we could not have enjoyed your visit as both Bessie & I have been entirely occupied during the last two weeks attending on dear Kate who was confined of a son on the 5th. She had a very <u>rapid time</u> & her recovery was progressing rather slowly when on Friday last, just a week from babys birth, she was taken ill quite suddenly with alarming symptoms which continued for several days. We had both Dr. McNabb & Dr. Burritt in consultation & I am most thankful to say she is now better but still very weak & requiring constant care both night and day. We are most fortunate in having both Louisa & Annie Stewart so close as they assist Bessie & "<u>take turns</u>" in night nursing. But it may be some time yet before dear Kate can regain strength enough to be able even to sit up which she has never attempted yet even in bed. Her two youngest children are staying here (<u>not</u> the baby) & we have little Bertha Brown also here for the benefit of attending school.

Arthur Mathias has also returned to us till he meets with some employment so that we have a full house & indeed these are such anxious times that I fear, if you should be able to pay us your intended visit, we should hardly be able to [enjoy] it as Bessie has her mind & time & hands all loaded at present. The Dr. says all depends on unremitting care to keep up Kates strength & to prevent the slightest excitement as her heart is very much affected and the slightest start or excitement might bring on those sad faintings again. She does not know I heard from you as we talk to her as little as possible but I am sure when she is well she will be rejoiced to hear of & from you & to see you if you can come some fine day <u>in summer</u>, for I fear we shall hardly feel at liberty to have you during the present moonlight or even in sleighing, for I suppose as this warm sunshine increases our snow will go & the roads will be very bad.

Our new baby is a very fine large strong little fellow & quiet too, notwithstanding his poor Mamas illness. He is very like both Cecil & Helen. Only think of Kate having <u>six</u> children! I have been wishing to write to your dear Mamma some time back but really have not had spirits or time as when I come home at night I am lazy & sleepy....

John Stewart has gone to the States to look for a farm & to try to raise some money as many farmers have gone from this neighbourhood & succeeded much better. The seasons are more moderate for agriculture & the crops fine & labour not so great as in Canada. But prices are high & some expenses are greater than here. When John has time to look round & judge better he will let us know more about it all as many here seem inclined to emigrate there. Have you any lambs yet. Robert has three within the last two days & so far they seem strong & well, poor little things. Our hens are not laying at all regularly. We only get an egg now & then but Louisas are laying very well & Kates pretty well. I think Louisa has geese but Robert has such objections to them that Bessie has not any nor has Kate I believe. They destroy the grain crops so much. I don't know how he will like Louisas if they trespass. They are very profitable as they sell well & the feathers are so nice for Pillows, &c, but if there is water near I believe they don't go so much into the fields. Annie & Louisa are both trying to make rag carpets. Poor old Betty is now taking care of Louisas house & family as she is obliged to stay so much with Kate & cutting & joining the rags is nice work for her.

We have been quite shut up with drifts lately. The River road was quite impassable for some time & is still very bad. Dear Ellen has gone to Toronto as she has been very poorly lately. I don't know if Mary has any of her young friends staying with her as we have had so little intercourse. Anna Hay too has been suffering from erysipelas in both her arms & a large boil on one which she fears is gathering again. It has been a tedious & painful trial to her and interferes sadly with her household cares and duties. I was much disappointed not seeing dear Kate when she was in Peterboro but our horses are very busy always as we have only <u>three</u>. Robert has been reducing his establishment & certainly his expenses every way he can & has not had any hired man for some months as Archy has gone on a farm of his own. Stewart (Bessies son) is able to help his

Left: *Betty Taylor ("Old Betty"), circa 1856. Photo credit: Sproule, Peterborough, Ontario.*

(Source: Jean Shearman fonds 05-013 Box 1 Folder 12. Courtesy Trent University Archives.)

Below: *Betty Taylor with William and Louisa Stewart's children, circa 1856. Photographer unknown.*

(Source: Jean Shearman fonds 05-013 Box 1 Folder 12. Courtesy Trent University Archives.)

Uncle a good deal & so is <u>Franky</u> but he goes now to school till the spring work requires him again. Edward is in Toronto & seems to like it very well. I think he is a very steady good boy.

I have only heard yet of the arrival of one of the copies of the Wild Flowers sent to my friends. Mrs. Rothwell [has] hers quite safe & is delighted with it which I am impatient to tell your Mamma. And now dearest I must conclude. Bessie is at home tonight & sends her love to you & kind regards to Mr. Atwood in which she is sincerely joined by your affectionate old friend & Mamma, F. Stewart.

1869: April 15[63]
To [Harriet Stewart], [Acton, Ontario]

Douro — 15th. April 1869

My very dear little Grand daughter

I wish to write you a long letter to show you in the only means in my power how much pleased I was with your very nice one which Aunt Dunlop gave me one day lately when I was at Malone. You are improving very much in writing and I think you will soon write as nicely as Mama.

But you should not wait for Papa to send your letters for he is too slow. I am glad you did not wait longer. Mamma is a much better medium for that purpose. Do you know Papa has not written to me since the 22d of last October! — six months very nearly! Don't you think if he were as far from you that you would write to him oftener. Dear Mamma has written me three letters since I had one from him.

You say you often talk about us so I can return the compliment with truth, for we <u>very</u> often talk of you all. I am glad you got my Christmas Gift safe. I have so many Grand children now that I can hardly remember birthdays and I am often sorry to find I have allowed some to pass over without even sending a letter of remembrance as I fear I have now allowed dear Mammas to pass bye and dear little Nora's. Oh how I should like to see you all and to kiss & <u>hug</u> you! ... I had some likenesses taken sometime ago but they were not approved of so I have not sent any home to my friends in "the Old Country" but I hope DV to be able to have some better to send in summer if I can. I have only been once in Peterboro since Christmas! or some time before it. I was at Aunt Dunlops one day lately and passed dear old Auburn. It always makes me very melancholy now to drive that way. Papa can tell you why.

And now I must remember that I must write to Mamma & if not too [ ] perhaps to Papa for I love both of them very much indeed. I hardly hope my dear children ever to see you again for I feel my days cannot be many in this world but I earnestly hope and believe we shall meet in a much happier one, never more to part. And meantime dear Harrie think of me as I do of you when in prayer & Believe me, Your Affectionate Grandma,

F. Stewart

1869: May 3[64]
To Frances Brown (Fan), [Peterborough, Ontario]

Monday 3d May 1869

My dear Fan, I am glad you took into your head to write to me. It is such a long time since you gave me that pleasure before. I feel very stupid and sleepy these dull dark days for I cannot take my turns on the Veranda or keep the door open as I do on nice warm days. Thank you for that hymn. It is very pretty. Do you know the meaning of Terrestrial and Celestial. Of course you do though you have not got any Globes, for you know the Globe representing our world or Earth is called the Terrestrial Globe and some Globes are made to show the Stars and they are called the Celestial Globes but they are very seldom used except in large schools where astronomy is taught....

I am sorry to say I often have pains in my back too but not like yours, for mine are from old age.

Have you any nice Sunday Book to read on Sundays. You should tell me sometimes what books you are reading and how you like them & what you think of them & what you like best in them. I have got two new books lately by post from Miss Wilson. One is travels in Italy & the other is a life of a Mr. Edgar, a gentleman that poor dear Aunt Matilda knew very well and she would have enjoyed reading it. But they are both in heaven now and very likely are together....

Now Aunt Bee has come to sit here so I must shut up my shop & say good bye. Ever your own loving Grandma — FS

1869: June 8[65]
To Frances Brown (Fan), [Peterborough, Ontario]

Tuesday 8th June 1869

My dearest Fan

I have been too long in writing to thank you for your two nice long letters which I have been wishing to answer sooner but have not one moment to spare. I am always trying to get on but some way I seem not to advance at all. For the last week I hardly sewed or knitted much. I have not felt very well lately & that makes one dull & slow & this cloudy weather & so many going away so far from us all, and poor Aunt Georgina so ill, altogether coming in one week seems too much for the poor old Mother and Grandmother of so many. And I have been thinking so much about them all that I could hardly think of anything pleasant except that I am sure God knows all & can help all who want his care or help if pray to Him and love Him and <u>Look</u> to Him & <u>trust</u> Him, & when one thinks of this it seems to take a great load off ones heart. And when I am sitting alone in the hall or in my room, these thoughts keep me from feeling lonely or too melancholy but sometimes I cannot help feeling melancholy. But I don't know why I am writing all this to you. How pleasant it is to have a fire these cool days and evenings. Have you got the stove out of the hall. I suppose you have long ago & the carpet on. I wonder when I shall get up there again. I did not like to go when Mother had no girl as I do so little to help her.

I must stop now as it is past 3 & I suppose you will be soon going.

Ever your old Grannie, FS

Thank you for the XL Psalm. Did you ever read the same Psalm in the Church of England Prayer book. Get Mothers Church of England Prayer book & read the last Psalm XL & tell me which you like best when you compare them. So goodbye again.

1869: July 21[66]
To Catharine Parr Traill, "Clinton Atwoods, Esq're, near Gores
Landing, Ont."

Peterboro, Wednesday
21st July 1869

My Dearest Mrs. Traill

Some weeks I have been intending to write to dear Annie to enquire how
you have been since your journey down there but many adverse causes have
come to present me from doing so. I grieve to say we have scarcely been free
from anxiety and illness in our family since winter but as this must be a letter more of a business nature than one of domestic details I will at once proceed to the business department. This days post brought me a letter from
my friend Mr. Edgeworth with some queries about plants which I think you
can answer better than I can & also a commission to procure some seeds of
the Pitcher Plant (Sarracenia Purpurea) and also seeds of the Sugar Maple.

He has written all his questions & directions on a separate paper
which I will enclose that you may see exactly what he wants as they are
for his friend Dr. Aitcheson who is anxious to introduce them into the
Himalaya District for cultivation & who is to leave England in Oct'r for
India, so that it is necessary if possible to have the package dispatched
about the middle of Sept'r, not later as he did not say what time in Oct'r
Dr. A. was to sail, but probably about the 1st.

I dare say you may be able to procure these seeds for me as you are
more in the habit of business of that kind than I am. I don't know if the
seeds will be ripe so soon but I look to you dear Friend for all necessary
information as well as the best way to pack them up secure from damp
&c &c. They want such a large quantity that I don't know where it can
be procured or found in such abundance but you or dear Kate will I am
sure let me know all particulars as soon as you can as I wish to answer his
letter & enquiries as soon as possible. Any expense there may be I shall
pay so let me know.

I long to hear how you have been since your removal to the Plains.
The air there always seemed to agree with you so much better than

Lakefield and you always enjoy so much being with dear Annie and Mr. Atwood. I hope soon to hear from you for tho' I may have appeared to have been idle about writing, I have constantly had you & your dear daughters in my mind & close to my heart, but really I am grown so slow & stupid that letter writing is now quite a task to me & my hand is grown so weak & shaky that sometimes I can scarcely write legibly. But I hope you will make allowance for all faults & deficiencies.

Ever since this year began we have been from one trouble to another & have had illness in our family. Dear Kate you know was for many weeks in a very low state, all March & into April. Since that dear Mary Brown has fallen into a very delicate state from having grown so rapidly. The Drs. think her spine is a good deal affected & also the lungs & heart. Dr. McNab has taken a very warm interest in her case & has her frequently staying in his house that he may study the case & use the treatment he finds best for her. She is not allowed to pursue her studies at school or to do anything in fact but to be as much out in the air as possible. Nothing can exceed the kindness she receives from all who know her. She is now staying at the McNabs & is better I hear. But we have a much deeper source of anxiety & sorrow in the illness of Henry's wife dear Georgina who has been laid down now for 7 weeks with a large inward tumour which began beneath the liver but now extends to the back & has been most painful & exhausting & the Drs. McNab & Burritt who are with her every day have given up hopes of her recovery. Yet the last two days she has appeared a degree stronger & more alive than she had been for three weeks past but we cannot depend much on this for the great trial will come when this abscess breaks & discharges which will we fear exhaust her small supply of strength. She is quite kept up by the nourishment she takes every hour, & sometimes sickness & other symptoms appear which are most alarming at the time, but she has got over.

Thursday morning

My dearest Friend. I began this letter yesterday & wrote [ ] under many difficulties. Now my time is short for I have been detained by visitors calling even tho' it is early & I expect to hear every moment that my Grandson or Bessie are come to take me home. I have been spending a very happy time for a week with dear Anna who desires me to be sure & give her love to you, Kate & Annie. She has heard three times from Fan, once from Ireland [where] she spent her first week with my sister and visited that wonderful place, the Giants Causeway, & twice from Scotland. She has been introduced to several of her relatives & was at a grand wedding of one of her cousins where there were 120 persons present & at a Dejeaner on the occasion. She writes in good spirits & seems to like all her friends.

I have had three visitors since I began this page & my hand shakes so much that I can hardly guide my pen. I am afraid you will find it rather a rambling production, for my brains seem all confused, having been so long living so very much alone as I have lately at Goodwood & plunging at once into Society & meeting so many old friends seems almost to bewilder me.

I had intended to write to Annie but I think I must wait till I am again in my quiet corner at Goodwood. Pray give her my fond love & kiss the dear children. I don't forget that I am in debt to dear Kate who wrote me a kind letter before you left Lakefield. I also wish to write to Jane Bird but not feeling sure of her whereabouts I have waited thinking I would write to Annie Dalye to enquire how they all were. But the illness of my dear daughter & having now the care of her baby, a dear boy of 16 months old, have taken up my time so much that I could not sit down to write to anyone till now that this commission from Mr. Edgeworth has made it necessary to apply to you my dear Friend for assistance as you are much more accustomed & more capable of such business than I am.

I find I must stop. I have written the last few lines when two young friends were talking to me & scarcely know what I am doing. Hoping it may not cause you any extra trouble or inconvenience & that you will pardon my so far encroaching on your kindness & patience.

I promised dear Anna to come to keep her company when her sons & Fanny had left her in her loneliness but dear Georgina's illness & having the Baby with us prevented me for some time. But lately two young ladies, the Misses Holland, have been with us & they are so fond of our baby they promised to take care of him while I spent a few days with dear old Anna which is such a treat to me.

Dear Kate Brown has not been as strong as I would desire since the summer. I can't complain of the hot weather for it has been but a few days. But she has been obliged to let her maid go home to help her parents some time ago & has not since been able to hear of one. They cannot be had here-abouts and she is quite unable for the work of her household with that great heavy child on her hands constantly, for he is restless & fretful & she has not been well. I feel very anxious about her & also about dear Annie Stewart who is now in daily expectation of her confinement, the 8th! Did you know John is away in the States? He is well & she hears from him every fortnight. Tommy is now settled with a farmer near his Uncle & seems very happy.

I must stop, dearest Mrs. Traill. Forgive this scrawl & never doubt the fond love for you & all your belongings. Your affect' friend,

F. Stewart

1869: September 17[67]
To Annie Atwood, Gore's Landing, Ontario

17th Sept'r 1869
Friday

My dearest Annie

You don't know how great I was disappointed in not seeing you when you were in Douro. You had been some days in our neighbourhood before I heard of your arrival & then I hoped you would be able to give us at least one day before you left, but by a letter from your dear Mother I found you were kept in a state of great anxiety almost during your whole visit by the illness of your children, which grieved me very much. I hope they & yourself have been much better since your return home & that you were none the worse of your short & anxious sojourn at Lakefield & found Mr. Atwood quite well & all your household affairs prospering on your return....

I have nothing to say of ourselves but a list of sickness. Here at Goodwood seems the only part of the country exempt from the sad trouble of illness. Four of my daughters in law are now ill & under medical treatment, Anna who will I trust soon be better but dear Ellen is a great sufferer & has had some severe pain in one of her eyes, in addition to her usual state of weakness & suffering from other causes. I have not seen her for some weeks as I never go out now & she has not been able to drive so far though she is out every day for a short drive on smooth roads. Mary

Dunlop was with us for some days lately which was quite a treat. She is a very nice companion.

I am very much grieved that we are so separated from my dearly loved friend, your dear Mamma. It seems so strange never to be together now but some way we have never been like our <u>old</u> Selves since our burning, & also having the school in this house makes a difference at least for the mornings as the drawing room is occupied by the music pupils & the dining room is the school room, so that I sit generally <u>in the hall</u>.

It seems long since I have heard from you. How does your dairy succeed this year. Have you made much butter or have you any sale for it nearer than Cobourg. It is a tolerable price now. Have you many sheep and lambs & how has your wheat turned out. You know I am always interested in your rural affairs. Have you a good servant! If you have you are better off than we are for ours has gone home to help her father & poor Kate has had such a creature as I am sure she w'd have been better almost without any, except that she could milk & churn but she could neither wash nor bake or [ ], & she broke & wasted more than her wages could repay. So at last Kate sent her away & she is far from able for the household work as her baby is very restless & cross.…

Indeed dear Annie we think of scarcely anything now but illness, so many are suffering. Louisa too is <u>very</u> ill but I hope with care may be restored in time. So you see it is hard to make out a cheerful letter & you must forgive this vile scribble written in haste & if you can spare time indulge me with one of your interesting letters. With kind regards to Mr. A. & all my friends in your neighbourhood. Believe me as ever, your own old loving <u>Mamma Stewart</u>.…

1869: November 17[68]
To Frances Brown (Fan), [Peterborough, Ontario]

Wednesday 17th Nov'r 1869

My dearest darling Fan

I am going to write you a long letter in return for yours which I liked so much and thank you for as much.

I think it is a very good way to read over the chapter of Scripture one has heard in Church after one comes home as it fixes it in our mind. I agree with you that that verse is a very beautiful one. How pleasant it is if one's mind is anxious or troubled about any thing to remember that the Lord knows all our sorrows and troubles, and <u>feels for us</u> and <u>with us</u> more even than our dearest friends can and we can <u>trust</u> Him without any fear of His forsaking us or deceiving us....

I have been thinking a great deal about old times as it is one of my memorable days, because on this day <u>65 years ago</u> when I was a very small bit of a girl my kind old friend Mr. Edgeworth took me up in his arms and kissed me to bid me Good bye as he was going away home to his own house. Well just then he said "Oh I think I will take you home with me. Put on your bonnet & get yourself ready. Where are your clothes?" He ran up stairs to my Aunts room where I was getting ready & he just took up a bundle of my clothes out of my drawer in his arms & stuffed them into a bag in his carriage & got a stool for me to sit on & away we drove. There were in the carriage Mr. & Mrs. Edgeworth and Miss Beaufort & Charlotte Edgeworth. We had 40 miles to drive, up hills & down hills & through two or three towns & it was quite dark when they got home. It was quite a mild warm damp day not like today at all. I staid there nearly six months & came home to my Uncles at Allenstown on the 20th of April 1805 having gone on the 17th Nov 1804. Oh it was such a nice happy time. So I always went there every year afterwards for a month or some weeks till I was married 11 years afterwards & now every one of those who were with me then both at Allenstown & Edgeworthstown are dead & gone except my one old self & one or two cousins who were wee children then. So I think I have made out as long a letter as yours. I send you a little poem I met with in a newspaper which took my fancy. I hope you may not be quite <u>disgusted</u> and wearied with this letter.

Aunt & Uncle Dunlop were here yesterday from about 4 till 10. I was wishing father & mother had come in too. We played 5 games of whist, Uncle Dunlop & Mary Mathias against Molly & me. We got 3 games & they two. So I think I may stop now & am your ever fondly loving Grandma,

F. Stewart

1869: December 25[69]
To [Harriet Brown], [Peterborough, Ontario]

Christmas day
1869

My own dear Harriette

I hope you are very well and very happy today and as merry as people generally are at this sociable season.

I have been some weeks intending to write to you so that you should have my good wishes and loving remembrance on this day but I have not been very well for sometime nor in very good spirits and you know people cannot write cheerful or pleasant letters unless they feel quite well and happy. One cause of my feeling dull was having been disappointed in my wish to send you <u>all</u> my very dear little Grandchildren some little presents but I found I could not manage it so I wrote to dear Mamma I fear a very dull & discontented sort of letter, for I felt so, & whenever I do so it makes me feel sick. But I have had a cheerful day for Aunt Kate & Uncle Robert and their six children spent the whole day here from a little past 11 in the morning till near 10 at night.

The servants of both families were allowed to go home to see their own friends. I am sorry to say none of our party were at Church for it threatened rain and we are 5 miles from our Church. Early in the morning about 3 oclock Mary & Caroline Mathias and Mary Brown went to Uncle Roberts house & sung two nice hymns just near their bedroom window. One was Hark! the Herald Angels Sing and the other hymn was Heavenly Home! Heavenly Home! Precious name to me. I dare say you know this last one. Of course you do the first one.

Their voices sounded very nice in the stillness of that hour. We had no Christmas tree this year but on the evening before 18 of my grandchildren & their mothers were here & had a merry evening with various games & they dressed up & acted charades, some of the older ones. Oh I should have liked so much to have your dear Papa & Mama & you my five dear children here along with ours. Aunt Louisas 5 were here but she could not come as she is staying in Peterboro. Aunt Annie and 7 of her children were here but dear Uncle John is far away in Illinois. Aunt Kate and her six were here besides Aunt Bee's 4 & our nieces & Uncle Robert so we had a large party.

I think Harriet is writing a few lines to you. She is a very nice little girl. She is not at all <u>fat</u> but is tall & thin. She & Aunt Lou's little <u>Birdie</u> are very fond of each other & go out on a little hand sleigh & slide down a little hill in our lawn. Papa will explain to you how they go.

I hope dear Harrie you may have & had a very merry Christmas & New Year for both will be "bye gones" when this reaches you. I have a headache today but I don't think it is very bad. So dear I hope you will soon write to me & believe me that though I have not been able to send you presents or to prove the truth of my words I am always your very loving Grandma,

F. Stewart

[1869][70]
To Ellen Dunlop, Peterborough, Ontario

[1869] Friday afternoon.

Dearest Ellen

As your dear girls seem undecided about staying tonight or going home, I will prepare a few lines as our [ ] are so uncertain. I was truly glad to see them & particularly dear Mary who seems <u>greatly</u> improved in health, strength & spirits since the last time I saw her. I do hope she may not find any bad effects from this long walk. I fear too much for both of them. We wish them to stay tonight but Mary says you would be uneasy if they did. However, if we can we will keep them. Too much fatigue is very bad for dear Mary & I don't think you would have any uneasiness about her. She says she will go right off to bed when she goes home. I am grieved to hear of dear Ivans illness & fear it may go hard with him. Surely these are startling times, so many leaving us in sickness & death, so many warnings that the <u>present</u> moment is all we can [ ] on. It seems wonderful the troubles & trials now going forward in both public & private affairs, & yet the outside objects around us so very beautiful, surpassing former years in richness & [ ] & so early when we anticipated a late & backward Spring.

I hear poor Mr. Fortie also is ill & on Saturday he was apparently quite well & at Mrs. Browns funeral. I am so sleepy today that I cannot keep my eyes from closing as you may perceive by my mistakes & blots & all other causes, my arm for one, which is stiff from rheumatism. I think the East wind is the cause of both.

I send you & Anna <u>six letters</u> between you, which you can exchange & return when read, but in writing to the writers of them or any of our friends don't mention that I sent you the letters or that you read them for I know they so much dislike having them sent round — & certainly one doesn't like it ones self. I am glad you enjoyed your visit to [Frank's] so much. I think you should leave home again & make use of the time when you can have Anna to look after the household. I am afraid the poor girls find us very dull, as Mary B. was obliged to go in the morning to help Annie all day with her packing & Mary M. had her school to attend to. But she is come home now. Oh see my ink is too thick. I must water it. You will <u>think</u> I am ill by this horrid writing & sleepiness, but I got up too early this morning & waited longer than usual for breakfast, which always makes me sleepy & weak all the day afterwards. But I am quite well & my nose has never attempted to bleed since the last day of that week when it bled so much, 3 weeks ago.

Poor Jack & his family are to move into town for a few days & they think of starting on their long journey on Wednesday next, the 2nd June. The 1st of June <u>48</u> years ago we sailed from Belfast for Canada! 48 years is a good space out of the 76 I have been in this world. I must write a wee bity to dear old Nan. When the roads get a little smoother I hope you will able to come out here but indeed dearest I do not wish you to come till you can do so without pain or danger of breaking down.

I see a change in darling Henry lately. He seems anxious about Darcy & is wishing he could manage to have him home if he could get some one to keep house for him & take [over for] them both. But I don't know where he can get any one to do. I don't know a girl fit to undertake the charges. I am <u>greatly</u> disappointed at his not getting the place [Jose] so kindly wished he should have, but that is now all over. I had such hopes the old Capt. would do it for me.

Oh this pen blots & my eyes close so I must stop. I send you Mary Wilsons last letter I don't think you saw, & 2 of Aunt Kates, & to Anna I send Mrs. Traills, Mrs. Bellinghams & 2 from Bessy Rothwell. I have not got any old country ones since. I had one I send from Mrs. Strickland. Perhaps you may see her. Tell me what you think of Gates so far. It is a [ ] book & some parts very good & at some too flighty. Goodbye dear. Anna wishes to read it too. Ever your own, F.S. I wish I could send these dear girls home in the Buggie but I have no horse or driver.

1870: October 24[71]
To Harriet [Stewart], [Acton, Ontario]

Douro — 24th Oct'r 1870

My dearest Harriet

Our trees were very beautiful a week or two ago. The weather was most delightful and so warm that we sat out on the veranda by [moonlight] but now we have quite high [ ] and frost every night. [ ] shocks of Earthquake have been [ ] all over this Province on Thursday last particularly. We did not <u>feel</u> it here but we heard a great noise like thunder only not the sharp crashing sound that thunder has but a <u>rumbling</u> sound which continued for some minutes. Aunt Bee & Aunt Kate & Mary Mathias and I all heard it going on & thought it was distant thunder. Afterward when we heard of the Earthquake we concluded it must have been connected with that as it was about the same hour and it was a very cool day.

Did I tell you in my last letter that I had two dear little birds, <u>Canadian canaries</u>. One of them was tamer that the other and I called it Petsey. It sung very sweetly and [ ] nice little coaxing ways. [ ] its cage just outside the [ ] everyday but one day last week I found it lying dead in the cage and its poor little head taken off!! So then I recollected having seen a Jay flying about amongst the trees near the house and I am sure it killed my dear little Petsey! I was very sorry. The other little bird was so frightened it could not eat & sat without moving for some hours and its poor little heart kept beating quite hard. It was very sick & very dull for several days

& is only just now beginning to recover but it has not sung at all. I am sure it feels lonely after the other.

Harriet Brown wishes you would write to her soon. I think you would be very fond of her. She is such a nice little girl. Mary Mathias teaches her every day. She is very good natured & merry and runs & jumps about. We have a good many apples now & Harriet helps to gather them. She sends her love & so does Aunt Bee and your own very fond Grandma

F. Stewart

Pray write to me again and to Harriet.

1870: December 1[72]
To Annie Atwood, Oaklands, Thorndale Rice Lake Plains, Ontario

Thursday 1st Dec'r 1870

My Dearest Annie

I am sure you must think me very unkind and neglectful in not having written to you during all the long time when you were so ill and under such dreadful afflictions. It seems cold and commonplace to assure you that I often thought of you and intended to write, but I was very poorly, all the hot weather, in consequence of my nose bleeding violently for many days & then a threatening of Dropsy, which altogether exhausted my strength & made me so shaky and weak that I really hated to begin a letter, & I am only now getting some letters answered which have been in my desk for many months. But indeed dearest Annie you & all your dear relations in this neighborhood have been constantly in my mind. I had a letter from your dear Mother some time ago, kind & loving as usual. She still suffers very much from lumbago. But how can she be well when her mind is (as it must be) loaded with anxiety about her two dearest sons surrounded as they are there by dangers of so many kinds. So far Willie had escaped smallpox & as he seems to understand the treatment so well, we may hope he may escape that most wretched of all maladies. I have heard of dear Kate having been at Malone & in Peterboro lately but we seem more out of the reach of our friends than ever as I have not had the use of my own horse for nearly a year past. She was completely used up, poor thing, & just lived walking about the Barnyard. She is not there now & I don't know what they have done with her but she is not able to work at all & so I have not been able to go out much, as you know what it is to depend on farm horses for ladies recreation! Indeed our young horses are so frisky that I don't like going out with them but now sleighing will I hope enable us to have a little more liberty. Our present set of horses are not fit for lady drivers & that is another difficulty as Bessies two eldest boys are always working for Robert & of course we must not take them for our indulgence....

I am now such a bad correspondent my hands tremble so much that some times I cannot write at all. But when I am well I feel stronger & steadier. You know I am very old & have become much more infirm within the last few years and my deafness has encreased so much that I am very stupid. Bessie of course cannot sit much with me as she has not had any servant for three months or more & her family is not small even tho' her two big boys generally take their dinner & tea at Roberts.

I am happy to say our darling Kate is better but far far from well or strong yet. She has been staying in town with Louisa for three weeks & came back last Saturday certainly a good deal better but still very far from strong & looking so pale & thin that you would hardly know her. However, she is fortunate in having a very good servant at last. And Caroline Mathias lives with them & helps her a great deal in attending to the children & sewing as well as in household cares & is a cheerful pleasant companion so that Kate is better off now than almost anyone I know. Here I am happy to say we are all well but there is much [very] fatal fever in the country & [more] especially in town. Every day we hear of two or three deaths. We have got an excellent Doctor in our good old Dr. McNabbs place. Dr. & Mrs. Burritt are quite an acquisition to our Society & from poor Kates tedious illness we have become quite intimate & sociable....

Believe me as ever Your Loving Mamma, F. Stewart...

[1870: winter]⁷³
To Annie Atwood, Gore's Landing, Ontario

Douro, Sunday Evening

My dearest Annie

Your dear Mother has been some time at the Homestead but I fear, though she has much comfort there and enjoyed the company of your dear Aunt, yet the pain in her back is not much better. I fear till this very changeable weather is over we cannot expect much change for the better in her pain. It is very trying to her not only from the great suffering but that it prevents her from writing which is of so much consequence to her. She must also be very anxious about your brothers in these times of trouble in the NW but I hope it may soon be settled. I am sure there seems disturbance & rebellion on every side & in every part of the world. But of course all is known by Our Almighty Good[ness] who knows best what we require & who orders all things right. Of this we can have no doubt. Last year was a continuous season of anxiety and sorrow to me & my family, & so far this year is beginning very gloomily as dear Ellen Dunlop has been very ill for some weeks past & tho' better is still suffering severe pain from some affection of the Spinal nerves. She is very weak and is going through a course of blisters which always depresses the spirit and exhausts strength. How very providential that dear Anna Hay is now living with her and has taken all the housekeeping on herself besides attending to dear Ellen.

Another invalid on our hands just now is poor Robert Brown who had a bad fall one day last week & hurt his back very much. He is better and can now walk a little but it gives him great pain to move & he is not able to go out or to attend to his outdoor affairs, which is very trying to his spirits as he has no <u>hired man now</u>, old <u>Archy</u> having settled on a farm of his own near Haliburton. Bessies two sons, Stewart & Franky, help their Uncle & have done all he requires during the summer and fall. Eddie is in Toronto and very well & seems quite happy. He and Tom Hay are in the same shop & board together with a very respectable nice family & have many kind friends there. When Bessie was lately in Toronto she spent a day with Mrs. John Hilton (Miss Foulis). She has five boys, very fine children but all very <u>large</u> & <u>wild</u>, almost too powerful for her, but she seems happy enough tho' they are in very narrow circumstances & she don't keep any servant. Bessie says she looks thin and care worn, but just the same dear little warmhearted creature. As ever, they were both very kind....

I hope dear Annie your house is warm & comfortable. We have very changeable & disagreeable weather & very <u>dark</u> & cloudy but we have plenty to do & plenty of Books to read & we manage to pass our time wonderfully, cheerfully considering the anxieties all parents must have & many other sources of trouble just at present. But yet we sh'd not complain for we have many great blessings & more comforts than many more deserving....

Ever your attached old friend, F. Stewart

Kind remembrance to Mr. Atwood.

1871: April 6[74]
To J. McNabb (Mack) Stewart, Peterborough, Ontario

Thursday 6th April 1871

My dear Mack

A long time ago I think I said I would make you a scrap book. I suppose you may forget that but I have been making it up by <u>little bits,</u> a bit now and another time a little bit more, and at last I have got it done and I send it to you. I am afraid when you see this parcel you will think there is something very nice in it and that you will be greatly disappointed when you find such a shabby Book but perhaps you may find some story or something in it that will amuse you some day or evening when you have a few spare minutes to look into it. I had a few lines yesterday from Aunt Annie to tell me that Uncle Jack had got the Turnip seed I sent by Express about ten days ago....

Give my love to them both & to Bun & Birdie, Kenny & Willie and a <u>big lump</u> for yourself with a kiss to Mamma & to Betty. I am dear Mc as ever your fond

Grandmamma.

F. Stewart

1871: July 14[75]
To Frances Stewart (Bun), Peterborough, Ontario

July 14th 1871

My dearest Bun

I am afraid you will think I have forgotten your Birthday but indeed I have not. I have been thinking of you very often & wishing I could have you here with me to give you a good [coax] & kiss but all our pleasant times seem gone by. I see no chance of seeing you unless Mamma can come & bring you with her. I don't believe I shall ever see Peterboro again. It seems like it but I can't help that & so dear I must write all my birthday wishes & send all the love I can in a letter which can never carry all I have to send. But I am sorry I have not got any present to send. I could not get into town or get any one to go so I could not get things I wanted & besides I have not got any money yet so I feel rather cross upon it. Still my dear Bun I wish you a great many happy years & returns of your Birthday. I wonder if Mary gives holidays. The other schools I find give 5 weeks which is too long I think.

The day after tomorrow the 18th will be poor Fanny Stewarts Birthday. She is far away out of our reach but I am sure she will think of us all & we will think of her. Tell Mama I wrote last week to Aunt Annie & gave her message. And now dear Bun go round & kiss Ma & Betty & the boys all for Grandma & get them all to kiss you in return for your own fondly loving Grandma,

F. Stewart

1871: July 17[76]
To Annie Atwood, Gore's Landing, Ontario

Douro, 17th July 1871

My dearest Annie

I am sure you think I have given you up as a correspondent so I think I will take up my pen and try to prove that this is not so. Besides, it is so long since any tidings [afar] from Rice Lake have reached me that I really do want to know how you all are. I suppose Mr. Atwood as all other farming gentleman is now busy at his harvest & I hope all his crops are turning out well. It is wonderful how well all seem in this neighborhood, notwithstanding the sad want of rain, which for a time made everything look brown & dried up & spoilt all the meadows so that hay will be very scarce this year. But the other crops all seem good tho' the straw is short....

Bessie was to have gone to spend some days with your dear mother on the following Sunday but little Harriet was taken ill with a feverish bilious illness which has been going through Kates family which put an end to poor Bees plans & anticipated enjoyment. The next week Mary Brown was laid down in the same way and so Bessie was again disappointed & now she don't know when she can go as Mary is far from strong & Bessie don't like to tax her strength too heavily by leaving all the responsibility & work of the household on her shoulders as she is still without a maid. It is impossible to get any now to come to a <u>farm</u>. They all hire in towns where they get $6 or $7 per month which is beyond dear Bessies means. It makes such a difference to her not having the farm. The [ ] (in produce) goes but a short way. Now her children are all grown into men & must have suitable clothing &c. But this farm is a perfect "<u>show</u>." It looks so nice & <u>well doing</u>. We have not a stump to be seen in the fields & all looks smooth & neat. Robert has indeed done his nephews justice in putting the land & fields all into the <u>best</u> order. I often wish it was not so far from all our friends. This is the only drawback for the house is most comfortable & convenient & the air pure & particularly healthful but we are sadly shut up from our friends & Society in general & during the last 18 months, since I have had no horse of my own, we seldom have a chance of going out except on Sundays. As Bee has not the farm I cannot afford to keep a horse, so I just manage to fill up my time between reading, writing, knitting, & sleeping. I am <u>knitting a quilt</u>, a great piece of work. I have not much sewing now so knitting takes its place.

I wish you were able to write me one of your nice letters telling me about <u>everything</u>, your home concerns & cows, horses, sheep, pigs, & fowl, & also potatoes, wheat, &c. Have you had the "<u>Potatoe Bug</u>" & are your potatoes good. The fields are rapidly changing colour now. Today Rob't is reaping at a neighbors with his reaping machine. It [ ] much time & labour. He has a mowing machine also & does a great part of the work now by <u>horse work</u> more than man work. Kate is, I am very happy to say, very well. She is better than for three or four years back but is thin & not very strong but able to do all that she requires. She has an excellent servant which is a good help & thank Goodness! no baby on hand which is best of all. Now dear, Goodbye. My time is up, so forgive [ ] & with kind regards to Mr. A. & love to the children & other friends, Believe me as Ever Your fondly attached Mamma Stewart, FS

If you see Jane Bird tell her we are looking out for her — love to <u>them</u>.

1871: September 25[77]
To Annie Atwood, Gore's Landing, Ontario

Douro 25th Sept'r 1871
near 10 Monday Night

My dearest Annie

I have just read your kind and most welcome letter which I received this evening and truly sorry I am to find you are still so weak. How often I wish you were nearer to us yet this seems a nonsensical wish because I have many very dear friends & even my own dear daughters who I see but seldom tho' living within a few miles of me....

I am sorry you have not a <u>comfortable</u> servant but you are fortunate to have <u>one at all</u>, to relieve you of the heavy part of the domestic work. Bessie has only just succeeded in getting one after being <u>a whole year</u> without any. She had engaged three at different times but they disappointed her as there was such a scarcity of girls that wages were exorbitant & they are so saucy about not having their meals with the family or require to have a horse & buggie to take them home every fortnight! This of course we could not promise as we have no horse for ourselves. Bessie & I are depending on the farm horses which now all belong to Robert as I have not had one for nearly two years. Consequently I can very very seldom get out & Bessie has to take <u>a chance</u> when anyone is going which puts her about greatly & prevents us from seeing our dear friends as formerly. But dear Annie you know this is a world of changes! — & we ourselves change as time passes & we find we are not what we were a few years ago.

We have had a long season of illness amongst our children both here & in Kates family. I am happy to say dear "Kitten" is much stronger than she was during the former three summers and one reason is that she has had a very good servant. Unfortunately she (the maid) she has been very ill & was obliged to go home for three weeks and Kate was nearly used up but last evening her servant came back, recovered in health & in good heart for working. She is a fine strong woman & very good natured to the children & trustworthy in every way. Robert looks very old & is much broken down. He wishes to give up farming & take some less laborious employment if he could procure anything suitable. But there lies the difficulty. Situations are so hard to get into & so many are seeking them that a person so little known and who has lived so long in retirement has but a little chance of succeeding. Their house is too small for their family now tho' it is not so numerous as you suppose. Her number is only six — Fanny, Jessie & Helen, Herbert, Cecil & Percy. They are all growing up fast & are useful & intelligent but are sadly backward in education since Mary Mathias has gone into Peterboro but we can't help that.

Kate has Henrys youngest child under her care but Caroline takes charge of him & little Helen which is some help to Kate, though now of course she is a good deal taken up about her own arrangements. As you have heard she is engaged to Henry Stewart but I don't think they can marry for some time as Henry has been most of the summer busy surveying on the continuation of the Midland railway near Orillia & Georgian Bay. His eldest boy is here & has lately been very ill from the "dregs" of Scarlet fever which the younger ones of both families have had followed by mumps.

I am happy & thankful to say our dear boy is now nearly as well as ever but he is looking very pale still. He is a very fine little fellow & one of the best children I ever saw. Bessie is as fond of him as if he was her own child. Our dear little Harriet is grown very tall & slight & is a very sweet child & a great comfort to her Mama, & so is Mary Brown who is quite the elder daughter of the family & a very fine girl in every way, both in character & appearance. Indeed I think her very superior to the [generality] of young girls of these days. I was very happy to see dear Kate at Annie Collins's wedding & we hoped to have had her here for some time but the children here had just got over scarletina & were ill with mumps & Kate was of course unwilling to bring her little Katie into the infection and I have not heard from either Kate or your dear Mama since but I have been dilatory about writing, for I am grown so stupid & slow both in thinking & acting that letter writing is now quite a task to me. I sit alone a great deal & when in the social circle my deafness keeps me from joining in conversation so that my mind is becoming dull tho' I still have many resources & even enjoy reading, tho my sight is far from good. But I have no reason to complain for few woman of my age (77) are as well as I am now for which I have reason to be thankful. I should much enjoy having dear Mrs. Traill with me for some time & still hope that in sleighing time (DV) we may have that great pleasure.

I must now come to our household affairs. Bessie has only two cows now as Robert has had the farm during the last four or five years & she can hardly make enough butter to enable her to lay by for winter as the dry summer burnt up all the pasture so that there has not been much dairy produce nor poultry either. The stock of hens was so reduced that we had to exchange eggs with some of our neighbors & now have about 30 young fowl. The crops have been very fair except hay which has failed everywhere. Stewart & Frank have done all the ploughing and all the farm work with their uncle for the last two years & he has had no hired man at all. They are very industrious & steady. Stewart is very tall & a very handsome fellow. Frank is not so tall nor so well looking but he is full of fire & makes us all laugh nearly to "high [striker]." Rolley is now in town in Mr. Erskines shop & boards with his Aunt Hay....

I am so tired writing I can hardly guide my pen, so will release you from the task of reading all this & only add my kindest regards to Mr. Atwood & kisses to the chicks in all which Bee joins with your ever affect' old Mama F. Stewart....

1871: October 1[78]
To Frances S. Brown, Sunnyside

1st Oct'r 1871

My dear Fan

I think I will send you a nice little bit of poetry which I think may be considered & called a hymn which I have copied out of *The Sunday* at home, and I took a notion you would like it tho' it looks rather long. I like to have some thing to write on Sunday so I also send you a scrap if you intend reading out scraps in the evening. I will (DV) give it to you on your return from church. Is Jessie to come home with you. I think she must be getting homesick, she so seldom likes being long from home. Do you know I am awfully sleepy. I have nodded two or three times over this. The house here is always so quiet & still. Even Dunbar never makes any noise like what other boys do & dear wee Rolley is too far off to hear the noise.

Oh dear I was asleep just when I was writing the words "to hear" in the 4th line back & I dreamed that someone said "Rolley has gone to Washington to see the President! & to be examined for the new situation" & I was just thinking why he went off so far & did not come to say Goodbye when I awoke, & now I will stop as I have been asleep again. Goodbye dear, Ever your own Grannie.

Oh see all the wee marks where my pen wandered to & had a wee dance to itself tho' it is Sunday. Goodbye dear. I am your own fond G once more & for ever,
F. Stewart

1871: December 10[79]
To Anna Maria Stewart (Birdie), [Peterborough, Ontario]

10th Dec'r. 1871

My dear Birdie

I send you a nice letter I had from Frances for I am not going to call her Bun anymore if I can remember it and as Aunt Annie has another Lizzie

Stewart, I think it much nicer to call her Frances, don't you think so? Now Nannie dear I want you to write to me. I have letters very often from all my grandchildren in Illinois and also from Aunt Kates children tho' they are not so far from me. But even Harriet and Dunbar write to me and I want you to write to me sometimes too for I am very fond of having letters from my friends. So pray tell Fannie Hay to take this hint. Anna Collins writes to me very often and I think Fannie should too. Tell her I wish often to hear what she is doing and thinking about as I know nothing about her and it seems as if she was a stranger & not a dear granddaughter.

Please take care of Franceses letter and hymn & return them when you have an opportunity & with love to all & <u>Jeff too</u>.

I am your ever loving

Grandma,

F. Stewart

Love to Rolley.

1872: January 9[80]
To Frances Stewart (Bun), "At Mr. Andersons"

Tuesday Evening
9 Jan'y 1872

My dearest Frances

You see I don't call you Lillie because I don't think you look like a Lily unless you have changed since I saw you. I have been long wanting to write to you but some way or other these days have been both darker & shorter than usual and I am every day growing older and slower in doing & thinking and more particularly in writing. But still I felt that your very nice letter deserved a good answer. I assure you my own dear Bun, it gave me very great pleasure to have a letter from you and it is so beautifully written. I hope you will try to keep up your writing for you write better than any of the girls I have round here and I was quite surprised to see you could write and spell so well. Try & write some every day & don't get the way of scribbling that all the other girls have for it is so <u>ladylike</u> to be able to write nicely. So dear write to me whenever you can that I may see you are not going back.

Thanks also for that hymn, the LVIII Paraphase. It was sung at your dear dear Papa's funeral & it always brings that day back to my heart and mind. I never can forget it. I hope you are very happy. I am sure you must be so as Mr. & Mrs. Anderson are so kind and have been so kind to Tom & so fond of dear Willie. Oh how I would like to see you all again and give each of you a big squeeze, close to my heart, with half a dozen kisses....

We had a very quiet Christmas it seemed, but a small party without your two families. Indeed we often miss you all & wish you were not so far away but we can't help that and hope to meet where there will be no more parting or sorrow. I heard from Min that you were all out skating on Christmas Day. I don't think any of our folks skated any that day but the boys go out in the evenings sometimes....

I wonder when Mamma will be home. How does she like Chicago. I think I will write to her tonight if I don't grow too sleepy. So I will now shut up this and turn my attentions to her, but am always & ever,

Your own loving Grandma,

F. Stewart....

[*Frances added the following notation about the addressee*] "Miss Stewart at Mr. Andersons, commonly called Bun or Lillie or Frances — by me."

[*in pencil in another hand*] Thursday Sept. 29th 1881

1872: January 10[81]
To Frances Brown (Fan), [Peterborough, Ontario]

10 Jan'y 1872

My dearest Fanny

I have often intended to write you and Jessie to thank you for your nice Christmas presents. Indeed I feel vexed & ashamed at not having done so much sooner for I have often looked at both the pretty edgings and your nice box which you sent the chrochet pieces in, all so very neat & nicely done & I hope to have it all sewn on my new chemises very soon as I have had one chemise half made for a long time which I must soon finish as my old ones are going to stripes. They split up the back & sides every time I wear them. So as the days grow longer I hope to be more alive & get more done if I do not get sick. I am so afraid of getting sick. This is the time of year I generally get one of my bad colds & I think if I get one now it would be sad trouble to everybody for all seem to have plenty to do but we must be thankful that when we hear of so much sickness & deaths in so many families we are all kept so well in both houses. I hope it may long continue so & that soon we shall all get more settled.

So in the meantime we must try & trust in God to guide us all in the right way and leave all our cares in His hands — Psalm xxxvii — 5, and all will be right. I must now go to tea so goodbye for this time.

Sunday — 14th Jan'y 1872

Do you know, my own dear Fan that I don't think I have written to you this year! Or since before Christmas! I seem to have just awakened from a long dream. Everything & every body seems so unsettled and uncomfortable since Christmas day which could not be called a happy one though we all seemed merry enough in the evening when the games were going on. But dear child, tho' we cannot help feeling all this very much yet we must feel sure that all is guided by a loving Father who knows best what we require and who will never send us more than He will enable us to bear if we only "<u>trust</u> in Him" and pray to Him to enable us to bear all and submit to all in the full assurance that "He holds the Helm" and guides the storm. And when He sees it right He can say "Peace be still" & give us peace or else strength to bear it all. Every event of our lives if <u>laid out for us</u> from before we are born till we cease to breath & He knows the end, before we can see the beginning! But we may pray to Him <u>to guide us</u> and to lead us and show us our way, through the thorns and tangles that seem so thick & painful but which (when passed) we can look back upon and trace His goodness and mercy to us. And sometimes He lets us see why He sent these trials and when they cause us to look into our own hearts perhaps we may find something wrong which He took this way of removing.

Well dear Fan I have just been writing the thoughts that often pass through my mind and they seem often to put every other subject out of their way but today they came down on this piece of paper & I hope you are not tired of it but being Sunday it seems more suitable than any nonsense would be. I wonder if you are writing to me today. I hope you are. I want to know so much about you but some way I have not seen you much lately & one day that you came up to see me (I believe it was last Sunday) I was asleep & so missed that pleasure which I was very sorry for.

Sunday evening 8 oclock — Just when I had written so far this morning they all came home from church and then dinner came and then I grew lazy & put off finishing this & now they have been trying to sing but did not get on well. Poor Aunt Bee did her best but Stewart did not care to sing much & there was no other singers but Harriet & Dunbar ...

1872: January 17[82]
To Anna Maria Stewart (Birdie), "at Mrs. Hays,"
[Peterborough, Ontario]

Wednesday
17th Jan'y 1872

My dear Birdie

You were a very good girl for writing to me. I liked your letter very much and I am very glad you have promised to write to me every Friday. I hope you will do so. I hope Anna's cold is better. I think she is very wise not to go out these cold days till her cold is gone.

I think Bud was a foolish fellow to drive so carelessly as to break the Harness. I wish Watch would stay up here as we have no dog at all. Watch comes here for a day or two and then he goes away for a week or more. We have no dog and I often wish for one. I like to hear dogs barking & it seems so dull not to hear a dog sometimes.

Oh do you know I was fast asleep.

Dear Birdie, do you know I am very apt to go to sleep when I am writing or reading and I am always vexed at being so lazy. And so my letter has been neglected but I can't help it. My eye was sore but it is nearly well today and now it is so near dinnertime that I must put all my papers and pens and ink away as I am rather more inclined to eat than to write just at present but I hope you will write to me soon again. I have not had a letter from Illinois for a long time. I think Fannie Hay had one from Mama. And now dear Goodbye.

Believe me your very fond

Grandma, F. Stewart

DIED.

MANN—In Smith, on the 24th ultimo, Aaron Mann, Esq., in the 40th year of his age.

STEWART—At Goodwood, near Peterborough on the 24th ultimo, Frances Browne, relict of the late Hon. Thos. A. Stewart, in the 78th year of her age.

Newspaper notice of Frances Stewart's death. Peterborough Review, *March 1, 1872: 3.*

CONCLUSION

❦

"That day I sat at my window all day watching in hopes of seeing her coming,"[1] wrote Frances Stewart. The above, a simple statement, haunting in its intimation of the loneliness Frances felt as she waited, was expressed in a letter that Frances sent to Annie Atwood on July 17, 1867. Anticipating a visit by Annie's mother, Catharine Parr Traill, on her way home from a visit with Frances's daughter Ellen, the aging widow had been disappointed to learn that Catharine had taken another route, travelling by stage directly from Peterborough. Frances keenly awaited the arrival of visitors, often unable to call on even her closest friends and family, having to count on others for a means of travel. One can only wonder what she thought about as she gazed from her window watching for her friend Catharine to appear.

A certainty that she would never see her Irish loved ones, so far away and many deceased by that time, did it feel a cruel extension of her pervading sense of loneliness not to have even a passing glimpse of her new-world friend? That a deep feeling of closeness existed between the two is easily recognized in Catharine's pronouncement, "This dear and much valued friend is associated with my own earliest experiences in the forest wilderness and with some of my happiest days beneath the pines of Douro."[2] How Frances must have yearned for the companionship of her long-time friend!

Frances's life is one of which we fortuitously have ample evidence. The letters, of which there are many, provide a tremendous source of information from which we are able to extrapolate meaning and formulate hypotheses about the woman who wrote them. Critical to arriving at reasonably sound postulations about Frances's life, too, is the understanding of the context in which they were written. The historical boundaries of the period allow for a range of stories to emerge and a concentrated analysis of any of the themes represented in Frances's writings could profitably contribute to an understanding of the author. What might one learn about her, for example, from an in-depth study of her relationship with her husband, Tom, or their servants? Through what lens did she perceive her surroundings as Tom and his helpers cut a home in the wilderness, burning massive piles of forest debris and eventually turning the soil to plant their crops? As she made small beginnings, sowing the home seeds sent lovingly from Ireland, did she reflect on the remnants of stumps about her, partially dislodged from the forest floor and a symbol of the lives Tom aspired to build for their children in the new world? Was Frances, even for a while, able to forget her beloved Ireland? How did she go about her daily activities, living with a despondent husband who sometimes intimated to her that she didn't match up to his expected standards? Was she weak and submissive at such times, or calm and assertive? Were the hustlings and bustlings of day enough to loosen the tight rein of loneliness that enveloped her during the small hours of the night while she wrote her letters and waited for the bread to rise? The reader will never have concrete answers to such questions; any suggestion of Frances's undocumented thoughts as she conducted her daily life will remain mere speculation.

Frances's moments of writing were, in a sense, a detachment from reality, a time to reflect, synthesize, and communicate feelings. While the letters essentially suggest the lonely existence of a stoic and principled pioneer, they also serve to convey the representation of a life that Frances would have others believe existed. She would have considered those who would be reading her letters, not only the intended recipients, but the many others, too, to whom the letters would most surely be circulated. Insightfully alluding to her consideration of this possibility, she complains to her daughter Ellen about the complications that could arise should a dispatch of letters that she had sent to Ellen and her sisters be circulated for general consumption: "I send you & Anna six letters between you, which you can exchange & return when read, but in writing to the writers of them or any of our friends don't mention that I sent you the letters or that you read them for I know they so much dislike having them sent round — & certainly one doesn't like it ones self."[3]

In light of such a passage, one must consider the possibility for the skewing of reality in the process of committing a rendition of it to paper and the intrinsic role that the intended recipient may play in the construction of the written text. Frances would never have let her privileged correspondents in Ireland know, for example, of the unending menial tasks that she must have performed. The complexities associated with text are manifold: regardless of Frances's intended meaning, as readers examine the letters they will attempt to fill in the gaps and impose meaning, acts that have the potential to imbue the author with imagined qualities reflective of the readers' own values and assumptions.

The letters that Frances wrote after leaving Ireland reveal an enormous upheaval in the life of one so inadequately equipped for the hardships of pioneer life. Immensely important, the letters, both those sent and those received, represent the only tangible means by which she could continue her relationship with loved ones in Ireland. Above all, Frances's letters provided evidence to the loved ones that she was alive, though heartbroken and homesick. As Ellen gathered them for the production of *Our Forest Home* after Frances's death, she remembered her mother's emotional response to the arrival of the long-awaited posts from the homeland: "How often I saw my mother read her Home letters & weep as if her heart would break."[4] David Gerber, claiming for the importance of letters in nurturing and maintaining relationships, writes that, "Intimate conversations, the ordinary, world-making discourse of individuals, would no longer suffice to provide anchors for the individual, so writing ... had to suffice to accomplish the goal of achieving continuity."[5]

Taken together, the exceedingly confusing layers of originals, handwritten copies, extracts, and manuscript variations that were compiled for the two editions of *Our Forest Home* are a tremendous record of female immigrant experience. They comprise a resource that is deeply enhanced by the complementary collection of letters that Frances received. The complementary letters alone would necessitate another volume! Frances pensively wrote in 1859, "I often think I don't know any person in Canada amongst the hundreds who have left their homes & friends who is so fortunate as I am in hearing so constantly from those dear ones who I left so many many years ago who still retain me in their home circle by constant intercourse on paper."[6]

One wonders whether Frances understood the value for posterity of these written exchanges. Carl Ballstadt, Elizabeth Hopkins, and Michael Peterman point out that she took a steady interest in the writings of her friend Catharine Parr Traill, sometimes "helping her with copying, and when the occasion called for it, finding subscribers for her books."[7] One wonders, therefore, whether Frances's attentiveness to these tasks reflected an interest in publishing something herself, or whether the earlier missives by friends and family in Ireland had heightened her awareness of the possibilities. What would she think if she knew that her letters are still being read in the twenty-first century!

Of the thousands of immigrants who arrived in the new world during the nineteenth century, textual legacies providing first-hand accounts of their experiences are rare. While Frances's privileged past meant an education that in turn resulted in the execution of letters that reflected a life, it is the person herself at the heart of the private exchanges who has captured the imagination of readers. I have read her letters with one set of eyes, partially positioned in childhood memories of the tiny hamlet of Maynooth, Ontario, where numerous stories about the earliest inhabitants, often heartily told with humour, abound. These stories, in fact, have *become* the people they portray, and will continue along this ever-fluid path with each retelling. Each and every person will read Frances's letters through a unique lens and, as in the past, she will continue to be reconstituted. Heather MacNeil asserts that cultural texts are in a "continuous state of *becoming* [emphasis mine], as they are resituated and recontextualized in different environments and by different authorities,"[8] a statement that fittingly describes the history of Frances's letters and their variant layers.

Revisiting "Our Forest Home" affords readers the opportunity to learn about Frances Stewart through her own first-hand accounts of her immigrant life. Understanding that her life was rooted in memories of her earlier years in Ireland, one is able to appreciate the basis for her unrealistic class expectations and the enduring melancholy she suffered. Ultimately — with the passage of time — faith in a divine being and the unwavering encouragement and praise of relatives and acquaintances in Ireland gave rise to Frances's quiet acceptance of the unlikely space and place she inhabited in nineteenth-century Canada.

APPENDIX 1

☯

The following is a full transcription of the "Land Grant for Thomas Alexander Stewart, York, 1822." (Page 31)

To His Excellency Sir Peregrine Maitland Lieutenant Governor of the Province of Upper Canada & Major General Commanding His Majesty's Forces therein &c &c &c

In Council
The Petition of Thomas Alexander Stewart now of York
Humbly sheweth

That your Petitioner is a native of Ireland, and emigrated from White Abbey in the County of Antrim, Ireland, in the month of June last, with his family of a wife, three children and two servants.

That your Petitioner has been for many years employed in the Linen, Flour and Cotton Business, and is well acquainted with the Mechanism used in those trades, and with mechanicks in general.

That your Petitioner emigrated to this Province with a full determination to establish himself thereon as an agriculturist, combined with any application of machinery he might find for his advantage, and has vested a great portion of his property in machinery and tools for every mechanical employment which he thought could be wanted in a new settlement, which, together with four years stock of made up wearing apparel he brought out with him, and with his ready money he estimates to be upwards of five hundred pounds sterling.

That your Petitioner has taken the Oath of Allegiance (Certificate whereof inherto annexed). That your Petitioner is anxious to settle in one of the townships mentioned in the notice from the Office of the Hon'ble Executive Council of the 7th of November last as for grant to actual settlers on certain terms & conditions, and his means enabling him to make large improvements and it being his wish to do so, He humbly prays that your Excellency will be pleased to grant him Twelve Hundred Acres for location in one of the townships above referred to, and on the Terms & Conditions as to Fees & Settlement Duties as mentioned therein.

And your Petitioner as in duty [ ] will ever pray

Thomas Alex'r Stewart.
York 3rd September 1822

NOTES

✑

PREFACE

1. E.S. Dunlop, ed., *Our Forest Home: Being Extracts from the Correspondence of the Late Frances Stewart* (Toronto: Printed by the Presbyterian Printing and Publishing Co., 1889).
2. Frances Stewart fonds, TUA, 94-006.

INTRODUCTION

1. Thomas Alexander Stewart (1786–1847).
2. Frances Stewart fonds, TUA, 94-1001, Frances Stewart to Catherine Browne [et al], March 11, 1823.
3. David A. Gerber, *Authors of Their Lives: The Personal Correspondence of British Immigrants to North America in the Nineteenth Century* (New York: New York University Press, 2006), 67.
4. Gerber, 3.
5. Bernadine Dodge, "Across the Great Divide: Archival Discourse and the (Re)presentations of the Past in Late-Modern Society," *Archivaria* 53 (2002): 19.
6. Jennifer Douglas and Heather MacNeil, "Arranging the Self: Literary and Archival Perspectives on Writers' Archives," *Archivaria* 67 (2009): 25.
7. Joan Sangster, *Earning Respect: The Lives of Working Women in Small-Town Ontario, 1920–1960* (Toronto: University of Toronto Press, 1995), 12–13.
8. Sangster, 12.

9. Anthony Giddens, *Modernity and Self-Identity: Self and Society in the Late Modern Age* (Stanford, CT: Stanford University Press, 1991), 54.
10. Stewart fonds, TUA 78-008 Letter #269, Frances Stewart [excerpts, bound with ribbon], May 27, 1826.

PART 1 — IRELAND: THE FIRST CHAPTER IN THE LIFE OF FRANCES STEWART, 1794–1822

1. Frances Stewart's commonplace book is located at TUA, 98-005. It is thought to include some poems written in the hands of Richard and Maria Edgeworth. It also includes poems by Mary Traill (daughter of Thomas and Catharine Parr Traill), and one of Susanna Moodie's poems, "The Canadian Woodsman," copied over at Auburn in August 1842, and appearing to be in Frances's hand. Many of the entries focus on loneliness and the death of children. According to Cinthia Gannett, the commonplace book is an "early ancestor to the journals of readings, quotes, observations, notes, and drafts that educated people, particularly scholars, writers, and artists, have kept for centuries." (Gannett, 109).
2. Stewart fonds, TUA, 78-008 Letter #70, Harriet Beaufort to Frances Stewart, December 3, 1812.
3. Stewart fonds, TUA, 78-008 Letter #59, Francis Beaufort to Frances Browne [Stewart], October 13, 1805.
4. M. Wilson, niece of Thomas Alexander Stewart, refers to the linen and cotton mill owned by Thomas and his brother John as White Abby Mills in an undated, typed copy of her memoirs located in the Jean Shearman fonds, TUA, 05-013.
5. Basil Hall, *Travels in North America in the Years 1827 and 1827*. Vol. 1. (Edinburgh: Printed for Robert Cadell, Edinburgh, and Simpkin and Marshall, London, 1830), 321. A letter dated April 21, 1828, from Thomas Alexander Stewart to Basil Hall is published in this book, pages 307–23.
6. Stewart fonds, TUA, 78-008 Letter #67.
7. Stewart fonds, TUA, 78-008 Letter #65.
8. Stewart fonds, TUA, 78-008 Letter #79.
9. Stewart fonds, TUA, 78-008 Letter #85.

PART 2 — UPPER CANADA: IMMIGRATION AND GENTEEL EXPERIENCE IN THE CANADIAN BUSH, 1822–1847

1. Marilyn Silverman, *An Irish Working Class: Explorations in Political Economy and Hegemony, 1800–1950* (Toronto: University of Toronto Press, 2001), 7.
2. Michael J. Wagner, "Gentry Perception and Land Utilization in the Peterborough — Kawartha Lakes Region, 1818–1851." (Master's thesis, University of Toronto, 1966), 1.
3. Selena M. Crosson, "Pilgrim Sisters: Exploring Female Friendship in Upper Canada in the Life of Frances Stewart (1794–1872)." (Master's thesis, Trent University, 2005), 100.
4. Stewart fonds, TUA, 78-008 Letter #91, Frances Stewart to Harriet Beaufort, July 1, 1822.
5. *Ibid.*
6. *Ibid.*
7. *Ibid.*
8. Silverman, 7.
9. Captain Charles Rubidge was a land agent who assisted Peter Robinson in settling the Irish immigrants in Peterborough in 1825. He also assisted other immigrant groups in 1831 and 1839 and was appointed Peterborough's Immigrant Agent by Lord Seaton, Governor General of Canada, in 1831.
10. Stewart fonds, TUA, 78-008 Letter #105, Frances Stewart to Maria Waller, December 14, 1822.
11. Stewart fonds, TUA, 78-008 Letter #210a, Frances Stewart to Betty Taylor, June 6, 1851.
12. Stewart fonds, TUA, 78-008 Letter #90, Frances Stewart to Catherine Kirkpatrick, July 23, 1822.
13. William John Keith, *Literary Images of Ontario* (Toronto: University of Toronto Press, 1992), 19.
14. *Ibid.*, 20.
15. Elizabeth Jane Birch, "Picking Up New Threads for Kathleen Mavourneen: The Irish Female Presence in Nineteenth-Century Ontario." (Master's thesis, Trent University, 1998, circa 1997), appendix ii.
16. Stewart fonds, TUA, 78-008 Letter #94, Frances Stewart to Maria Waller, October 30, 1822. This letter is a variant copy and has not been reproduced in this volume.
17. Mrs. Bethune moved to Cobourg, Newcastle District, from New York about 1817, a few years after the death of her husband, Reverend John Bethune.

18. Stewart fonds, TUA, 78-008 Letter #97, Frances Stewart journal, January 14, 1823. This journal is a variant copy and has not been reproduced in this volume.

19. Mary Lucyk Heaman, "Auburn Excavation Preliminary Report," Peterborough: Borden Site Designation: BbGn-1 (Unpublished paper, 1973), 50. A copy of this report is located in the Jean Shearman fonds, 05-013, TUA.

20. John J. Mannion, *Irish Settlements in Eastern Canada: A Study of Cultural Transfer and Adaptation* (Toronto: University of Toronto Press, 1974), 173.

21. Sydney Bellingham fonds, TUA, 69-1003, Sydney Bellingham memoirs [spring 1824]. Photocopy.

22. Elizabeth Shearman Hall and Jean Shearman, *A Sense of Continuity: The Stewarts of Douro*. Revised edition. (Toronto: Pro Familia, 1993), 67.

23. Stewart fonds, TUA, 78-008 Letter #121, Harriet Beaufort to Frances Stewart, July 26, 1826.

24. Silverman, 485.

25. Stewart fonds, TUA, 78-008 Letter #103, Harriet Beaufort to Frances Stewart, November 23, 1823.

26. Stewart fonds, TUA, 78-008 Letter #131, Frances Stewart to Honora Edgeworth Beaufort, April 6, 1829.

27. Stewart fonds, TUA, 78-008 Letter #122, Frances Stewart to Maria Waller, August 2, 1826. This letter is incomplete and has not been reproduced in this volume.

28. Some of the references to food in this chapter appear in "Culinary Themes in the Writings of Frances Stewart, Genteel Pioneer of Douro Township," an article by the author published in *Culinary Chronicles: The Newsletter of the Culinary Historians of Ontario*, Autumn 2005, No. 46.

29. Stewart fonds, TUA, 78-008 Letter #98, Frances Stewart to Maria Noble, February 24, 1823.

30. E.S. Dunlop, ed., *Our Forest Home: Being Extracts from the Correspondence of the Late Frances Stewart*. Second edition. (Montreal: Gazette Printing and Publishing Co., 1902), 19.

31. Misao Dean, *Practising Femininity: Domestic Realism and the Performance of Gender in Early Canadian Fiction* (Toronto: University of Toronto Press, 1998), 23.

32. Barbara Maas, *Helpmates of Man: Middle-Class Women and Gender Ideology in Nineteenth-Century Ontario*. Kanada-Studien, vol. 4 (Bochum: Universitätsverlag Dr. N. Brockmeyer, 1990), 117.

33. Stewart fonds, TUA, 78-008 Letter #114, Frances Stewart to Harriet Beaufort, February 1824. Frize is coarsely woven woolen cloth with a shaggy nap on one side. This item is a fragment and has not been reproduced in this volume.

34. Stewart fonds, TUA, 78-008 Letter #131, Frances Stewart to Honora Edgeworth Beaufort, April 6, 1829.
35. Frances Stewart correspondence, TPL. TRL, Baldwin Room, S215 A, Catharine Parr Traill to Frances Stewart, November 17, [1844].
36. Elizabeth Jane Errington, *Wives and Mothers, School Mistresses, and Scullery Maids: Working Women in Upper Canada, 1790–1840.* (Montreal and Kingston: McGill-Queen's University Press. 1995), 35. (See Errington Chapter 2, Notes 43, 44, and 45 for sources of quotations within the quotation).
37. Maas, 102.
38. Sir Frances Beaufort collection, Huntington Library, FB 1603, Frances Stewart to Francis Beaufort, December 10, 1826.
39. *Ibid.*
40. Nancy Christie, "A 'Painful Dependence': Female Begging Letters and the Familial Economy of Obligation," in *Mapping the Margins: The Family and Social Discipline in Canada, 1700–1917,* eds. Nancy Christie and Michael Gauvreau (Montreal and Kingston: McGill-Queen's University Press, 2004), 82.
41. *Ibid.*, 92.
42. *Ibid.*, 87.
43. *Ibid.*, 88.
44. Wagner, ii.
45. Shearman Hall and Shearman, 68.
46. *Ibid.*, 67.
47. John J. Mannion, "Irish Imprints on the Landscape of Eastern Canada in the Nineteenth Century: A Study of Cultural Transfer and Adaptation." (Ph.D. dissertation, University of Toronto, 1971), 74.
48. Wagner, 56.
49. Stewart fonds, TUA, 78-008 Letter #197, Frances Stewart to Maria Waller, December 7, 1846.
50. Wagner, 53.
51. Stewart fonds, TUA, 78-008 Letter #115, M. Waller to Frances Stewart, March 20, 1824.
52. Stewart fonds, TUA, 78-008 Letter #269, Frances Stewart to Harriet Beaufort, May 27, 1826.
53. Stewart correspondence, TPL. TRL, Baldwin Room, S215 A, Frances Stewart to Mary [ ], January 3, 1852.
54. Stewart fonds, TUA, 78-008 Letter #88. A journal of the 1822 voyage to Upper Canada and subsequent early days in the colony; "Miss Beaufort" inscribed on the back suggesting that Frances may have sent this copy to Harriet Beaufort; includes a passage entitled "The Young Emigrants by Mrs.

Traill." *The Young Emigrants* was published in 1826, suggesting that at least part of this journal was compiled after 1826 and perhaps after Catharine became friends with Frances in 1832 upon arriving from England.

55. Stewart fonds, TUA, 78-008 Letter #91 [journal entries]. Includes notation "Extract from F.S. July 21 1822 No. 1, M.N. [Maria Noble?] to Miss Beaufort." Includes a detailed version of the journey up the St. Lawrence en route to Upper Canada; 78-008 #88 and #88b comprise other variant journal extracts.

56. Stewart fonds, TUA, 78-008 Letter #89. Letter is torn and some text is missing; 78-008 Letter #90 (not reproduced in this volume), which appears to be an extract copied from #89, has been used to reconstruct the missing text; #90 may have been copied by Kate as the address includes her known location, "Clongill Rector."

57. Stewart fonds, TUA, 78-008 Letter #95.

58. Stewart fonds, TUA, 78-008 Letter #96. Fragment.

59. Stewart fonds, TUA, 78-008 Letter #105.

60. Stewart fonds, TUA, 78-008 Letter #106. A notebook or journal fragment regarding "Indians"; document consists of several small pages sewn together; several words have been crossed out, suggesting that this may have been a notebook in which Frances jotted notes about her subject. Tiny indistinct diagrams accompany Frances's descriptions of the clothing worn by the Aboriginals she encountered.

61. Stewart fonds, TUA, 78-008 Letter #98. Includes a red wax seal with the initials *FB* in ornate script.

62. Stewart fonds, TUA, 94-1001 Letter #1.

63. Traill family collection, LAC, MG 29, D81, v.7A. This document, entitled "Extracts from Canadian Letters," is written in Frances's hand. Because it is located in the Traill family papers at LAC, it may be assumed that Frances composed this script, which relates to the October 23, 1823, death of her daughter Bessie, for Catharine Parr Traill. As Catharine arrived in Upper Canada in 1832, and Frances did not know her beforehand, the date "1823" assumedly reflects the date of Bessie's death, not the date that the document was written. A poem entitled "Elegy on Little Bessy Stewart" is located in Frances's Commonplace Book (TUA, 98-005). Written in Frances's hand, it was composed by "SRB, Douro" in 1829. A copy, also in Frances's hand, is located in the Traill family papers along with the account of Bessie's death. Note that Frances commonly uses two different spellings of the child's name.

64. Stewart fonds, TUA, 74-1005 Letter #2. "Extracts."

65. Stewart fonds, TUA, 78-008 Letter #268. "Extracts," bound with ribbon.

66. Stewart fonds, TUA, 78-008 Letter #269. "Extracts," bound with ribbon.

67. Sir Francis Beaufort collection, Huntington, FB 1603. This item is repro-
    duced by permission of The Huntington Library, San Marino, California.
68. Stewart fonds, TUA, 78-008 Letter #126.
69. Stewart fonds, TUA, 78-008 Letter #129. This item is a copy made by
    Frances's daughter Bessie, a few months after her mother's death in 1872;
    as the following note on the copy suggests, the original was returned to
    its owner, Mrs. Wilson, after Bessie had copied it: "Copied May 27th 1872
    from Mrs Wilson's letter sent to us to read and return to her. She loved the
    writer too much to part with her letter as long as she lives. I will always keep
    this beside me to read & study.... I trust each of my dear children may read
    this when I am gone as I know how deeply they adore her memory. Bessie
    Brown, Goodwood."
70. Stewart fonds, TUA, 78-008 Letter #132. The penciled date, 1829, appears
    to have been written in another hand; a seal of black wax is well preserved
    and depicts an oval with a shamrock in the middle and the words *Erin
    Favour Win.*
71. Stewart fonds, TUA, 78-008 Letter #131.
72. Stewart fonds, TUA. 78-008 Letter. #148.
73. Stewart fonds, TUA, 74-1006 Letter #6. Photocopy only.
74. Stewart fonds, TUA, 78-008 Letter #178.
75. Stewart fonds, TUA, 78-008 Letter #197. Incomplete.
76. Stewart fonds, TUA, 78-008 Letter #204. Includes a red wax seal depicting
    a circle with the script *FS.*

PART 3 — THE FINAL CHAPTER: WIDOWED LIFE IN THE DEVELOPING NATION, 1847–1872

1. Stafford F. Kirkpatrick fonds, TUA, Stafford Kirkpatrick to Alexander
   Kirkpatrick, July 9, 1845. Stafford Kirkpatrick (1809–1858) was the brother
   of George Kirkpatrick, husband of Frances's sister Catherine.
2. Douglas McCalla, *Planting the Province: The Economic History of Upper
   Canada, 1784–1870* (Toronto: University of Toronto Press, 1993).
3. Alison Prentice, Paula Bourne [et al], *Canadian Women: A History*. Second
   Edition (Toronto: Harcourt Brace, 1996), 70.
4. Stewart correspondence, TPL. TRL, Baldwin Room, S215 A, Frances
   Stewart to [Harriet Beaufort], November 15, 1850.
5. *Ibid.*
6. Dunlop, 1902. 139.

7. Sally Chivers, *From Old Woman to Older Women: Contemporary Culture and Women's Narratives* (Columbus: Ohio State University Press, 2003), 99.

8. Stewart correspondence, TPL. TRL, Baldwin Room, S215 A, Frances Stewart to [Harriet Beaufort], November 15, 1850.

9. Stewart fonds, TUA, 92-1002, Letter #1, Frances Stewart to unknown, August 1, 1854.

10. Stewart fonds, TUA, 78-008 Letter #215a, Frances Stewart to Mary Martha Noble Sutton, November 10, 1856.

11. Stewart correspondence, TPL. TRL, Baldwin Room, S215 A, Frances Stewart to (an aunt), October 7, 1851.

12. Stewart fonds, TUA, 92-1002 Letter #9, Frances Stewart to Harriette [Harriet Brown], December 25, 1869.

13. Traill family collection, LAC, Frances Stewart to Annie (Atwood), September 25, 1871.

14. Stewart fonds, TUA, 74-1005 Letter #3, Frances Stewart to Maria [ ], April 11, 1854.

15. Stewart fonds, TUA, 78-008 Letter #200, Frances Stewart to Reverend Robert Taylor, September 20, 1847.

16. *Ibid.*

17. Crosson, 166–67.

18. Joyce C. Lewis, "Frances Stewart," in *Portraits: Peterborough Area Women Past and Present*, ed. Gail Corbett. (Peterborough: Portraits' Group, 1975), 67.

19. Stewart fonds, TUA, 78-008 Letter #129. This quotation is Bessie Brown's (1872) postscript on her own copy of a letter that had been sent originally by her mother, Frances Stewart, to a cousin, Mrs. Wilson, June 3, 1828.

20. Stewart fonds, TUA, 78-008 Letter #200.

21. Stewart fonds, TUA, 78-008 Letter #201. A copy, in another hand.

22. Stewart fonds, TUA, 78-008 Letter #205. Incomplete.

23. Stewart fonds, TUA, 78-008 Letter #206. Incomplete.

24. Stewart fonds, TUA, 78-008 Letter #208. Incomplete.

25. Stewart fonds, TUA, 74-1006 Letter #7. Photocopy only.

26. Stewart correspondence, TPL. TRL, Baldwin Room, S215 A. Incomplete.

27. Stewart fonds, TUA, 78-008 Letter #209a. Written prior to Louisa's marriage to William Stewart.

28. Stewart fonds, TUA, Letter 78-008 #210a.

29. Stewart fonds, TUA, 78-008 Letter #255. Incomplete.

30. Stewart correspondence, TPL. TRL, Baldwin Room, S215 A. A stamp with the words *God Bless You* is attached to the original on the concluding page.

31. Stewart correspondence, TPL. TRL, Baldwin Room, S215 A.

32. Stewart correspondence, TPL. TRL, Baldwin Room, S215 A. Incomplete.
33. Stewart fonds, TUA, 74-1006 Letter #5. Photocopy only.
34. Stewart fonds, TUA, 74-1005 Letter #3. Incomplete.
35. Stewart fonds, TUA, 92-1002 Letter #1. "Extracts." This letter has a glued strip overlay down one side of one page which covers some words, making them illegible. On the last page, in another hand, the following is written: "Dear Kate send this back for our travellers to see. M.S."
36. Stewart fonds, TUA, 78-008 Letter #214a.
37. Stewart fonds, TUA, 78-008 Letter #215a. Fragment.
38. Stewart fonds, TUA, 78-008 Letter #215. Damaged; as the edges of the letter are missing, some information has been lost.
39. Stewart fonds, TUA, 92-1002 Letter #2.
40. Stewart fonds, TUA, 92-1002 Letter #3. Fragment.
41. Stewart fonds, TUA, 92-1002 Letter #4. Fragment. Written after Charles Stewart's wedding of August 9, 1860.
42. Stewart fonds, TUA, 97-023 Folder 4.
43. Stewart fonds, TUA, 78-008 Letter #217.
44. Stewart fonds, TUA, 78-008 Letter #218a.
45. Traill family collection, LAC, MG 29, D81 v. 1. An incident described in the letter dated May 20, 1866, helps to establish the date of this letter; approximately twelve lines of this letter are partially obliterated and the text is missing.
46. Traill family collection, LAC, MG 29, D81 v.1.
47. Traill family collection, LAC, MG 29, D81, v. 1.
48. Stewart fonds, TUA, 92-1002 Letter #5.
49. Traill family collection, LAC, MG 29, D81, v.1.
50. Stewart fonds, TUA, 78-008 Letter #220a.
51. Traill family collection, LAC, MG 29, D81, v.1.
52. Traill family collection, LAC, MG 29, D81, v.1.
53. Traill family collection, LAC, MG 29, D81, v.1.
54. Traill family collection, LAC, MG 29, D81, v.1.
55. Stewart fonds, TUA, 78-008 Letter #278.
56. Traill family collection, LAC, MG 29, D81, v.1.
57. Traill family collection, LAC, MG29, D81, v.1.
58. Traill family collection, LAC, MG 29, D81, v.1. This letter indicates that Annie had named her daughter Katharine Stewart after her mother Catharine Parr Traill, and Frances, i.e. "Dearest Annie you were very very kind to think of joining my name with your dear Mothers for your little daughter."
59. Stewart fonds, TUA, 92-1002 Letter #6.
60. Stewart fonds, TUA, 92-1002 Letter #7.
61. Traill family collection, LAC, MG 29, D81, v.2.

62. Traill family collection, LAC, MG 29, D81, v.2.
63. Stewart fonds, TUA, 92-1002 Letter #8.
64. Stewart correspondence, TPL. TRL, Baldwin Room, S215 A.
65. Stewart fonds, TUA, 78-008 Letter #221.
66. Traill family collection, LAC, MG 29, D81, v.1.
67. Traill family collection, LAC, MG 29, D81, v.2.
68. Stewart fonds, TUA, 78-008 Letter #222.
69. Stewart fonds, TUA, 92-1002 Letter #9.
70. Stewart-Dunlop fonds, TUA, 94-007/1/7 Letter #6.
71. Stewart fonds, TUA, 92-1002 Letter #10. Some words are not transcribed as a small corner of the letter is missing.
72. Traill family collection, LAC, MG 29, D81, v.2.
73. Traill family collection, LAC, MG 29, D81, v.2.
74. Stewart fonds, TUA, 78-008 Letter #222a.
75. Stewart fonds, TUA, 78-008 Letter #222b.
76. Traill family collection, LAC, MG 29, D81, v.2.
77. Traill family collection, LAC, MG 29, D81, v.2.
78. Stewart fonds, TUA, 78-008 Letter #223.
79. Stewart fonds, TUA, 78-008 Letter #223a.
80. Stewart fonds, TUA, 78-008 Letter #224a. A small section of the letter is missing.
81. Stewart fonds, TUA, 78-008 Letter #225. A page is missing.
82. Stewart fonds, TUA, 78-008 Letter #225a. This is the last extant letter that Frances wrote before her death on February 24, 1872.

CONCLUSION

1. Stewart fonds, TUA, 78-008 Letter #278, Frances Stewart to Annie Atwood, July 17, 1867.
2. Carl Ballstadt, Elizabeth Hopkins, and Michael Peterman, eds. *I Bless You in My Heart: Selected Correspondence of Catharine Parr Traill.* (Toronto: University of Toronto Press, 1996), 13.
3. Stewart fonds, TUA, 94-007/1/7 Letter #6, Frances Stewart to Ellen Dunlop (1869): photocopy only.
4. Kirkpatrick papers, PRONI, D/1424/3/49, Ellen Dunlop to George Kirkpatrick, October 29, 1888. Quote reproduced with permission of the Deputy Keeper of the Records, Public Record Office of Northern Ireland.
5. Gerber, 57.

6. Stewart fonds, TUA, 92-1002, Letter #2, Frances Stewart to "Aunty," April 4, 1859.
7. Ballstadt et al, 131.
8. Heather MacNeil, "Archivalterity: Rethinking Original Order," *Archivaria* 66 (2008): 2.

BIBLIOGRAPHY

PRIMARY SOURCES

Beaufort, Sir Francis collection. Huntington Library.
Bellingham, Sidney fonds. Trent University Archives (photocopy).
Executive Council Office of the Province of Upper Canada fonds. Library and
    Archives Canada.
Kirkpatrick papers. Public Record Office of Northern Ireland.
Kirkpatrick, Stafford F. fonds. Trent University Archives.
Rubidge, Captain Charles fonds. Trent University Archives.
Shearman, Jean fonds. Trent University Archives.
Shearman, Jean, and Elizabeth Shearman Hall fonds. Trent University Archives.
Stewart, Frances correspondence. Toronto Reference Library, Baldwin Room.
Stewart, Frances fonds. Trent University Archives.
Stewart-Dunlop fonds. Trent University Archives.
Stewart family books. Trent University Archives.
Stewart family fonds. Trent University Archives.
Traill family collection. Library and Archives Canada.

SECONDARY SOURCES

Ballstadt, Carl, Elizabeth Hopkins, and Michael Peterman, eds. *I Bless You in My
    Heart: Selected Correspondence of Catharine Parr Traill.* Toronto: University
    of Toronto Press, 1996.

Bell, Duncan. "Introduction." In *Memory, Trauma, and World Politics: Reflections on the Relationship Between Past and Present.* Edited by Duncan Bell. Basingstoke, UK: Palgrave MacMillan, 2006.

Birch, Elizabeth Jane. "Picking Up New Threads for Kathleen Mavourneen: The Irish Female Presence in Nineteenth-Century Ontario." Master's thesis, Trent University, 1998, circa 1997.

Chivers, Sally. *From Old Woman to Older Women: Contemporary Culture and Women's Narratives.* Columbus: The Ohio State University Press, 2003.

Christie, Nancy. "A 'Painful Dependence:' Female Begging Letters and the Familial Economy of Obligation." In *Mapping the Margins: The Family and Social Discipline in Canada, 1700–1917.* Edited by Nancy Christie and Michael Gauvreau. Montreal and Kingston: McGill-Queen's University Press, 2004.

———. "'The Plague of Servants': Female Household Labour and the Making of Classes in Upper Canada." In *Transatlantic Subjects: Ideas, Institutions, and Social Experience in Post-Revolutionary British North America.* Edited by Nancy Christie. Montreal and Kingston: McGill-Queen's University Press, 2008.

Crosson, Selena M. "Pilgrim Sisters: Exploring Female Friendship in Upper Canada in the Life of Frances Stewart (1794–1872)." Master's thesis, Trent University, 2005.

Dean, Misao. *Practising Femininity: Domestic Realism and the Performance of Gender in Early Canadian Fiction.* Toronto: University of Toronto Press, 1998.

Delafosse, F.M. *Centenary History: St. John's Church Peterborough, 1827–1927.* Peterborough, ON: The Review Press, 1927.

Dodge, Bernadine. "Across the Great Divide: Archival Discourse and the (Re)presentations of the Past in Late-Modern Society." *Archivaria* 53 (2002): 16–30.

Douglas, Jennifer, and Heather MacNeil. "Arranging the Self: Literary and Archival Perspectives on Writers' Archives." *Archivaria* 67 (2009): 25–39.

Dunlop, E.S., ed. *Our Forest Home: Being Extracts from the Correspondence of the Late Frances Stewart.* Toronto: Printed by the Presbyterian Printing and Publishing Co., 1889.

———. *Our Forest Home: Being Extracts from the Correspondence of the Late Frances Stewart.* Second edition. Montreal: Gazette Printing and Publishing Co., 1902.

Edmison, John Alexander, ed. *Through the Years in Douro (Peterborough, Ontario), 1822–1967.* Peterborough: A.D. Newson, 1967.

Errington, Elizabeth Jane. *Wives and Mothers, School Mistresses, and Scullery Maids: Working Women in Upper Canada, 1790–1840.* Montreal and Kingston: McGill-Queen's University Press, 1995.

Gannett, Cinthia. *Gender and the Journal: Diaries and Academic Discourse.* SUNY Series, Literacy, Culture, and Learning. Albany, NY: State University of New York Press, 1992.

Gerber, David A. *Authors of Their Lives: The Personal Correspondence of British Immigrants to North America in the Nineteenth Century.* New York: New York University Press, 2006.

Giddens, Anthony. *Modernity and Self-Identity: Self and Society in the Late Modern Age.* Stanford, CT: Stanford University Press, 1991.

Guillet, Edwin C. *Pioneer Days in Upper Canada.* Toronto: University of Toronto Press, 1933.

———, ed. *The Valley of the Trent.* Toronto: The Champlain Society for the Government of Ontario, 1957.

Hall, Basil. *Travels in North America, in the Years 1827 and 1828.* Edinburgh: Printed for Robert Cadell, Edinburgh; and Simpkin and Marshall, London, 1930.

Heaman, Mary Lucyk. "Auburn Excavation Preliminary Report," Peterborough, ON: Borden Site Designation: BbGn-1 (unpublished paper), 1973.

Jones, Elwood. 2004. "The Naming of Peterborough." *Heritage Gazette of the Trent Valley* 8, No. 4 (February 2004): 5–8.

Keith, William John. *Literary Images of Ontario.* Toronto: University of Toronto Press, 1992.

Lewis, Joyce C. "Frances Stewart." In *Portraits: Peterborough Area Women Past and Present.* Edited by Gail Corbett. Peterborough, ON: Portraits' Group, 1975.

Maas, Barbara. *Helpmates of Man: Middle-Class Women and Gender Ideology in Nineteenth-Century Ontario.* Kanada-Studien, vol. 4. Bochum: Universitätsverlag Dr. N. Brockmeyer, 1990.

MacNeil, Heather. "Archivalterity: Rethinking Original Order." *Archivaria* 66 (2008): 1–24.

Mannion, John J. "Irish Imprints on the Landscape of Eastern Canada in the Nineteenth Century: A Study of Cultural Transfer and Adaptation." Ph.D. dissertation, University of Toronto, 1971.

———. *Irish Settlements in Eastern Canada: A Study of Cultural Transfer and Adaptation.* Toronto: University of Toronto Press, 1974.

Martin, Norma, Donna S. McGillis, and Catherine Milne. *Gore's Landing and the Rice Lakes Plains.* Cobourg, ON: Hayne's Printing, 1986.

McCalla, Douglas. *Planting the Province: The Economic History of Upper Canada, 1784–1870.* Toronto: University of Toronto Press, 1993.

Montreal Gazette. "Port of Quebec: Arrived," July 27, 1822.

Needler, G.H. *Otonabee Pioneers: The Story of the Stewarts, the Stricklands, the Traills, and the Moodies.* Toronto: Burns & MacEachern, 1953.

Peterborough, Land of Shining Water: An Anthology. Peterborough, ON: City and County of Peterborough, 1967.

Peterborough Review. "Died," March 1, 1872.

Prentice, Alison, Paula Bourne [et al]. *Canadian Women: A History.* Second Edition. Toronto: Harcourt Brace, 1996.

Sangster, Joan. *Earning Respect: The Lives of Working Women in Small-Town Ontario, 1920–1960.* Toronto: University of Toronto Press, 1995.

Shearman Hall, Elizabeth, and Jean Shearman. *A Sense of Continuity: The Stewarts of Douro.* Revised edition. Toronto: Pro Familia, 1993.

Silverman, Marilyn. *An Irish Working Class: Explorations in Political Economy and Hegemony, 1800–1950.* Toronto: University of Toronto Press, 2001.

Vibert, Elizabeth. "Writing 'Home': Sibling Intimacy and Mobility in a Scottish Colonial Memoir." In *Moving Subjects: Gender, Mobility, and Intimacy in an Age of Global Empire.* Edited by Tony Ballantyne and Antoinette Burton. Urbana, IL: University of Illinois Press, 2009.

Wagner, Michael J. "Gentry Perception and Land Utilization in the Peterborough-Kawartha Lakes Region, 1818–1851." Master's thesis, University of Toronto, 1966.

Index

❦

Irish immigration, 52, 112–13, 116, 139–41

Keith, William John, 55
Kirkpatrick, Catherine (née Browne) (*Kate*), 13–14, 39, 47–48, 73–77, 85, 97–104, 120, 134, 145, 161–66, 182, 187, 190, 199, 278, 279
Kirkpatrick, Rev. George, 14, 97–98, 279
Kirkpatrick, Stafford, 13, 137, 149, 198, 279

Langton, Miss [Anne], 38, 133
Langton, Mr. [John], 133
Lewis, Joyce, 155
Logging, 89

Maas, Barbara, 60, 62
MacNeil, Heather, 35, 268
Maitland, Sir Peregrine, 52, 76, 271–72
Malone (*see* Family property)
Mannion, John J., 57, 64
McCalla, Douglas, 149
McCauley, Mr., 86–88
McNabb, Dr. John, 12, 171, 175, 177, 223, 233, 240, 250
Mills, 42–43, 86, 131, 144–45, 182, 274
Moodie, Susanna, 17, 38, 59–60, 274
Mountain, Bishop and Mrs., 74–76, 104
Muchall, Mary (née Traill), 13, 212, 222–24, 226–27, 232, 274
Mud Lake, 96, 100

Napoleonic Wars, 39, 42, 51

Otonabee River, 30, 52, 95–96, 99–100, 104–05, 113–14, 144–45, 179, 182

Peterman, Michael, 268
Porter, David, 140–41, 176
Porter, William, 140, 176
Pregnancy, labour, and birth, 55, 65, 102, 110–11, 146, 152–53, 177, 184–86, 200, 221, 227, 229, 233, 242
Prentice, Alison, 150

Reade, Dr., 13, 112, 115–16
Regatta, 132–33
Reid, Maria (née Stewart), 13, 57, 82, 96, 102, 109, 116, 139, 188, 205
Reid, Robert, 13, 37, 42–43, 49, 52, 54, 56–57, 66, 69–70, 78–79, 81, 83, 86, 95–96, 99–100, 102, 104, 109, 113–14, 118–19, 131, 139–40, 160, 179, 182, 188
Robinson, Peter, 13–14, 52, 112, 115, 275
Roger, Rev. J.M., 14, 137–38, 143, 155, 157, 159, 206
Rubidge, Charles and Mrs., 14, 54, 86, 108–10, 223, 275

Sangster, Joan, 35–36
Scott's Mills, 95, 102, 111–12
Servants and staff, 11, 30, 49, 52, 54, 58–59, 63, 71, 79, 81–82, 92, 94, 100, 107, 109–10, 112, 114–16, 138, 140–42, 145–46, 150, 163–65, 168, 170, 175–77, 181–82, 192, 197, 213, 218, 228, 230–31, 234–35, 238, 241–43, 245, 247, 250–56, 271
Settlement duties, 85, 272
Shearman, Jean, 11, 22, 57, 64
Silverman, Marilyn, 54, 57–58
Sowden, Mr., 93
Spousal abuse, 134–35

OF RELATED INTEREST

Pearls and Pebbles
by Catharine Parr Traill
edited by Elizabeth Thompson
978-1896219592
$21.95 / £14.99

Published in 1894, *Pearls & Pebbles* is an
unusual book with a lasting charm, in which
the author's broad focus ranges from the
Canadian natural environment to early
settlement of Upper Canada. Through Traill's
eyes, we see the life of the pioneer woman,
the disappearance of the forest, and the
corresponding changes in the life of the Native
Canadians who have inhabited that forest.

Much to Be Done
Private Life in Ontario from Victorian Diaries
by Frances Hoffman and Ryan Taylor
978-1550027723
$21.99 / £11.99

Victorian Ontario included people from all
walks of life, from homeless beggars to wealthy
gentry. In *Much To Be Done* we glimpse how life
was lived in nineteenth-century Ontario, not
only in the grand mansions, but also in the farm
houses and streets where our ancestors lived. It
promotes a historical understanding which links
people of today with the Ontario of the past.

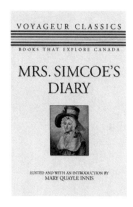

Mrs. Simcoe's Diary
by Mary Quayle Innis
978-1550027686
$22.99 / £12.99

Elizabeth Simcoe's diary, describing Canada from 1791 to 1796, is history written as it was being made. Created largely while she was seated in canoes and bateaux, the diary documents great events in a familiar way and opens our eyes to a side of Canadian history that is too little shown.

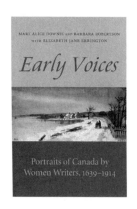

Early Voices
Portraits of Canada by Women Writers, 1639–1914
Edited by Mary Alice Downie and Barbara Robertson
978-1554887699
$28.99 / £16.99

This selection of writings by twenty-nine Canadian women presents a unique portrait of Canada through time and space, and a range of voices, from high-born wives of governors general to a fisherman's wife in Labrador. All of which demonstrate how women's experiences helped shape this country.

Available at your favourite bookseller.

DUNDURN
www.dundurn.com

What did you think of this book?
Visit *www.dundurn.com* for reviews, videos, updates, and more!